"The book's greatest strength lies in its stimulating and provocative examples. Readers are treated to a host of insights from cognitive science, culture high and low, the rough-and-tumble world of litigation, and the lofty perches of appellate advocacy and judging."

Ross Guberman, Author, Point Made: How to Write Like the Nation's Top Advocates *and President, Legal Writing Pro*

"Professors Berger and Stanchi have combined their respective interests in rhetorical theory and cognitive science to produce an extremely engaging book about legal persuasion. This volume will be immensely helpful to advocates, but it also provides scholars with concrete examples that illuminate and advance deep insights."

Francis J. Mootz III, Dean and Professor of Law, McGeorge School of Law, University of the Pacific, USA

"Every law student, law teacher, attorney, judge, and – dare I say politician? – should read Berger and Stanchi's brilliant new synthesis of rhetorical theory and cognitive science. Both accessible and sophisticated, its clear succinct explanations and examples will help you think more clearly, advocate more effectively, and decide more wisely."

Kate O'Neill, Professor Emeritus, University of Washington School of Law, USA

LEGAL PERSUASION

This book develops a central theme: legal persuasion results from making and breaking mental connections. This concept of *making connections* inspired the authors to take a rhetorical approach to the science of legal persuasion. That singular approach resulted in the integration of research from cognitive science with classical and contemporary rhetorical theory, and the application of these two disciplines to the real-life practice of persuasion. The combination of rhetorical analysis and cognitive science yields a new way of seeing and understanding legal persuasion, one that promises theoretical and practical gains. The work has three main functions. First, it brings together the leading models of persuasion from cognitive science and rhetorical theory, blurring boundaries and leveraging connections between the often-separate spheres of science and rhetoric. Second, it illustrates this persuasive synthesis by working through concrete examples of persuasion, demonstrating how to apply this new approach to the taking apart and the putting together of effective legal arguments. In this way, the book demonstrates the advantages of a deeper and more nuanced understanding of persuasion. Third, the volume assesses and explains why, how, and when certain persuasive methods and techniques are more effective than others. The book is designed to appeal to scholars in law, rhetoric, persuasion science, and psychology; to students learning the practice of law; and to judges and practicing lawyers who engage in persuasion.

Linda Berger is the Family Foundation Professor of Law at the University of Nevada, Las Vegas, William S. Boyd School of Law. Professor Berger has been a leader in building the discipline of legal writing. Her recent scholarly work blends interdisciplinary study with rhetorical analysis, drawing on research findings from analogy, metaphor, and narrative studies in order to examine the persuasiveness and effectiveness of written and oral communication.

Kathryn M. Stanchi is the Jack E. Feinberg '57 Professor of Litigation and Affiliated Professor of Gender, Sexuality and Women's Studies at Temple University Beasley School of Law. She is recognized as the leading scholar to bring persuasion science into the literature of legal persuasion. Her scholarship often focuses on the intersection of persuasion, rhetoric, and feminism. She has published and lectured extensively on this and related topics.

Law, Language and Communication
Series Editors
Anne Wagner, *Université du Littoral Côte d'Opale, France* and
Vijay Kumar Bhatia, *formerly of City University of Hong Kong*

This series encourages innovative and integrated perspectives within and across the boundaries of law, language, and communication, with particular emphasis on issues of communication in specialized socio-legal and professional contexts. It seeks to bring together a range of diverse yet cumulative research traditions in order to identify and encourage interdisciplinary research.

The series welcomes proposals – both edited collections as well as single-authored monographs – emphasizing critical approaches to law, language, and communication, identifying and discussing issues, proposing solutions to problems, and offering analyses in areas such as legal construction, interpretation, translation, and de-codification.

Other titles in the series

Synesthetic Legalities: Sensory Dimensions of Law and Jurisprudence
Edited by Sarah Marusek
ISBN 978-1-4724-8295-2

Multilingual Law: A Framework for Analysis and Understanding
Colin D. Robertson
ISBN 978-1-4094-2188-7

Shari'a in the Secular State: Evolving Meanings of Islamic Jurisprudence in Turkey
Russell Powell
ISBN 978-1-4724-7954-9

Language and Culture in EU Law: Multidisciplinary Perspectives
Edited by Susan Šarčević
ISBN 978-1-4724-2897-4

Towards Recognition of Minority Groups: Legal and Communication Strategies
Edited by Marek Zirk-Sadowski, Bartosz Wojciechowski and Karolina M. Cern
ISBN 978-1-4724-4490-5

The Ashgate Handbook of Legal Translation
Edited by Le Cheng, King Kui Sin and Anne Wagner
ISBN 978-1-4094-6966-7

Legal Lexicography: A Comparative Perspective
Edited by Máirtín Mac Aodha
ISBN 978-1-4094-5441-0

LEGAL PERSUASION

A Rhetorical Approach to the Science

Linda L. Berger and Kathryn M. Stanchi

Routledge
Taylor & Francis Group

LONDON AND NEW YORK

First published 2018
by Routledge
2 Park Square, Milton Park, Abingdon, Oxon OX14 4RN

and by Routledge
711 Third Avenue, New York, NY 10017

Routledge is an imprint of the Taylor & Francis Group, an informa business

© 2018 Linda L. Berger and Kathryn M. Stanchi

British Library Cataloguing-in-Publication Data
A catalogue record for this book is available from the British Library

Library of Congress Cataloging-in-Publication Data
Names: Berger, Linda L., author. | Stanchi, Kathryn M., author.
Title: Legal persuasion : a rhetorical approach to the science /
    Linda L. Berger, Kathryn M. Stanchi.
Description: Abingdon, Oxon [UK] ; New York : Routledge, 2017. |
    Series: Law, language and communication | Includes bibliographical
    references and index.
Identifiers: LCCN 2017009322| ISBN 9781472464521 (hardback) |
    ISBN 9781472464552 (pbk.)
Subjects: LCSH: Communication in law. | Semiotics (Law) |
    Forensic oratory. | Persuasion (Rhetoric) | Law—Methodology. |
    Law—Language.
Classification: LCC K213 .B43 2017 | DDC 340/.14—dc23
LC record available at https://lccn.loc.gov/2017009322

ISBN: 978-1-4724-6452-1 (hbk)
ISBN: 978-1-4724-6455-2 (pbk)
ISBN: 978-1-315-11299-2 (ebk)

Typeset in Galliard
by Apex CoVantage, LLC

Infinity icon © LovArt/Shutterstock

To lawyers who use rhetoric to pursue the possible. LLB
To Frank, who taught me so much about persuasion. KMS

CONTENTS

PREFACE

When we got together to write this book, we had in mind an overview of legal persuasion that combined our different areas of expertise. Kathy Stanchi has been writing for years about the insights persuasion science provides for the thoughtful and deliberate legal advocate. Linda Berger has been examining classical and contemporary rhetorical theories and using rhetorical methods and rhetorical criticism to analyze lawyers' arguments, especially in written briefs and opinions. When we decided to write together, we realized that although we had approached the subject of legal persuasion from different directions, we had arrived at the same place: legal persuasion results from making and breaking mental connections. We thought that a book exploring the rich interdisciplinary potential of rhetoric and science would be a novel and useful approach to persuasion and would have much to offer the practice and study of law.

In that sense, this book is a true collaboration. While we each took primary responsibility for certain chapters that were within our specific areas of expertise, we both made our marks on every part of this book. Both of us were pleasantly surprised at the true synergy that our collaboration created when we considered and edited the chapters outside our usual areas of expertise. We believe that synergy makes the book a real integration of rhetorical theory and science. Thus, the order of authors reflects the alphabetical order of the letters of our last name. For better or worse, every part of this book is truly both of ours.

Our initial approach was to chart a middle course that included a strong foundation in the theory of persuasion but also a true grounding in the practical. The book's organization reflects this approach in that each chapter takes the time to explain and describe the theory and also includes case studies as examples of the theory as applied. As legal writing professors, we know that a firm grounding in theory is essential to the ability to make advocacy decisions in the wide diversity of contexts that confront the legal advocate. As much as practicing lawyers like to disclaim theory, they use it every day. As just one example, virtually every litigator will tell you that they start their case planning with a "theory of the case" that is meant to guide their strategic decision making throughout the litigation. Persuasion theory works similarly; it is an overarching set of principles that lawyers can translate into practical strategic decisions. This book is meant to help with that translation, both by bringing together in one source some of the leading persuasion theories and by showing how those theories have been used by legal advocates in past cases.

Our idea to combine theory with practice, however, presented the problem of audience. Who is the intended audience of the book? Practicing lawyers? Law professors? Students? We thought that those groups, and members of the public in general, would be interested in how persuasion works in legal settings. As we wrote, we recognized that we were writing to all these different audiences. That broad target for the book presented some tone and communication issues – speaking simultaneously to law professors, practicing lawyers, and students was often a tightrope walk for us. We very much did not want to "dumb down" the theory, but we did want it to be understandable to everyone in our audience. We often erred on the side of simplifying, but sometimes we included complex theoretical details because of a desire for thoroughness or accuracy. We recognize that in attempting to walk this tightrope of audience, we might have occasionally missed the mark.

But if nothing else, the premise of this book is that lawyers should be thinking about theory, and theoreticians should be thinking about the practical, and everybody should be thinking about how to educate the next generation. We believed that the hiccups resulting from our wish to follow this integrated approach were worth it to break new interdisciplinary ground for legal advocacy. We hope the result is challenging, useful, informative, and interesting.

ACKNOWLEDGMENTS

Everything we do starts with our students, and so we start by thanking our students for helping us explore, develop, and test the concepts in this book. Their understanding, responses, challenges, and feedback have been invaluable.

We owe special thanks to the careful and hard-working research assistants who helped us find useful examples in lawyers' briefs, judicial opinions, and many other sources, including Brent Resh, Tam Tran, Michael Ahlert, Dina Kopansky, and Sara Mohammed. Sabrina Mercado, Jasmine Greene and Shauna Pierson provided editing assistance at the final stages. We are especially grateful to Brent Resh for organizing and preparing the chapter bibliographies.

Among our colleagues, Amy Sloan was the first to encourage us to view this book as primarily a work of scholarship, and we thank her for that encouragement. We gained many valuable insights and helpful suggestions from Amy and the other reviewers of the initial proposal: Laura Little, Greg Mandel, Ann McGinley, Richard K. Neumann Jr., and Jean Sternlight. We received consistent and very welcome support from our law librarians, our deans, and our law schools, UNLV's Boyd School of Law and Temple's Beasley School of Law.

The University of Washington's Whiteley Center at Friday Harbor in the San Juan Islands provided a serene and beautiful setting at a critical moment in the writing of the book: our appreciation to the Whiteley Center and to Tom Cobb and Kate O'Neill for suggesting that we apply for a writing retreat there.

Finally, to our colleagues at our own law schools and across the country, our friends, and our family members who put up with our talking about this book for more than four years: we are grateful for you and feel very fortunate to have you in our lives.

PART I

Introduction

1

MAKING CONNECTIONS

Making connections is the critical concept that unites persuasion science with rhetorical theory and the real-life practice of persuasion. Connections are critical because most things in life are ambiguous: what we read, hear, and see is open to interpretation. When we sit in a restaurant and a person with a pad and pencil approaches us, we expect that he wants to take our order rather than wanting to interview us, take a bet on a horse race, or draw our picture. (Winter 2003). Our expectation is based on the connections our brain made between the individual we observed and the setting, the timing, the individual's dress, our past experiences, and a host of other factors. When the same waiter asks us if we want to hear *what's fresh*, we expect him to describe today's best offerings from the menu rather than the air, the water, or the flowers. Our scripts for eating in a restaurant, acquired through experience, set up our usual expectations.

Still, because both words and observations hold out the potential for alternatives to be considered, they are open to interpretation, and that openness makes persuasion possible. Sometimes the advocate will want the decision maker to assume that the person with the pad and pencil is a waiter, but sometimes lawyers must persuade us that our initial view, our first impression, is mistaken or incomplete. By attempting to influence the decision maker to keep searching for clues, or to go back to search for alternative scenarios, lawyers can influence their audiences to make certain mental connections and to turn away from others.

In the chapters that follow, we explain and illustrate how lawyers can make the right choices to influence connections. For example, we explore the reasons why lawyers might decide to use one rather than another metaphor or analogy as well as how lawyers should select an especially appropriate storyline or characterization, fit their arguments into a comfortable organizational structure, or choose specific words and phrases for particular purposes.

To persuade an audience member is to help her connect the pieces of the puzzle in order to see a particular picture. If, for example, a lawyer wishes to argue that driving while intoxicated is a "violent felony," the lawyer may initially confront a problem of "connection."[1] People have schema or stock images of what a "violent felony" is, and for most of us, those schemas do not include drunk driving. The lawyer's job is to lead the reader to connect the "violent" results of drunk driving with the relatively passive action of driving a vehicle. The lawyer must also weaken the associations the reader may have between "violent felony" and stereotypical violent crimes such as assault or murder.

As this example shows, the connections in our minds are formed by common cultural understandings as well as by our personal experiences. Many of our cultural understandings and personal experiences have been with us for a long time, and they are well settled in our minds. For most situations, we must choose from among a number of possible connections stored in memory. If the advocate is to succeed in reinforcing the more favorable connections and in severing the less favorable ones, she must engage in advocacy that is vivid and memorable enough to replace the lived experience.

It is easy to say that persuasive advocacy should function as a virtual lived experience for the reader. But how can the advocate guide the reader so that the experience unfolds in that way? That is the question this book seeks to answer.

The advocate's first job is to make connections with the members of her audience. Both persuasion science and rhetorical theory suggest that one thing will in fact lead to another: agreement on premises will lead to agreement on conclusions; agreement on a first, small step will encourage agreement on later, bigger ones. Thus, when legal persuasion is effective, an initial link, a recognized commonality, will lead to a series of subsequent connections: between individuals and categories, legal problems and their settings, argument opportunities and timing, initial arguments and next steps, turning points and resolutions. Even breaking connections depends on making connections. To sever connections, the advocate guides audience members to see alternative cues that link the current situation with perspective-shifting images, stories, or analogies.

The cognitive science view of thinking lends itself to the idea that we see, interpret, and talk about new information and concepts through the filters and frames we have already constructed, that we go through a process of comparing new things to the things we already know: What is *this* like? Into what category does it fit? Is it so unusual that we need to create a new category? After we compare, we argue about the comparisons, either with ourselves or with others: Is *this* new thing more like this option or more like that one? How is it like this? How is it like that? What difference does our choice make?

The purpose of the book is not only to explore how persuasion works, but also and more practically to examine how to construct legal arguments that will effectively connect with particular audiences in specific situations. By taking a rhetorical approach to persuasion, we have integrated research findings from cognitive science with classical and contemporary rhetorical theory, and we have then applied both to the taking apart and the putting together of effective legal arguments. The combination of rhetorical analysis and cognitive science yields a new way of seeing and understanding legal persuasion, one that promises theoretical and practical benefits.

---

1 This example is taken from a Supreme Court case, *Begay v. United States*, 553 U.S. 137 (2008).

First, the book brings together the leading models of persuasion from cognitive science and rhetorical theory. In the process, it blurs the boundaries and leverages the connections between the often-separate spheres of science and rhetoric. Second, the book illustrates persuasive synthesis by working through concrete examples of persuasion from real-life legal contexts. Finally, the book assesses and explains why, how, and when certain persuasive methods and techniques are more effective than others. This assessment and explanation is based not only on our study of rhetorical concepts and persuasion research but also on our testing of what we have found by working through in-depth analyses of actual legal arguments.

The rhetorical approach

Many of the commonplace strategies and techniques used by today's legal advocates derive from Aristotle's *Rhetoric*. First, of course, Aristotle described the well-known modes for inventing persuasive arguments: ethos, logos, pathos, and kairos. (Corbett and Connors 1998). As a mode of invention, *ethos* suggests that the advocate consider arguments based on the knowledge, experience, credibility, integrity, or trustworthiness of the speaker. Ethos may emerge from the character of the advocate herself, from the character of another actor within the argument, or from the sources used in the argument.

Pathos suggests arguments based on building common ground between listener and speaker, or listener and third-party actor. Common ground may emerge from shared emotions, values, beliefs, ideologies, or anything else of substance. *Logos* suggests arguments based on the syllogism or the syllogistic form, including arguments based on enthymemes and analogous cases. As we will discuss later in the book, more flexible argument frames based on metaphor, analogy, and story also draw on the persuasive power of packaging, that is, the audience's inclination to accept an argument that is delivered in a familiar and recognizable organizational package. *Kairos* suggests that the advocate constructing arguments take into account the appropriateness of timing and setting. For example, the "right moment" for an argument is when social conditions make the argument compelling despite its lack of precedential support, as in the *Brown v. Board of Education* (1954) decision that separate but equal schools are inherently unequal.

In addition to these modes of invention centered on different kinds of persuasive appeals, Aristotle categorized a still-helpful laundry list of topics for argument. Applying the "topoi," or the step-by-step process of invention outlined by classical rhetoricians, can be helpful to advocates when they are reading an opinion to examine how the arguments were constructed or generating arguments in support of a given position. As Aristotle pointed out, some topics for argument are inevitable in certain situations. In legal reasoning, advocates know in advance that they must make certain moves: arguing that a particular situation falls within the language of a statute or rule (plain meaning or legislative intent), that this situation is analogous or distinguishable on the facts or the reasoning from a precedent case, or that applying the rule to this situation would further or undermine the policies underlying the rule.

In classical rhetoric, once arguments had been invented, selected, and arranged, the writer or speaker selected a fitting "style" and put them into words. (More contemporary rhetoricians view the whole question of word choices and writing style as an integral part of the blended construction of persuasive arguments.) Classical rhetoricians identified a number of figures of speech, including schemes and tropes. Schemes are a deviation from the ordinary pattern of words, and tropes are a deviation from the ordinary meaning of a word. Many of these style techniques are used to complement and implicitly support other persuasive approaches. For example, the schemes of balance, such as parallelism and antithesis, draw on some of the same psychological influences as priming and syllogistic organization while schemes of unusual or inverted word order, such as anastrophe (inversion of the natural or usual word order), parenthesis, and apposition may contribute to arguments designed to break connections with the status quo.

As for contemporary rhetoric, a grasp of each individual *rhetorical situation* gives the advocate a way to analyze the opposing arguments and the underlying precedent that is essential to crafting responsive arguments. (Bitzer 1968). The key to rhetorical situation analysis is to precisely identify the trigger or the prompt for the advocacy. Different prompts evoke different audiences and impose different constraints on the rhetorical response. In Bitzer's term, a rhetorical situation is marked by an imperfection or problem that encourages the speaker or writer to construct an appropriate argument designed to persuade the relevant audience, that is, an audience with the ability to resolve the problem. For example, in *Walker v. City of Birmingham* (1967), the lawsuit that challenged an injunction against the 1963 Easter civil rights march in Birmingham, Alabama, the justices had very different views of the "imperfection" that called for a rhetorical response.

In *Walker*, Birmingham had denied a parade permit to the civil rights marchers, including the Rev. Dr. Martin Luther King, and then the city obtained an injunction forbidding the marchers from proceeding without a permit. The marchers violated the injunction by marching anyway and were arrested. The Supreme Court was asked to decide that the injunction violated the Constitution. For Justice Stewart, the problem was the marchers' disobedience of an injunction; for Justice Brennan, the problem was the unconstitutional city ordinance under which the injunction was issued. Thus, Justice Stewart described one incident that occurred during the Easter Sunday civil rights march as menacing: "Some 300 or 400 people from among the onlookers followed in a crowd that occupied the entire width of the street and overflowed onto the sidewalks. Violence occurred." (*Walker* 1967). Justice Brennan characterized the same incident as much less disruptive: "The participants in both parades were in every way orderly; the only episode of violence, according to a police inspector, was rock throwing by three onlookers." (*Walker* 1967).

At the core of most modern rhetorical theories of persuasion is Kenneth Burke's concept of *identification*. (Burke 1969). In Burke's concept, identification is both literal and figurative, the sharing of something of substance between speaker and listener. Burke suggested that individuals form their identities through physical objects, work, family, friends, activities, beliefs, and values; they mentally share "substance" with the people and the things with whom they associate; and they mentally separate themselves from other people and things. The shared substances forge identification, and persuasion results: "You persuade a man only insofar as you can talk his language by speech, gesture, tonality, order, image, attitude, idea, identifying your ways with his." (Burke 1969). According to Burke, identification can work in several ways: as a means to an end (we have the same interests); through antithesis (we have the same enemies); and through identification at an unconscious level (we have the same unspoken values).

When it comes to what the classical rhetoricians referred to as style, we assume that the lawyer's writing style, word choices, tone, and mechanics will be designed to meet the needs of her audience and situation. Persuasive arguments will be accurate enough not to mislead (though often depicted from a particular perspective); they will be as brief (or as extended) and as clear (or as nuanced) as fits the audience, situation, and purpose. We also assume that "readability" matters, that is, that all other things being equal, the brief that is more easily read and understood, that helps the reader see where the writer is going, and that keeps the reader on track will be more effective than briefs that are hard to understand. Research mostly backs up this assumption. (Spencer and Feldman 2016). And this assumption makes sense from both rhetorical and persuasion science vantage points. Readability enhances the speaker's credibility (ethos), speaks to the listener's values and interests (pathos), and contributes to our intuitive sense that an argument is logical and valid (logos) because it hangs together.

The science of persuasion

Scientific research into persuasion and human decision making spans a number of fields, and the findings that support much of the guidance provided in this book emerge from cognitive and social psychology. Psychological studies of judicial and juror decision making have proliferated over the last two decades, but little of the persuasion science research has specifically addressed legal persuasion or legal audiences. Nonetheless, the findings provide guidance that helps advocates make more thoughtful decisions under differing circumstances. In addition to better understanding the communication process that leads to persuasion, the science of persuasion has provided concepts and labels that will allow us in this book to identify specific approaches and techniques and to illustrate their use in particular legal documents. (Stanchi 2006).

Contemporary persuasion science has been traced to the studies undertaken by psychologist Carl Hovland when President Franklin D. Roosevelt asked him during World War II to study how to effectively persuade soldiers to engage in continuing battle. (Hovland et al. 1953). The following decades of research led to Richard Petty and John Cacioppo producing an integrated model of persuasion. This model was used to describe how likely it was that audience members would deliberate and reflect on various arguments presented to them. In the Elaboration Likelihood Model (ELM), the thinking involved in decision making was ranked somewhere along a continuum from deep thinking to little active thought. The central route to persuasion – linked to important issues highly relevant to the audience member – required the audience member to carefully consider the information provided, clarify the arguments on both sides, and then make a deliberate and informed choice. On the peripheral route to persuasion, on the other hand, audience members were influenced by more superficial cues (font style, grammar errors, the likeability of the advocate) that produced changes in beliefs and attitudes without the audience member having gone through a recognizably deliberative or reflective process. (Petty and Cacioppo 1986a, 1986b). The influence of this model of thinking can be seen most notably in Daniel Kahneman's delineation between the decision-making processes he labels as System 1 (fast and intuitive) and System 2 (slower and more reflective). (Kahneman 2011).

Although the extent to which an audience may be open to persuasion depends on the surrounding context, including how much the audience member cares about the issue, there are a number of offsetting considerations. These factors affect whether the audience member will deliberate carefully or whether she will use a decision-making shortcut. (Reilly 2013). Audiences in general, and judges in particular, simply may not have enough time to carefully deliberate. And in life as well as judging, there are non-obvious shortcuts, including reliance on the judgment of others around the decision maker. (Cialdini 2006; Mullins 2014).

In addition to identifying the so-called central and peripheral routes to persuasion, persuasion scientists described a tug of war between the speaker's overtures of persuasion and the audience's response of resistance. Various techniques were described that would affect the audience member's motivation and thus increase or lessen her resistance to a particular message. For example, the inoculation technique proposed to inject audience members with a weakened version of the opposing arguments in order to stimulate longer-term resistance to those arguments by in effect preempting the attacks. (McGuire 1964).

Cognitive scientists also revealed that all decision making is affected by a range of unconscious cognitive biases, mostly reflecting the mind's tendency to make the quick-and-easy connection. Along with his long-time research partner Amos Tversky, Kahneman was a pioneer in exploring these biases, notably including such framing effects as loss aversion (the preference for avoiding loss as opposed to acquiring gains) and the representativeness heuristic (the tendency to judge the likelihood of something based on what we think is a "typical" case). Cognitive bias is one area in which legal scholars have begun to pay attention to the methods and findings of psychology, thanks in large part to the work of Jeff Rachlinski, who has published a series of important and informative articles examining whether judges are susceptible to the same cognitive biases as layperson decision makers. (Guthrie et al. 2001, 2007).

Finally, any description of the most influential findings of modern persuasion science would include the tools identified by Robert Cialdini based on his own extensive fieldwork. (Cialdini 2006). Most often applied to negotiation, these tools are of significant use to written advocacy as well. For example, the concept of persuading others through the use of reciprocity can be seen when advocates make concessions that ease the way toward identifying the more important issues and arguments. Cialdini's finding that audiences are influenced by commitment and consistency can be seen in the argumentation techniques that begin in small agreement and build in steps to eventually reach broader agreement. Similarly, the concern for consistency is illustrated in studies indicating that polling jury members in public while they are deliberating may result in their being less willing to change their positions, a result that may mean more hung juries over time. (Mullins 2014).

Some caution is necessary in applying the methods and findings of persuasion science to legal persuasion and decision making. As already mentioned, few of the persuasion studies addressed legal decision making or explored the ramifications of applying to lawyers or judges the lessons learned from research studies in which other kinds of audiences were tested. (Stanchi 2006). Moreover, legal audiences may react differently to persuasive messages than other audiences do. Lawyers and judges are often thought to be most comfortable with traditional approaches to legal reasoning and argumentation. And this might suggest that the legal audience is more likely to be persuaded by conventional techniques than by approaches that challenge or deviate from tradition. (Stanchi 2006).

A note about audience

Throughout this introduction, and throughout the book, we refer to "audience" and the importance of connecting with "audience." To write a coherent account of persuasion, we had to consider the legal audience collectively and somewhat monolithically even though the audience for legal advocacy can of course vary widely. We tackle the judicial audience (as opposed to the non-law-trained audience) in Chapter 3, because we believe that law training can affect a person's view of what is persuasive. But the book does not venture beyond the distinction between law-trained and non-law-trained. How an administrative judge reacts to an argument may be very different from how a legislative aide reacts to a lobbying attempt, and different federal or state judges on the same court can react quite differently to different arguments depending on a whole host of diverse characteristics ranging from age, gender, and race to personal experience and beyond.

That said, we believe that there are significant commonalities in the way that human beings respond to advocacy and that it is possible to generalize about what "works" to persuade and what does not. If we didn't believe that, we couldn't have written a book! We believe that the principles explored in this book can be used to inform legal advocacy of all kinds, before all manner of legal audiences, both law trained and not. As always, the advocate must be judicious and careful about choosing tactics, as not all tactics will be effective with all audiences. But an overarching goal of this book is to help advocates choose more wisely by explaining in more depth why some tactics are effective and others not. This will help the advocate choose among tactics, regardless of the particular legal audience the advocate is facing.

We acknowledge that most of our examples – though not all – come from written briefs, and mostly appellate briefs, which means that most of the examples are focused on the law-trained audience. But we stress that the book is meant for lawyers of all stripes – appellate lawyers, trial lawyers, transactional, and beyond. Our choice of examples is largely due to availability and accessibility – appellate briefs are widely published and the cases tend to be well known. Trial transcripts, administrative briefs, and other legal documents are a bit more difficult to come by. And trial tactics are quite a bit more difficult to excerpt effectively as compared with written advocacy. In our view, it is easier for a reader to see an example pulled from a discrete paragraph in a brief: with only a short explanation, the reader can see the use of the tactic in that discrete paragraph without having to read the entire document. This is harder to do with a trial transcript, even an opening or closing argument, because so often the tactics are interwoven with the "big picture" of the trial in a way that makes them difficult to sever without losing meaning.

That is all to say that although the book is meant to be a general primer on legal persuasion, we recognize that not all of the tactics will be usable in all contexts or with all audiences. We acknowledge that as part of the rich study of persuasion. We trust our readers to use the deeper explanations and rationales we provide to generalize from the examples. We hope that by combining examples with deep explanation of the reasons the tactics work, we will give advocates the information they need to make their own, fully informed choices about when to use the tactics and before which audiences to employ them.

How the book is organized

Because it provides the basis for our conclusion that making connections is the crux of persuasion, the book begins with a short overview of thinking and decision making, drawing on a blended version of cognitive science and rhetoric. From there, we address the setting for legal persuasion, going into some detail about what studies have found to be characteristic of the judicial audience in particular. To understand the setting for persuasion, the advocate must also explore other aspects of the context for specific legal arguments, including the complexities of matching an individual argument to the right time and place.

Following the rhetorical roadmap, we move next to the process of constructing arguments, or what classical rhetoricians called invention. The chapters clustered together in this section first explore how analysis can uncover pre-existing stories, stereotypes, and images that affect decision makers. The chapters in this section then move to the process of creating effective fact and law stories as well as metaphors and factual analogies.

In the next cluster, we consider what the classical rhetoricians called "arrangement" or the techniques of persuasion that are based on order and on making connections among parts of arguments, first priming, and then syllogisms and case analogies. The final cluster considers the ways in which the tone of our arguments can affect persuasion.

Cases & briefs

Begay v. United States, 553 U.S. 137 (2008).
Brown v. Board of Education, 347 U.S. 483 (1954).
Walker v. City of Birmingham, 388 U.S. 307 (1968).

Bibliography

Bitzer, L.F., 1968, 'The Rhetorical Situation', *Philosophy and Rhetoric*, 1, 1–14.
Burke, K., 1969, *A Rhetoric of Motives*, rev. edn., University of California Press, Los Angeles.
Cialdini, R.B., 2006, *Influence: The Psychology of Persuasion*, rev. edn., Harper Business, New York.
Corbett, E.P.J. and Connors, R.J., 1998, *Classical Rhetoric for the Modern Student*, 4th edn., Oxford University Press, Oxford.
Frost, M., 1990, 'Brief Rhetoric – A Note on Classical and Modern Theories of Forensic Discourse', *Kansas Law Review*, 38, 411–431.

Guthrie, C., Rachlinski, J.J. and Wistrich, A.J., 2001, 'Inside the Judicial Mind', *Cornell Law Review*, 86, 777–830.

Guthrie, C., Rachlinski, J.J. and Wistrich, A.J., 2007, 'Blinking on the Bench: How Judges Decide Cases', *Cornell Law Review*, 93, 1–44.

Hovland, C.I., Janis, I.L. and Kelly, H.H., 1953, *Communication and Persuasion: Psychological Studies of Opinion Change*, 1st edn., Yale University Press, New Haven.

Kahneman, D., 2011, *Thinking, Fast and Slow*, Farrar, Straus and Giroux, New York.

McGuire, W. J., 1964, 'Inducing Resistance to Persuasion: Some Contemporary Approaches', in L. Berkowitz (ed.), *Advances in Experimental Psychology*, vol. 1, pp. 191–229, Academic Press, New York.

Mullins, A.E., 2014, 'Subtly Selling the System: Where Psychological Influence Tactics Lurk in Judicial Writing', *University of Richmond Law Review*, 48, 1111–1156.

Petty, R.E. and Cacioppo, J.T., 1986a, 'The Elaboration Likelihood Model of Persuasion', in L. Berkowitz (ed.), *Advances in Experimental Social Psychology*, vol. 19, pp. 124–207, Academic Press, New York.

Petty, R.E. and Cacioppo, J.T., 1986b, *Communication and Persuasion: Central and Peripheral Routes to Attitude Change*, Springer, New York.

Reilly, P., 2013, 'Resistance Is Not Futile: Harnessing the Power of Counter-Offensive Tactics in Legal Persuasion', *Hastings Law Journal*, 28, 1171–1228.

Spencer, S.B. and Feldman, A., 2016, 'The Relationship Between Brief Clarity and Summary Judgment Decisions', viewed 18 October 2016, from https://ssrn.com/abstract=2807045

Stanchi, K.M., 2006, 'The Science of Persuasion: An Initial Exploration', *Michigan State Law Review*, 2006(2), 412–456.

Winter, Steven L., 2003, *A Clearing in the Forest: Law, Life, and Mind*, University of Chicago Press, Chicago, IL.

2

THINKING AND DECISION MAKING

Starting to persuade

Even the best plan rarely survives "contact with the enemy." (Heath and Heath 2007). Taking such real-life lessons into account, this book meshes planning with action, persuasion science with rhetorical experience. Think about how Google's mapping application tells you the shortest route from point A to point B. Remember that the plan does you little good when the Memorial Day parade overwhelms ordinary traffic patterns and turns all the busy streets in your neighborhood into one-way thoroughfares. In traffic, as in legal persuasion, the chances of navigating successfully are boosted when you can draw on a combination of science and experience.

How we think

Thinking as chunking

Because of their role in thinking and decision making, storytelling, metaphor-making, and analogizing form the core of communication. This is aptly illustrated in cognitive science's depiction of the mind in the statement that *the mind is a computer* and the resulting inferential leap that thinking is akin to information processing. Even though we understand that the metaphor is not literally true, its widespread use for decades has come to affect and even govern our ability to think about thinking.

According to researchers in the cognitive sciences, we learn by constructing mental images and frameworks over time, then by calling up from memory those that are most accessible or those that seem most comparable whenever we encounter new information. Thinking thus becomes primarily a process of comparison: we see and we understand new data by making connections between what we encounter in the world and the knowledge structures that exist in our memory. (Hofstadter 2001; Gentner et al. 2001).

From this perspective, the critical step in thinking is our ability and propensity to recognize patterns – in other words, to make connections. As we learn, we sort and "chunk" new information into schemas or knowledge structures that we embed in memory. Once we have built up these memory banks, we search through them whenever we confront new information, looking for the knowledge structures (or categories) that will help us perceive and interpret what we've seen. Our often-unconscious choice of which category is the best match affects our view of the new information; it "filters" what we see and "frames" the way that we understand it.

When we encounter new information in the world, why do we "chunk" pieces together and then slot them into preexisting categories in our minds? In a short story by Jorge Luis Borges, the protagonist, Funes, remembered every detail, "not only every leaf of every tree of every wood, but also every one of the times he had perceived or imagined it." To manage this torrent of memories, Funes "decided to reduce each of his past days to some seventy thousand memories, which would then be defined by means of ciphers." He changed his mind when he realized that the project would be both interminable and useless. Although Funes was only nineteen, "by the hour of his death he would not even have finished classifying all the memories of his childhood." (Borges 2001).

Chunking – putting things into categories – helps make understanding possible. In his focus on the details, Funes could not understand that a category such as *dog* included many different individual animals and that a dog who looked different from one side would fall into the same category as the same dog seen from the front. As Borges wrote, "To think is to forget differences, generalize, make abstractions. In the teeming world of Funes, there were only details." (Borges 2001).

This ability to think generally and abstractly in order to construct categories is also necessary to memory. Douglas Hofstadter concluded that babies do not remember events because they are not yet far enough along in the "relentless, lifelong process of chunking." Without a "repertoire of concepts" in their minds, babies "look at life through a randomly drifting keyhole," able to make out only the smallest and nearest aspects of what they see before them. (Hofstadter 2001).

This view of cognition assumes that people naturally and intuitively reflect about what has happened to them in the past. Based on their reflection, they construct stories and frameworks out of the details of their lives and the world. As we grow older, our frameworks become more nuanced and sophisticated. Because incoming stimuli rarely fit exactly a mental category that already exists, more advanced chunks become necessary. When we recognize that the new information does not fully match a prior category, we try to pick out new patterns, often forming additional abstract concepts. As it became clear, for example, that violent abuse involving personal relationships occurred not only in marriages and not only when the husband was the abuser and the wife was the victim, the category of intimate partner violence came to replace the former category of domestic violence, which itself had replaced even older concepts such as wife battering. Category construction and abstract thinking thus grow out of our ability to analogize, or to engage in what Hofstadter terms:

> the mental mapping onto each other of two entities – one old and sound asleep in the recesses of long-term memory, the other new and gaily dancing on the mind's center stage – that in fact differ from each other in a myriad of ways.
>
> *(Hofstadter 2001)*

Thinking as arguing

Aristotle defined rhetoric as "an ability, in each particular case, to see the available means of persuasion." (Kennedy 1991). This conception of rhetoric works in tandem with cognitive science. The blend with cognitive science is even more appropriate given contemporary rhetoricians' broader definition of "rhetoric" as the study of all the ways in which humans use symbols to communicate. (Foss et al. 2002). Though not yet the prevailing view, the potentially rich relationship of rhetoric and cognitive psychology is recognized by experts. Some authors claim that much of social psychology can be viewed as an effort to empirically test classical rhetorical concepts. (Billig 1996). Moreover, research into the psychology of persuasion has been described as the new rhetoric (Brewster Smith 1981), and Aristotle has been called the "world's first published social psychologist." (Aronson 2011).

Expanding the cognitive science explanation that human thinking is primarily a matter of categorizing, the rhetorical perspective values both the ability to analogize (and categorize) and the ability to differentiate (and particularize). Both strategies are essential if we are to engage in argument. While cognitive social psychologists suggest that we need to categorize in order to simplify, rhetoricians recognize that we need to be able to differentiate and particularize in order to manage the complexities of individual situations. Fortunately, any new bit of information can be considered either as a potential particularity or as a potential member of a category. For example, the government official who usually follows a standard routine to process individual requests may treat an otherwise run-of-the-mill request with particularity when the request is made by a relative or friend or when it will involve an unusually large financial gain.

From this rhetorical perspective, human thinking develops not by information processing – as the computer model suggests – but in a more complex and recursive way through direct interactions between the human thinker and the world. (Epstein 2016; Searle 1990). Recursively, individual thinkers move back and forth between categories and particular instances. (Billig 1996). Thinking's main component becomes "a form of internal argument, modeled on outward dialogue." In this view, thinking follows Protagoras's direction that for every question there are (at least) two opposite answers. From there, the crucial rhetorical activities can be seen as justification of one position and criticism of another. And for the rhetorician, these rhetorical activities can be understood only within the context of an individual situation.

Cognitive scientists and rhetoricians agree that selection – whether conscious or not – is involved in thinking. Sometimes selection appears to be an efficient shortcut; at other times, it takes the form of a destructive cognitive bias. Either way, selection is inevitable because our capacity to perceive can never encompass the entire picture. Our ability to explain and describe falls short of the full story. Some things must always be brightly lit, and others eclipsed. Moreover, according to Michael Billig, whenever selection is involved, we are already engaged in particularization because we are treating one category out of many categories as being uniquely appropriate. So "our basic cognitive processes [do not] merely function to provide psychological stability and order. They also provide the seeds of argumentation and deliberation." (Billig 1996). When, for example, we notice a stranger in our neighborhood, we sort through and select among many possible categories into which she might fit, using only the very imperfect and partial information available to us. Is she a visitor, a salesperson, a worker, a tourist, the new neighbor, or a potential criminal? This thinking process may assure us (sometimes without basis) that we are correct in our categorization or it may prompt us to seek out more information to make a more reflective choice.

How we decide

Intuitive and deliberative decision making

Our audiences are many; we encounter them in an array of rhetorical situations; and they make different kinds of choices. Though many differences exist, we ask all of them to decide. And when it comes to describing decision making, most psychologists now focus on systems of intuition and deliberation that interact with one another, sometimes in recursive or repetitive fashion. As the name suggests, intuitive processes are mostly automatic and unconscious (much as the categorization model of thinking suggests) while deliberative processes are more effortful and reflective (much as the internal argument model of thinking describes). (Berger 2013).

For convenience, researchers have labeled these processes as System 1 (thinking "fast" or intuitively) and System 2 (thinking "slow" or reflectively). In a typical short-hand description, System 1 "is rapid, intuitive, emotional, and prone to bias," while System 2 "is more deliberate, more reflective, more dispassionate, and (it is said) more accurate." These processes and labels have become well known through Daniel Kahneman's book, *Thinking, Fast and Slow.* (Kahneman 2011).

Among the best known of Kahneman's experiments is the "Linda problem," designed to show how predispositions affect our judgment and overcome our knowledge of statistical probabilities. In the Linda problem, Kahneman posits that "Linda is thirty-one years old, single, outspoken, and very bright. She majored in philosophy. As a student, she was deeply concerned about issues of discrimination and social justice and also participated in antinuclear demonstrations." The researchers ask a combination of questions, concluding with:

> Which alternative is more probable?
> Linda is a bank teller.
> Linda is a bank teller and is active in the feminist movement.

A majority of those answering usually choose the second option, which, according to typical deductive logic, is the incorrect answer. The second option is incorrect because the group of people who are bank tellers must be larger than the group of people who are both bank tellers and feminists. Kahneman explained the wrong answers as stemming from a logical error he describes as "representativeness": the most coherent and plausible explanation is that a person with those personality attributes most likely would be a feminist and so if she was a bank teller, she had to be a feminist too. (Kahneman 2011).

While Kahneman studied error in decision making, and his studies focused on questions with right or wrong answers, another school of thought studied successful problem solving prompted by expert intuition. This kind of "intuition," scientist Gary Klein discovered, was not a gut reaction. (Klein 1999, 2009). Instead, this "intuition" depended on an initial flash of recognition and went on from there to testing the options. A "cue" in the current situation alerted the problem solver to an analogous pattern in a past experience, allowing the expert to select among and draw upon past or known experiences to come up with potential solutions, usually in the form of alternative, but still parallel, patterns or paths. Gathering information by extracting stories from a range of experts, Klein found that in real-life complex situations, experts relied on this kind of expert intuition to identify workable options to test.

A recent prototype of this kind of expert intuition is well known:

> On January 15, 2009, at 3:25 p.m., US Airways Flight 1529, an Airbus 320, took off from LaGuardia Airport in New York on its way to Charlotte, North Carolina. Two minutes after the takeoff, the airplane hit a flock of Canadian geese and lost thrust in both of its engines. The captain, Chesley B. "Sully" Sullenberger III, and the first officer, Jeffrey Skiles, safely landed the airplane in the Hudson River at 3:31 p.m. All 150 passengers plus the five crew members were rescued.
>
> *(Klein 2009)*

Captain Sullenberger had been flying airplanes for almost forty years. He had been an Air Force fighter pilot and a glider pilot as well as a commercial airline pilot; he had participated in many airline crash investigations; he was involved in developing and teaching techniques for managing airplane emergencies. Sullenberger's decision making followed the process suggested by Klein's intuitive decision-making model. He first considered the option of returning to LaGuardia, but realized that the airplane would not make it that far; he then considered the option of finding another airport, but almost immediately decided that was too far as well. So he settled on the third option, landing in the Hudson River.

In a joint project, Kahneman and Klein agreed that intuitive expertise existed under conditions such as those affecting Sullenberger: the expert had accumulated a great deal of repeated experience and had received accurate feedback on most prior occasions. (Kahneman and Klein 2009). The difference in their descriptions was emphasis. Klein projected a two-step process in which intuitive matches are brought to mind for reflective testing; we can see this in the Sullenberger example above. Kahneman viewed System 2 thinking as a constant monitoring mechanism that exists to correct intuitive thinking. Under this model, Sullenberger's first and strongest instinct might have been to return to LaGuardia, but his System 2 thinking overrode that as unlikely to succeed.

Following Kahneman, Jonathan Haidt has suggested that emotions – often related to System 1 thinking – do more to drive decision making than is commonly acknowledged. Haidt concluded that the "emotional dog" wags the "rational tail"; in other words, our "reasoning" is often employed to justify the decisions we reach on the basis of what he termed an unreflective emotional response. In one experiment, more than 70 percent of people refused to sign a contract to sell their soul to the researcher for $2, even though the contract itself said that it was not real or binding. Haidt used the label "moral dumbfounding" to describe this phenomenon of stubbornly maintaining one's initial judgments based on an immediate emotional response despite logical arguments to the contrary. (Haidt 2012).

We like to think of ourselves as being reflective and analytical. But most experts agree that we have no choice but to accept our need for intuitive decision making to get through the day. Like Funes with his billions of details, we could not act if we had to reflect every time we encountered a traffic light: what does "red" mean at this street? Is it different from what it meant at the last street?

The point is to try to distinguish situations in which our intuitive decisions lead us astray from those in which we have enough experience to rely on our judgment to call up options for testing. This translates into advocacy. Advocates who are thoughtful in their persuasive choices recognize the distinction between valuable uses of experienced intuition by decision makers and the harmful application of stereotypical thinking. They know that decision making most often blends the processes of intuition and reflection. And they craft their advocacy strategies with those principles in mind.

How we argue

Arguing about categories

Imagine that the President calls a military engagement a "rescue mission" rather than an "invasion." One name calls up one category, and the other label suggests an entirely different picture with its associated network of meanings. As this example illustrates, the categories that we use for thinking and decision making do not suddenly appear with accurate labels already stuck to their backs nor are their boundaries or centers well defined.

Advocacy thus encompasses our selection of categories and our designation of their defining characteristics. When we create and name categories, we are drawing on two of the primary sources of persuasive arguments: the ability to "name" things and the ability to "negate." We can argue that the category of dogs (naming) includes a poodle but not a wolf (negating). (Billig 1996). According to rhetoricians, as we categorize, we move back and forth between categorization and particularization. Through this process, we create arguments about what the category should be called, what its boundaries are, and what its core or essence is. For example, the category of "mother" might encompass birth mothers, stepmothers, adoptive mothers, women who play a parenting role, caregivers, parents of any gender, family leaders, founders, or predecessors. Its essence might be found in biology, actions, emotions, history, culture, or relationships. When the word "mother" is used in a statute, advocates might argue that the intended or understood meaning should encompass any or all of these individuals and characteristics.

From the cognitive science perspective, the use of categories is efficient, whether categorizing happens consciously or unconsciously. By helping us chunk, categories help us sort. As in the waiter example in Chapter 1, making connections between what we perceive and the frameworks we have already constructed in our minds eases comprehension and action. The scripts and schemas that accompany the category help us focus on what's important. They help us "place" items in time and place. They lead to inferences and assumptions. (Chen and Hanson 2004).

Because mental categories are embedded not only through individual experience but also through shared history, language, and culture, the legal advocate may be able to persuade by taking advantage of easy matches. Ready-made labels categorize complex situations and intuitively suggest simple responses. When a judge confronts a deadbeat dad, the solution that comes to mind is to make the father financially responsible (even in circumstances where that is an impossibility because he is, for example, incapacitated or imprisoned). When a lower-level hourly employee is said to suffer from burnout, the natural response is to reduce the employee's working hours (even in circumstances where the reduction in pay makes the employee's living conditions impossible).

For the purposes of persuasion, advocates have several alternatives for making arguments based on categories. First, the advocate may argue about the construction of a category: What is the category's label? What does it include? What is the characteristic that determines what items fit and what items do not? Second, the advocate may argue about what categories match a particular situation. Many potential matches exist, but some will be favored. As will be discussed in later chapters, advocates may consciously choose to prompt persuasive connections to particular categories.

∞ Case study: arguments about categories in California v. Carney

The Fourth Amendment requires the police to get a warrant before they search your home. The U.S. Supreme Court has recognized an automobile exception to the warrant requirement for two reasons. First, automobiles are easily moved and thus their drivers and occupants might flee before the warrant could be obtained. Second, extensive state regulation of automobiles – along with the public's ability to see inside the vehicles when they are traveling on public streets and highways – means that the owner and those inside the car have lesser expectations of privacy than residents inside their homes. *California v. Carney* (1985) raised a classic category argument to be resolved by the U.S. Supreme Court: Should a motor home be considered a home or an automobile? The majority held that the motor home's mobility made it more like a car, and thus it fell within the exception to the requirement that police get a warrant before conducting a search. At the same time, the dissent contended that this particular motor home, outfitted with furniture and curtains, should be viewed as a home, particularly because any exception to a general rule of constitutional protection should be narrowly interpreted. The justices argued back and forth in the way that category arguments typically proceed: What categories might be relevant? What does the category of automobiles contain? How about the category of homes? What characteristics are most important? Which category fits this situation best?

Arguing from inconsistency

When we consider one of our colleagues to be a competitor for a promotion in the workplace, we may disapprove of her tendency to spend weekends working at the office on tedious and mundane details. But when we are working collaboratively with her on a particular project, our impression of her work habits will be much more favorable. We can resolve the resulting cognitive dilemma by explaining to ourselves that the current project is critically important and outside the normal routine, thus justifying our revised interpretation.

Cognitive scientists suggest that one of our major motivations is to avoid the mental discomfort created by conflicting impressions. We would like to maintain a consistent outlook on the world. So we channel the contrary sense perception in a way that alleviates our discomfort. According to the cognitive dissonance theory proposed by Leon Festinger, when two thoughts are inconsistent, we work to align our thoughts with our actions or our actions with our thoughts. (Festinger 1957).

As a result, arguments may be based not only on actual inconsistencies but also on the criticism that a position is or appears to be inconsistent. That criticism sets in motion the rhetorical motive to respond or to defend.

Earlier in the argument creation process, rather than being something to avoid, ambiguity and inconsistency serve as the rhetorical breeding ground for arguments. Thus, instead of avoiding inconsistencies, the rhetorician often ends up deliberately searching for them. Only when individual circumstances are different – when inconsistencies exist – are imaginative resolutions and new insights possible.

∞ Case study: arguments from inconsistency in Boykin v. Alabama

Just as *California v. Carney* is a classic example of an argument about categories, *Boykin v. Alabama* (1969) is a prototype for arguments from inconsistency. In *Boykin*, the defendant pleaded guilty to a series of armed robberies in Mobile, Alabama, and (incomprehensibly to many people today) was sentenced to death. The record did not show that the judge had asked Boykin whether he entered his plea knowingly and voluntarily nor did it show that Boykin was aware of his constitutional rights to trial by jury and to confront his accusers. Pursuant to Alabama law, a jury trial was held to determine Boykin's punishment. Boykin offered no testimony or evidence before the jury determined that he should be sentenced to death. The Supreme Court of Alabama affirmed the death sentence, but three justices dissented on the grounds that because the trial court record was silent as to the plea, it did not show that the petitioner entered his plea knowingly and voluntarily.

In the U.S. Supreme Court, Justice William Douglas delivered the opinion of the majority, holding that a silent record is insufficient to show that a guilty plea has been made voluntarily. It is simply inconsistent, he determined, to assume without some affirmative statement in the record that the defendant had knowingly and voluntarily entered a guilty plea. In the analogous situation of a confession made outside the courtroom, Justice Douglas pointed out that the prosecution must prove that the confession was voluntary before it may be admitted. When a guilty plea is entered inside the courtroom, Justice Douglas concluded that the Constitution required a similar showing of voluntariness.

Summary

Thinking involves a back-and-forth of generalizing and particularizing: chunking new information into categories and arguing about individual situations. Similarly, decision making takes place automatically and unconsciously as well as reflectively and deliberately. Advocates who understand the general nature of intuitive and deliberative decision-making systems can be more selective about their persuasive strategies and approaches, crafting different responses to different rhetorical situations.

Cases & briefs

Boykin v. Alabama, 395 U.S. 238 (1969).
California v. Carney, 471 U.S. 386 (1985).

Bibliography

Aronson, E., 2011, *The Social Animal*, 11th edn., Worth Publishers, New York.
Berger, L., 2013, 'A Revised View of the Judicial Hunch', *Legal Communication & Rhetoric: JALWD*, 10, 1–45.
Billig, M., 1996, *Arguing and Thinking: A Rhetorical Approach to Social Psychology*, 2nd edn., Cambridge University Press, Cambridge.
Borges, J.L., 2001, 'Funes the Memorious', transl. J.E. Irby, in J. Rasula and S. McCaffery (eds.), *Imagining Language: An Anthology*, pp. 320–325, MIT Press, Cambridge, MA.
Brewster Smith, M., 1981, 'Foreword', in R.E. Petty, T.M. Ostrom and T.C. Brock (eds.), *Cognitive Responses in Persuasion*, 1st edn., pp. xi–xii, Psychology Press, New York.
Chen, R.C. and Hanson, J.D., 2004, 'Categorically Biased: The Influence of Knowledge Structures on Law and Legal Theory', *Southern California Law Review*, 77, 1103–1253.
Epstein, R., 2016, 'The Empty Brain', *Aeon*, viewed from https://aeon.co/essays/your-brain-does-not-process-information-and-it-is-not-a-computer
Festinger, L., 1957, *A Theory of Cognitive Dissonance*, Stanford University Press, Stanford, CA.
Foss, S., Foss, K. and Trapp, R., 2002, *Contemporary Perspectives on Rhetoric*, 3rd edn., Waveland Press, Prospect Heights, IL.
Gentner, D., Bowdle, B., Wolff, P. and Boronat, C., 2001, 'Metaphor Is Like Analogy', in D. Gentner, K.J. Holyoak and B.N. Kokinov (eds.), *The Analogical Mind: Perspectives From Cognitive Science*, pp. 199–255, MIT Press, Cambridge, MA.
Haidt, J., 2012, *The Righteous Mind: Why Good People Are Divided by Politics and Religion*, Pantheon, New York.
Heath, C. and Heath, D., 2007, *Made to Stick: Why Some Ideas Survive and Others Die*, Random House, New York.
Hofstadter, D.R., 2001, 'Epilogue: Analogy as the Core of Cognition', in D. Gentner, K.J. Holyoak and B.N. Kokinov (eds.), *The Analogical Mind: Perspectives From Cognitive Science*, pp. 499–538, MIT Press, Cambridge, MA.
Kahneman, D., 2011, *Thinking, Fast and Slow*, Farrar, Straus and Giroux, New York.
Kahneman, D. and Klein, G., 2009, 'Conditions for Intuitive Expertise: A Failure to Disagree', *American Psychologist*, 64(6), 515–526.
Kennedy, G.A., 1991, *Aristotle On Rhetoric: A Theory of Civic Discourse*, Oxford University Press, Oxford.
Klein, G., 1999, *Sources of Power: How People Make Decisions*, MIT Press, Cambridge, MA.
Klein, G., 2009, *Streetlights and Shadows: Searching for the Keys to Adaptive Decision Making*, MIT Press, Cambridge, MA.
Searle, J.R., 1990, 'Is the Brain's Mind a Computer Program?', *Scientific American*, January, 26–31.

PART II

Setting

Audience, timing, and location

When we talk about "setting," we mean much more than just place or location. The setting for legal persuasion is the context for the argument, or the world within which the argument takes place, including not only the "where," but also the "who" and the "when." Thus, when we talk about setting, we include audience and timing.

Because there are many settings for legal advocacy, it is crucial to any advocate's planning to assess her audience and to consider how the time and place of the dispute may affect the chances for communication and persuasion. Chapter 3 will focus on the "who" of the setting, concentrating especially on judges. As Chapter 3 will describe, decision-making studies indicate that judges are affected by many of the same influences as the rest of us, and so persuasion that is sensitive to underlying attitudes and beliefs and blends together appeals to reason, emotion, and values will likely be more effective. In Chapter 4, we focus on timing and location by exploring the rhetorical concept of *kairos*. Kairos differs from chronological time in its emphasis on the most opportune time to make a particular argument – and on the idea that there is an essential moment in time that captures the heart of the problem. Advocates should be aware of kairos as a means of identifying potential tipping points, but they also should recognize that turning points can be created through the lawyer's efforts.

3

THE JUDICIAL AUDIENCE

Any treatment of persuasion must concern itself with audience. The identity and characteristics of the target of the persuasion can influence and alter the process and substance of the persuasive message. In law, the question is complicated by the range and diversity of potential audience members; lawyers need to persuade jurors, single judges, panels of judges, and often other lawyers. All of these targets present different challenges for the legal advocate.

Throughout this book, we begin from the premise that all the targets of legal persuasion share certain decision-making attributes and that a solid understanding of those attributes can be gleaned from the science and theory of rhetoric and persuasion. In that spirit, our hope is that the principles outlined in the book will work effectively with most target audiences, whether judges, jurors, or others.

But, as lawyers, we also know that in many ways law is a unique culture with its own rules and conventions about what is relevant and persuasive. This unique culture, inculcated and reinforced by legal training and law practice, has to be considered in any discussion of legal persuasion.

With this in mind, Chapter 3 focuses on the judicial audience and what we know specifically about how judges decide and what persuades them. In doing so, we are mindful that, of course, different judges in different situations may decide in different ways and be persuaded by different approaches. The motivations and constraints on a federal district court judge are different from those of a Supreme Court justice or a New Jersey state appellate judge. Nevertheless, we believe that it is possible to outline a coherent set of guiding principles that allow us a starting point for determining what persuades the judicial audience.

What judges say

He was the second person to use the metaphor that day. But it is Chief Justice Roberts who is most often quoted as saying during his Senate confirmation hearing that *judges are umpires* whose role is limited to calling balls and strikes.

> Umpires don't make the rules, they apply them. The role of an umpire and a judge is critical. They make sure everybody plays by the rules, but it is a limited role. Nobody ever went to a ballgame to see the umpire.
>
> *(Roberts 2005)*

Justice Roberts's often-quoted view that what judges do is simply take the rules of law and apply them somewhat mechanically to the facts of given cases has been rejected by most legal thinkers. (Baum 2008; Simon 2004). Yet it endures especially in what judges say about what they do and in the language of judicial opinions. (Simon 1998). Judge Harry Edwards has famously said that the "law" and not the political preferences of judges controls legal decision making. (Edwards 1985). This view, sometimes referred to as the formalist view of decision making, sees law as a set of objectively verifiable rules that need only be identified and then applied to a given situation. Under this view, a judge's political views, emotions, experiences, and psychology do not influence the process.

Although psychologists warn that most people do not have a good sense of what truly persuades them because persuasion largely happens subconsciously (Cialdini 2006), we also know that the conventions of a discipline can be important because shared values are a key component of persuasion. (Smith 2008). Moreover, people are more comfortable and psychologically susceptible to being persuaded if they are confronted with material that is familiar and expected. There are certainly times when taking a decision maker outside her comfort zone can be persuasive – and we talk about some of those times later in the book. But those times are exceptions to the general rule that a recognizable, familiar approach is often the most persuasive.

When judges talk about what persuades them, the influence of the mechanistic "balls and strikes" view of legal analysis is apparent. As Professor Dan Simon eloquently puts it "even though legal formalism has been officially discredited, even scorned, its ghosts continue to whisper to us that any other type of judging is simply unlawful." (Simon 1998). Judges say they want lawyers to get to the point, lay out the law, and show how the law applies to the facts. (Robbins 2002; Voros 2011). Because of time constraints, judges report that they prefer lawyers to get to the disputed point early and use traditional "tried and true" organizational styles, such as syllogistic organization. (Robbins 2002; Voros 2011). Judges also consistently emphasize candor: they want lawyers to address opposing arguments and adverse authority honestly and forthrightly. (Voros 2011; Aldisert 2003).

Judges also tend to deny that politics and emotions influence them. (Edwards 1985; Scalia and Garner 2008). This traditional view of decision making as dispassionate and objective sees the rule of law as a mechanism for avoiding emotion's effects on decision making. (Bandes 2009; Maroney and Gross 2014).

Even if we suspect that judges may not be wholly accurate in describing what persuades them, we nevertheless must consider what judges say because they believe it.

In law, for example, that may mean tempering emotional arguments, even though it is beyond dispute that emotions drive decision making, because judges find overt emotional appeals inappropriate and may be annoyed by them. It may mean disclosing an adverse fact or authority, even if we think it is irrelevant, because the judge expects it.

Models of judicial decision making

But what judges tell us about what persuades them is only part of the story. Indeed, commentators across law, political science, and psychology have criticized as inaccurate the mechanistic "balls and strikes" approach described by judges.

The accounts of how judges decide are copious and often conflicting. Legal commentary in particular has varied and evolved, with the formalism of the classical view overtaken by legal realists who emphasized the primacy of experience over formal logic and critical legal scholars who focused on judging as largely result oriented. The psychological and political commentaries have been similarly varied, with some models emphasizing that decision making is driven by a judge's attitudes or values and others focusing on cognitive processes. We outline some of the principal theories here.

If a single theme can be drawn from current research and theories of how judges (and juries) make decisions, it is that the decision maker engages in "sensemaking" or in constructing plausible stories or frameworks that make sense of what they have been told. (Berger 2013; Pennington and Hastie 1991). These theories describe an unconscious process in which the decision maker's implicit knowledge and experience intuitively affect his or her perceptions and impressions, and those in turn add up to an increasingly coherent and cohesive whole. (Berger 2013).

As introduced in Chapter 1, most models agree that judicial decision making is a combination of intuitive and deliberative judgment, also called System 1 and System 2 thinking. (Guthrie et al. 2007; Kahneman 2011). Intuition, the judicial "hunch," can be useful for problem solving because it helps generate solutions to problems and helps test the efficacy of solutions by mentally simulating them. (Berger 2013). But intuition can also lead to inaccurate judgments and biases because it often relies on shortcuts such as stereotypes and heuristics. In other words, intuition allows judges to see the full range of solutions to a problem, but it can sometimes generate an inaccurate solution or judgment. When this happens, a judge may persist in that first "snap" judgment, and then look for reasons in the law and factual record to support it. (Simon and Scurich 2013; Haidt 2001). Or, the judge may reevaluate and reject the original System 1 judgment and override it by engaging in more deliberate System 2 thinking. (Guthrie et al. 2007).

Moreover, despite the traction of the unidimensional result-oriented view, more current models regard judicial decision making as a result of numerous complex motivations. Rather than being motivated purely by policy goals, judges decide through a complicated and multidimensional process involving the intersection of cognition, motivation, emotion, political preference, experience, and practicalities. For example, judges want to follow policy consistent with their views, but they also want to reach just decisions and make efficient use of their time. Their decision making may also be influenced by strategic thinking about how others will react to their decision – such as the need to curry the votes of other judges and concerns over being reversed by a higher court. (Baum 2008; Robbennolt 2005). Contextual practicalities such as time pressures and case management are also a consistent presence in judicial decision making, particularly for judges with a heavy case load. (Robbennolt 2005).

In this model, each goal and constraint creates a network of connected elements that can potentially influence decision making. (Robbennolt 2005). The goals and constraints include those that judges are consciously aware of and those that are more intuitive. In any given decision, some elements will have more strength or salience than others. Judges reach decisions by balancing all the most forceful or salient elements. In other words, decision making involves choosing a path based on a "holistic assessment of various competing actions and goals." (Thagard and Milgram 1995).

Complex decision making, such as that involved in judging, requires the processing of a multitude of facts, concepts, and values and the integration of them into a discrete choice. This process of reasoning – of consideration and integration of myriad factors – tends to turn complex cases with multiple competing arguments into more coherent, straightforward accounts. (Simon 2004). Although multiple and various motivations might color judicial decision making, it is likely that judges seriously consider only a few of those factors. (Simon and Scurich 2013). In other words, the reasoning process tends to turn complex problems into simple, obvious ones. As Justice Holmes said of the seemingly intractable problems he faced as a judge, "Always when you walk up to the lion and lay hold[,] the hide comes off and the same old donkey of a question of law is underneath." (DeWolfe Howe 1961).

As an illustration of how the cognitive tendency toward coherence leads to judges having more confidence in their ability to make the right decisions, consider an example. Often, a judge will find the set of arguments on one side more appealing than those on the other, even (or especially) in cases that are "close calls" with strong arguments on both sides. As the judge moves through the process of deciding the outcome, the judge's view of the legal materials (the facts, the authorities) changes and adjusts to better match up with the more appealing set of arguments. (Simon and Scurich 2013).

This process is neither linear nor conscious – it is recursive or "bidirectional." As the judge actively constructs mental models of the situation, the judge's perceptions of the evidence change. In other words, as a judge's reasoning tends toward a particular account, her view of the supporting legal materials alters in a way that brings her closer to making what appears to be the more coherent decision. She begins to view the chosen account as more clearly supported by the legal materials, which then leads to additional alteration of her view of the legal materials, and so on. The end result is that what once was viewed as a complex case becomes a straightforward and seemingly "easy" decision, one not compelled by the judge's political leanings or personal feelings but one that the judge confidently believes was compelled by the facts and authorities. (Simon 1998).

All these models emphasize slightly different aspects of the decision-making process, but for our purposes, the most important thing is that their description leaves ample room for the advocate to influence the course of decision making. For example, the advocate can make arguments that reinforce the "snap" System 1 judgment, or conversely, she can advance claims that encourage more reflective System 2 deliberation. She can make arguments that highlight or strengthen any one or more of the multiple goals served by the network of decision making, or she can construct arguments that appear to make one side's position more appealingly coherent.

∞ Case study: Justice Roberts's decision to uphold the Affordable Care Act

In *National Federation of Independent Business v. Sebelius* (2012), the first U.S. Supreme Court case challenging the Patient Protection and Affordable Care Act (ACA) (known as Obamacare), commentators were surprised that Chief Justice John Roberts voted with the majority to uphold the constitutionality of the Act. As a member of the Court's conservative bloc, Justice Roberts was widely believed to oppose the Act on policy grounds, and indeed in his majority opinion he explicitly disclaimed that the Court was endorsing the wisdom of the Act. In this case, therefore, Justice Roberts seemingly did not vote in accordance with his political beliefs or his "attitudes," thus undercutting the decision-making models that emphasize judges' tendency to decide cases based on the results they favor rather than through a process of deliberation.

But under the more complex models of decision making, we can see many different considerations that could have influenced Justice Roberts's vote. He may have been concerned about public perceptions of the Court's legitimacy, particularly after the politically divided and controversial decisions in *Citizens United* (2010) and *Bush v. Gore* (2000). He may have been thinking about his own legacy as Chief Justice and whether he would be remembered as presiding over a politicized court. He may have considered the conservative value of judicial restraint to be more important than the conservative opposition to sweeping entitlements. In terms of judicial restraint, he may have felt that his personal integrity required him to vote consistently with his confirmation hearing statements endorsing a limited judicial role in reviewing the enactments of Congress (psychologists call this "self-affirmation"). Justice Roberts also might have overridden his initial intuitive judgment about the ACA by thinking more deliberatively about the issue.

All of these feelings, and likely others, worked in various degrees to influence Justice Roberts's historic vote in *National Federation v. Sebelius*. And they all presented opportunities for the advocates in that case to influence the decision.

Cognitive bias

Judges are also susceptible to cognitive biases. As Jerome Frank noted, "[J]udges are human and share the virtues and weaknesses of mortals generally." (Frank 1973). This is so even though judges are specially trained and undoubtedly strive to make fair, unbiased decisions. The lure of cognitive bias, which hastens the decision-making processes of all human beings, is too strong to be overcome by even the most rigorous training. Judges may even be more vulnerable to some cognitive biases to the extent that they are overloaded with cases and must make decisions quickly, two conditions that can lead to an overreliance on ready-made frameworks and shortcuts. (Guthrie et al. 2001).

Among other biases, empirical studies have shown that judges are susceptible to anchoring bias, hindsight bias, and egocentric bias to the same extent as non-law-trained subjects. (Guthrie et al. 2001). Anchoring bias is the tendency to rely on an irrelevant piece of information in making a decision, such as beginning with the jurisdictional monetary limit for lawsuits in recommending settlement amounts. Hindsight bias leads judges to believe that they would have predicted the correct result even though no objective evidence exists to suggest that this is so. Finally, egocentric bias leads judges to overestimate how correct their decisions are: most judges predicted that they were less likely to be overturned than the "average" judge.

As already mentioned, judges are also susceptible to the "coherence bias." When they decide difficult issues, they tend to favor the more straightforward and visibly coherent accounts, smoothing over complexity. Like jurors, judges also tend to be unable to overlook inadmissible evidence that has come to their attention. (Wistrich et al. 2005). Finally, judges are just as unable to accurately assess credibility as are most other people: their determinations about whether people are lying are no better than chance. (Ekman 2009).

Some studies showed that judges are somewhat better able to resist framing effects and the representativeness heuristic than non-law-trained subjects, but they were still unduly influenced in these areas. In the study of framing effects, judges had to evaluate a settlement offer when it was framed as either a gain for the plaintiff or a loss for the defendant. In terms of financial outcome, the settlements were identical; the only difference was that one offer was framed as a gain for the plaintiff and the other as a loss for the defendant. Judges tended to favor the settlement offer framed as a gain, though somewhat less so than non-law-trained decision makers.

The representativeness heuristic describes the tendency to make categorical judgments and particularly to do so without paying attention to competing facts such as statistical information. This is the shortcut blamed for the wrong answers most people give to the Linda problem discussed in Chapter 2 (requiring the study subjects to say whether it is more probable that Linda is both a bank teller and a feminist than that Linda is a bank teller). For example, when judges were given a hypothetical problem in which they had to choose between an easy categorical judgment and a more deliberative evaluation of statistical evidence, a majority of the judges relied on the incorrect categorical judgment. Even so, however, the judges did choose the correct response with more frequency than subjects who were not law trained. (Guthrie et al. 2001).

Summary

In sum, analyzing the judicial audience's response to persuasive efforts is complex. Judges are very firm in their beliefs about what persuades them but likely wrong about some of the influencing factors and how those factors are weighed and compete with one another. This complicates things because advocates must simultaneously cater to the strong beliefs of the judicial audience (to avoid alienating the audience) while also crafting arguments that actually work. The important takeaways here are the following: (1) many judges firmly believe that emotion and politics have no place in legal decision making, even though the science is decisive that emotions, experiences, and culture are a critical part of decision making and persuasion; (2) judges are susceptible to the same cognitive biases as others although they may have expert experience that equips them to make better judgments about issues of legal reasoning and interpretation; (3) advocates should tailor arguments to connect with the shared expectations of the legal audience for particular sources of authority and frameworks of argument but should also take advantage of the knowledge that emotion and bias will play a key role in judicial decision making.

Cases & briefs

Bush v. Gore, 531 U.S. 98 (2000).
Citizens United v. Federal Election Commission, 558 U.S. 310 (2010).
National Federation of Independent Business v. Sebelius, 567 U.S. 1 (2012).

Bibliography

Aldisert, R.J., 2003, *Winning on Appeal: Better Briefs and Oral Argument*, 2nd edn., NITA, Boulder, CO.

Bala, N., Lee, K., Lindsay, R. and Ramakrishnan, K., 2005, 'Judicial Assessment of the Credibility of Child Witnesses', *Alberta Law Review*, 42, 995–1017.

Bandes, S.A., 2009, 'Empathetic Judging and the Rule of Law', *Cardozo Law Review De Novo*, 133–148.

Baum, L., 2008, *Judges and Their Audiences: A Perspective on Judicial Behavior*, Princeton University Press, Princeton, NJ.

Berger, L., 2013, 'A Revised View of the Judicial Hunch', *Legal Communication & Rhetoric: JALWD*, 10, 1–45

Cialdini, R.B., 2006, *Influence: The Psychology of Persuasion*, rev. edn., Harper Business, New York.

Cohen, J., 2014, *Blindfolds Off: Judges on How They Decide*, American Bar Association, Chicago.

Edwards, H.T., 1985, 'Public Misperceptions Concerning the "Politics" of Judging: Dispelling Some Myths About the D.C. Circuit', *University of Colorado Law Review*, 56, 619–642.

Ekman, P., 2009, *Telling Lies: Clues to Deceit in the Marketplace, Politics, and Marriage*, W.W. Norton & Co., New York.

Frank, J., 1973, *Courts on Trial*, Princeton University Press, Princeton, NJ.

Guthrie, C., Rachlinski, J.J. and Wistrich, A.J., 2001, 'Inside the Judicial Mind', *Cornell Law Review*, 86, 777–830.

Guthrie, C., Rachlinski, J.J. and Wistrich, A.J., 2007, 'Blinking on the Bench: How Judges Decide Cases', *Cornell Law Review*, 93, 1–44.

Haidt, J., 2001, 'The Emotional Dog and Its Rational Tail: A Social Intuitionist Approach to Moral Judgment', *Psychological Review*, 108, 814–834.

Holmes, O.W., in M. DeWolfe Howe (ed.), 1961, *Holmes Pollock Letters: The Correspondence of Mr. Justice Holmes and Sir Frederick Pollock, 1874–1932*, Harvard University Press, Cambridge, MA.

Kahneman, D., 2011, *Thinking Fast and Slow*, Farrar, Straus and Giroux, New York.

Klein, G., 1999, *Sources of Power: How People Make Decisions*, MIT Press, Cambridge, MA.

Maroney, T.A. and Gross, J.J., 2014, 'The Ideal of the Dispassionate Judge: An Emotion Regulation Perspective', *Emotion Review*, 6(2), April, 142–151.

Pennington, N. and Hastie, R., 1991, 'A Cognitive Theory of Juror Decision Making: The Story Model', *Cardozo Law Review*, 13, 519–557.

Robbennolt, J.K., 2005, 'Evaluating Juries by Comparison to Judges: A Benchmark for Judging?', *Florida State Law Review*, 32, 469–509.

Robbins, K.K., 2002, 'The Inside Scoop: What Federal Judges Really Think About the Way Lawyers Write', *The Journal of the Legal Writing Institute*, 8, 257–284.

Roberts, J., 2005, 'U.S. Chief Justice John Roberts' Opening Statement to the U.S. Senate Judiciary Committee at the Beginning of His Confirmation Process', *West Virginia Lawyer*, 42–43.

Scalia, A. and Garner, B.A., 2008, *Making Your Case: The Art of Persuading Judges*, Thomson West, Eagan, MN.

Simon, D., 1998, 'A Psychological Model of Judicial Decision Making', *Rutgers Law Journal*, 30, 1–142.

Simon, D., 2004, 'A Third View of the Black Box: Cognitive Coherence in Legal Decision Making', *The University of Chicago Law Review*, 71, 511–586.

Simon, D. and Scurich, N., 2013, 'Judicial Overstating', *Chicago-Kent Law Review*, 88(2), 411–431.

Smith, M.R., 2008, *Advanced Legal Writing: Theories and Strategies in Persuasive Writing*, 3rd edn., Wolters Kluwer, New York.

Thagard, P. and Milgram, E., 1995, 'Inference to the Best Plan: A Coherence Theory of Decision', in A. Ram and D.B. Leake (eds.), *Goal-Driven Learning*, pp. 439–454, MIT Press, Cambridge, MA.

Voros, F., 2011, 'To Persuade a Judge, Think Like a Judge', *Utah State Bar Journal: View From the Bench*, September, viewed 9 September 2016, from www.utahbar.org/utah-bar-journal/view-from-the-bench/to-persuade-a-judge-think-like-a-judge/

Wistrich, A.J., Guthrie, C. and Rachlinski, J.J., 2005, 'Can Judges Ignore Inadmissible Information? The Difficulty of Deliberately Disregarding', *Cornell Law Faculty Publications*, April, Paper 20, viewed 9 September 2016, from http://scholarship.law.cornell.edu/cgi/viewcontent.cgi?article=1019&context=lsrp_papers

4

KAIROS

Fitting time and place

Some arguments burst onto the scene at just the right time. The advocate finds a perfect fit between the argument and the occasion for making it. For other arguments, an appropriate setting – or the right fit of time and place – must be constructed. This is the heart of rhetoric, "the art which seeks to capture in opportune moments that which is appropriate and attempts to suggest that which is possible." (Poulakos 1983).

Constructing the appropriate setting to capture an opportune moment may take time. For example, it took 14 years for lawyers to win a grant of asylum for Rodi Alvarado, a Guatemalan woman who fled to the United States to escape domestic abuse. (*Matter of R.A.* 2009; Preston 2009). Alvarado's lawyers finally persuaded an immigration judge that it had been impossible for Alvarado to leave her husband and safely remain in her home country, and so she at long last qualified as a member of a discrete social group entitled to seek asylum. But it was not enough for Alvarado's lawyers to pursue their legal arguments for more than a decade. Those legal arguments finally connected with decision makers when the right moment arrived. And the right moment arrived because it had been constructed over decades by advocates and survivors of domestic violence within the United States telling stories and collecting data. By telling their stories in the media and through public interest organizations, domestic violence survivors in the U.S. had demonstrated that women were most at risk when they left the perpetrators of domestic violence. So what had once been widely accepted was now shown to be untrue: it was a myth to believe that the survivors could have left their assailants years or months earlier. With this new cultural understanding, Alvarado's asylum request was seen as "fitting." The opportune moment arrived when Alvarado's story rang true because it had become a familiar story within the larger culture.

Similarly, in the years leading up to the U.S. Supreme Court decision that laws barring marriage between partners of the same sex were unconstitutional, federal district courts across the country, one after the other, had handed down almost identical same-sex marriage decisions. Although these decisions seemed to follow one another without much effort, rather like dominoes, the seemingly rapid evolution of the law came about because societal and judicial minds had been changed over a long period of time by what Nan Hunter has characterized as a hybrid process of public relations, political action, and well-timed litigation.[1]

In contrast, inopportune moments can sink the best of arguments. In 1872, the first lawsuits raising questions about the meaning of the 14th Amendment came before the U.S. Supreme Court. Although the plaintiff's lawyer in *Bradwell v. Illinois* (1873) argued that both the equal protection clause and the privileges and immunities clause of the new amendment protected Myra Bradwell's right to pursue her chosen profession, the U.S. Supreme Court upheld Illinois' decision barring her from the practice of law. Earlier the same week, in the *Slaughterhouse Cases* (1873), the Court had upheld Louisiana's statute granting a monopoly to a single corporate slaughterhouse over a challenge from independent butchers. In both cases, the Court said the new equal protection clause applied only when the challenged inequality was based on race and that the privileges and immunities clause had nothing to do with the rights of citizens to practice their livelihoods. Given the worries of state governments that the Reconstruction Amendments had shifted the balance of power from the states to the national government, it simply was the wrong time to ask the Supreme Court to grant the national government sweeping new authority, even if that authority was exercised to protect the fundamental rights of all the nation's citizens. (Goldfarb 2016).

Openings and images

Thinking in terms of *kairos* can guide advocates in their search for opportune moments. In its ideal form, kairos captures or creates a turning point. When classical rhetoricians identified the persuasive modes of ethos, pathos, and logos, they distinguished kairos from the more familiar concept of chronos or linear time. While chronological accountings appear to link one event to the next – persuading the audience that one thing has followed another logically or for a particular reason – kairic moments are loaded with significance in and of themselves. (Sipiora and Baumlin 2002; Smith 1986; Poulakos 1983).

There are two components to the kairic sense of timing. First, the lawyer must recognize *the most opportune moment* in chronological time. The advocate uses the most opportune moment to construct an opening for telling the client's story. Second, the advocate must isolate *the most essential moment*, the optimum place in time within the problem setting itself. The advocate uses the essential moment to construct an iconic image that lies at the heart of a client's story. The opportune moment lies within the larger societal setting for making a particular argument, while the essential moment lies within the particular rhetorical setting of the argument. (Berger 2015b).

The value of developing a persuasive sense of timing that reflects both the most opportune and the most essential moments is supported by persuasion science research, especially the studies of priming and building step-by-step argument chains. Finding the right time for an argument may mean spotting emerging trends or small changes in the law or society that will provide the "prime" or the "foot in the door" to tip the audience's first response in favor of the argument.

The value of developing a kairic sense of timing is supported as well by contemporary rhetorical theory. Every legal argument takes place within a particular rhetorical situation, and every rhetorical situation presents a kairic moment that the speaker can discover

---

1 Professor Hunter made this point in a presentation at the UNLV Boyd School of Law in October 2016.

and use. (Bitzer 1968; Vatz 1973). A rhetorical situation exists when a problem calls out for a rhetorical response that is aimed at an audience which can solve or address the imperfection. The shape and name given to the problem affect the discovery of the kairic moment and the appropriate rhetorical response. For example, even within a chronological timeline, the persuasive lawyer may decide to begin his client's story with one event rather than another, and thus to create a different crisis or turning point. And rather than being stuck in a rigidly linear timeline, the persuasive lawyer may choose to open up the focus on critical moments of time rather than abide by chronological sequence. By seizing the moment that provides an opening for telling the story, the advocate may find a more receptive reader. By isolating the moment or moments that crystallize the essence of the situation, the advocate may help the reader make crucial persuasive connections.

Most opportune moments

As already mentioned, a recent example of kairos in its sense as the most opportune time for advancing an argument is illustrated by the lower court outcomes that followed Justice Antonin Scalia's comment in *United States v. Windsor* (2013) that there would be no turning back after the Supreme Court decision that the Defense of Marriage Act was unconstitutional. Many of the subsequent briefs and lower court opinions seized on his prediction that the ruling would be extended to overturn state statutes restricting same-sex marriage. (Alliance 2015). Advocates who filed those challenges were seen – in retrospect at least – to have seized the most opportune moment. Finding the most opportune moment often depends, as this example illustrates, on understanding your audience. In other words, the time was right to make this argument to these audience members: lower court judges being asked to decide an issue very similar to the question determined in *Windsor* seized upon the guidance despite its having been offered in sarcastic dissent.

∞ Case study: the right time to move from corporate free speech to corporate religious expression

Judges themselves often seem to be employing kairos to create both opportune and essential moments. An unusually obvious setup of such an opportunity occurred in *Citizens United v. Federal Election Commission* (2010). After scheduling the case for re-argument on the question of whether two prior cases should be overruled, the Supreme Court decided in *Citizens United* that the answer was yes, and that corporations should thereafter be treated as if they were individual speakers when it came to spending (because spending money was a stand-in for political speech or free expression) in political campaigns.

Once *Citizens United* had been decided, the most opportune moment for an argument to expand corporate rights to encompass religious expression appeared to be easily within grasp. As the Tenth Circuit Court of Appeals wrote, "the First Amendment logic of *Citizens United* – where the Supreme Court has recognized a First Amendment right of for-profit corporations to express themselves for political purposes" applies as well to religion. (*Hobby Lobby Stores, Inc. v. Sebelius* 2013).

Following suit, in *Burwell v. Hobby Lobby Stores* (2014), the Supreme Court decided that the drafters of the Religious Freedom Restoration Act (RFRA) intended for its protections to extend to corporations. In *Hobby Lobby*, employers challenged the Affordable

Care Act's requirement that they provide insurance to cover contraceptives. Before the U.S. Supreme Court ruled that corporations had "free speech" rights similar to those of individuals – that is, that corporations had a First Amendment right to spend money in political campaigns – it would have been difficult to pursue a lawsuit contending that corporations had statutory or constitutional rights to the exercise of religious freedoms. The decision in *Citizens United* carved out the opening that made the claim by Hobby Lobby's lawyers seem to appear at exactly the right time. Again, the timing was especially opportune for the most important audience – the Supreme Court justices.

∞ *Case study: Justice Roberts and the Voting Rights Act*

Among many other examples of the judicial creation of right moments, an opinion by Justice John Roberts stands out. Justice Roberts constructed an opening by crafting a compromise majority opinion on the Voting Rights Act (VRA) in *Northwest Austin Municipal Utility District Number One v. Holder* (2009). Through this means, Justice Roberts was later able to take advantage of an opportune moment to change the course of the Act. (Hasen 2012). Eight justices agreed to the compromise decision in *Northwest Austin*. Then, when *Shelby County v. Holder* (2013) came before the Court, Justice Roberts was able to rely on the earlier case, in which the majority had "expressed strong constitutional doubts about the Voting Rights Act but stopped just short of pulling the trigger." (Greenhouse 2013).

Justice Roberts's movement through the opening he created emphasized the crucial interplay of audience, time, place, and opportunity for action. First, the VRA was a one-in-a-million legislative response to a once-in-a-lifetime situation: it "employed extraordinary measures to address an extraordinary problem." The requirement that states get federal permission before enacting laws about voting was "a drastic departure from basic principles of federalism." Even more notable was that the requirement applied to only some states – "an equally dramatic departure from the principle that all States enjoy equal sovereignty." (*Shelby County* 2013).

Turning to the kairic setting he had created, Justice Roberts asked the timely question: even if voting discrimination still existed, the question of the moment was whether the current burdens are "justified by current needs." This question created the need for action. But Justice Roberts wrote as though his action was unremarkable. In his opinion, it was the dissent that was taking remarkable action by ignoring prior precedent: "the dissent refuses to consider the principle of equal sovereignty, despite *Northwest Austin*'s emphasis on its significance." Finally, the action Justice Roberts took was, in his opinion, fitting and proper for the occasion. The decision was no bigger than the opening that was created; it was only a small step: "Our decision in no way affects the permanent, nationwide ban on racial discrimination in voting found in § 2. We issue no holding on § 5 itself, only on the coverage formula." (*Shelby County* 2013).

Most essential moments

When we remember fairy tales, we often recall one vivid and lasting image rather than the connected events of the story. This is an example of kairos in the sense of capturing the most essential moment. When we think of Rapunzel, the unforgettable image is of "yards of hair tumbling down from the window in the tower." (Pullman 2012). We forget what happens before and after she lets down her hair.

Similarly, we remember the metaphor used to describe changing scientific accounts of the development of the universe, but little of the accounts themselves. "Only a century ago the universe was held to be eternal and unchanging. Then came the expanding universe and the Big Bang, an origin almost biblical in nature, like a girl bursting out of a cake." (Overbye 2013). This singular moment marks our changed understanding of the nature of things.

∞ Case study: the die was cast in Miranda's Interrogation Room 2

In its sense as the most essential moment, kairos is illustrated in the petitioner's brief filed in *Miranda v. Arizona* (1966). Miranda had been charged with kidnapping and raping an eighteen-year-old girl. According to the brief, "[o]n March 13, 1963, defendant was arrested at his home and taken in custody to the police station where he was put in a lineup consisting of four persons." (Brief for Petitioners 1966). After being identified by two witnesses, "Miranda was then taken to Interrogation Room 2 at the local police headquarters and there interrogated on both [this matter and an unrelated robbery]." Lest the reader fail to grasp the essential moment, the brief repeats the information with more detail: "After the lineup, it was Officer Cooley, who had arrested Miranda, who took petitioner to Interrogation Room 2." The brief pointed out that no one told Miranda of his right to counsel, and then returns again: "Here, Officer Cooley also testified as to interrogation in Room 2 of the Detective Bureau, and narrated extensively a confession he attributed to the petitioner." And yet again, the essential moment: "A written statement, obtained from Miranda while he was under the interrogation in Room 2, was then put into evidence." And finally, the argument itself:

> When Miranda walked out of Interrogation Room 2 on March 13, 1963, his life for all practical purposes was over. Whatever happened later was inevitable; the die had been cast *in that room at that time*. There was no duress, no brutality. Yet when Miranda finished his conversation with Officers Cooley and Young, only the ceremonies of the law remained; in any realistic sense, his case was done.
>
> *(Brief for Petitioner 1966)*

In the *Miranda* brief, Interrogation Room 2 became the actual physical place within a particular moment, a kairic space that captured the essence of Miranda's argument. Unless the Constitution required police to tell a criminal defendant that he had the right to have an attorney present during his questioning, the defendant's constitutional rights at trial would be virtually meaningless. The defendant's fate would rest on what he had said, without the benefit of counsel, while being interrogated by police, alone in a room for hours.

∞ Case study: the "urban danger" that necessitated handgun control in Heller

In his dissent in *District of Columbia v. Heller* (2008), Justice Breyer reviewed the question of whether the gun control statute would achieve its objective of saving lives. Taking the point of view of the legislature (in this case, the D.C. City Council) that adopted the statute thirty years earlier, Justice Breyer pointed to the committee report finding that handguns – whose registration was restricted under the law at issue – had "a particularly strong link to undesirable activities in the District's exclusively urban environment." (*Heller* 2008).

Continuing throughout the dissent, his emphasis is on the specific context of a uniquely "urban danger": "[U]rban areas, such as the District, have different experiences with gun-related death, injury, and crime than do less densely populated rural areas."[2] Justice Breyer also described the District's law as "tailored to the life-threatening problems it attempts to address" in an area that is "totally urban" and suffers from "a serious handgun-fatality problem." In his conclusion, he emphasized that "there simply is no untouchable constitutional right guaranteed by the Second Amendment to keep loaded handguns in the house in crime-ridden urban areas." (*Heller* 2008).

Although Justice Breyer dissented on a number of legal grounds from the majority's decision that the District's gun regulation was unconstitutional, the image of urban danger permeated his opinion. Though unacknowledged as the essence of his argument by the author, this image was at the heart of the rhetorical situation in which Justice Breyer determined that handgun regulation was not only constitutional but necessary. (Berger 2015a).

∞ *Case study: George Zimmerman's profiling of Trayvon Martin*

The potential for persuasion when an advocate focuses on the most essential moment within an individual rhetorical situation was illustrated in the trial of George Zimmerman for the 2012 murder of Trayvon Martin in Sanford, Florida. In his closing arguments, the prosecutor focused on the moment when "Trayvon Martin, an unarmed black teenager carrying nothing but snacks" first encountered "Mr. Zimmerman, who saw himself as a cop and Mr. Martin as a hoodie-clad criminal." If Zimmerman in effect profiled Martin as a criminal at first sight, then Zimmerman's actions were the product of his own mistaken assumptions rather than, as the jury saw it, the result of some later threat posed by Martin. The prosecutor's effort to portray everything that followed, including the fatal shooting, as arising out of this essential moment employed kairos. By centering on an initial profiling based on irrational stereotyping, the prosecutor attempted to capture and freeze the essence of the Zimmerman-Martin story. (Alvarez 2013).

∞ *Case study: Justice Alito and the creation of a religious corporation in Hobby Lobby*

For a judicial example of focusing on the essential moment, we turn again to the majority opinion in *Burwell v. Hobby Lobby Stores, Inc.* (2014). There, Justice Samuel Alito portrayed the crucial moments in time as having occurred decades before the lawsuit began. Even though these moments fell outside the chronological timeline

---

2 Katie Pryal pointed out Justice Breyer's reliance on the "urban danger" setting during the Rhetoric & Law Colloquium at the University of Alabama, Huntsville, in April 2014.

of the lawsuit itself, Justice Alito emphasized that the turning point in his reasoning occurred in the moments of creation of the two plaintiff corporations. Advancing the argument that a corporation takes on the religious beliefs of its owners, Justice Alito determined that RFRA barred laws that would require a closely held corporation to provide insurance for contraceptives in violation of its owners' religious beliefs.

To construct the image of a corporation with religious beliefs, Justice Alito focused on critical moments involving the families who owned and controlled those companies over the years. At the beginning of his recitation of the facts of the lawsuit, he wrote:

> David and Barbara Green and their three children are Christians who own and operate two family businesses. Forty-five years ago, David Green started an arts-and-crafts store that has grown into a nationwide chain called Hobby Lobby. . . . One of David's sons started an affiliated business, Mardel, which operates 35 Christian bookstores and employs close to 400 people.
>
> *(Hobby Lobby 2014)*

In Justice Alito's view, the owners of a corporation should be able to follow their religious beliefs even while acting on behalf of their businesses and in their roles as corporate officers. By conveying an image of these corporations as virtually indistinguishable from their owners, it went without saying that the corporations themselves had beliefs that would be affected by the legislation at issue.

Summary

As will be discussed in the storytelling chapters, lawyers often adjust the chronology of their stories to shift the audience's understanding of the plot or narrative arc and thus affect the audience's expectation of the most appropriate outcome. Kairos is a different kind of time shifting that depends on identifying turning points. Rather than shifting the audience's understanding of what should or will come next, the use of kairos may shift the readers' understanding of the current climate and setting. To use kairos, the advocate must learn how to sense the most opportune moment to advance a particular argument and how to isolate the essential moments that convey the heart of the problem.

Cases & briefs

Bradwell v. *Illinois*, 83 U.S. 130 (1873).
Burwell v. Hobby Lobby Stores, Inc., 134 S. Ct. 2751 (2014).
Citizens United v. Federal Election Commission, 558 U.S. 310 (2010).
District of Columbia v. Heller, 554 U.S. 570 (2008).
Hobby Lobby Stores, Inc. v. Sebelius, 723 F.3d 1114 (10th Cir. 2013).
In the Matter of R.A., 2009, Brief for Respondent, available at https://cgrs.uchastings.edu/sites/default/files/R-A-_brief_immigration_ court_08_19_2009_0.pdf
Miranda v. Arizona, 384 U.S. 436 (1966).
    Brief for Petitioner [Ernesto Miranda], 1966 Westlaw 87732.
Northwest Austin Municipal Utility District Number One v. Holder, 557 U.S. 193 (2009).

Shelby County v. Holder, 133 S. Ct. 2612 (2013).
Slaughterhouse Cases, 83 U.S. 36 (1873).
United States v. Windsor, 133 S. Ct. 2675 (2013).

Bibliography

Alliance for Justice, 2015, 'Love and the Law: Federal Cases Challenging State Bans on Same-Sex Marriage', viewed 24 September 2016, from www.afj.org/wp-content/uploads/2015/06/Federal-Marriage-Equality-Report-6.23.15-POSITIVE.pdf.

Alvarez, L., 2013, 'In Closing, Zimmerman Prosecutor Focuses on Inconsistencies', *The New York Times*.

Berger, L.L., 2015a, 'A Rhetorician's Practical Wisdom', *Mercer Law Review*, 66, 459–484.

Berger, L.L., 2015b, 'Creating Kairos at the Supreme Court: Shelby County, Citizens United, Hobby Lobby, and the Judicial Construction of Right Moments', *The Journal of Appellate Practice and Process*, 16(2), 147–181.

Bitzer, L.F., 1968, 'The Rhetorical Situation', *Philosophy and Rhetoric*, 1, 1–14.

Goldfarb, P., 2016, '*Bradwell v. Illinois* Rewritten Opinion', in K. Stanchi, L. Berger and B. Crawford (eds.), *United States Feminist Judgments: Rewritten Opinions of the United States Supreme Court*, Cambridge University Press, Cambridge.

Greenhouse, L., 2013, 'The Cost of Compromise', *The New York Times*, and reprinted in C. Barbour and M.J. Streb (eds.), 2014, *Clued in to Politics: A Critical Thinking Reader in American Government*, 4th edn., pp. 204–208, CQ Press, Los Angeles.

Hasen, R.L., 2012, 'Anticipatory Overrulings, Invitations, Time Bombs, and Inadvertence: How Supreme Court Justices Move the Law', *Emory Law Journal*, 61(4), 779–800.

Overbye, D., 2013, 'A Quantum of Solace: Timeless Questions About the Universe', *The New York Times*.

Poulakos, J., 1983, 'Toward a Sophistic Definition of Rhetoric', *Philosophy & Rhetoric* 16(1), 35–48, in J.L. Lucaites, C.M. Condit, C.M. and S.A. Caudill (eds.), 1999, *Contemporary Rhetorical Theory: A Reader*, pp. 25–34, The Guildford Press, New York.

Preston, J., 2009, 'U.S. May Be Open to Asylum for Spouse Abuse', *The New York Times*.

Pullman, P., 2012, *Fairy Tales From the Brothers Grimm: A New English Version*, Viking Penguin, New York.

Sipiora, P. and Baumlin, J.S. (eds.), 2002, *Rhetoric and Kairos: Essays in History, Theory, and Praxis*, State University of New York Press, Albany.

Smith, J.E., 1986, 'Time and Qualitative Time', *The Review of Metaphysics*, 40(1), 3–16.

Vatz, R.E., 1973, 'The Myth of the Rhetorical Situation', *Philosophy and Rhetoric*, 6(3), 154–161.

PART III

Invention

Stories, metaphors, and analogies

As a legal advocate, there are some things you cannot control. You cannot change the facts and only rarely can you change the law. But you can think about the facts from different points of view. You can research the law thoroughly and carefully to uncover new angles and perspectives. And though you are limited in your construction of persuasive arguments by the available raw materials, you can draw on vast amounts of contextual information – historical trends, cultural settings, policy rationales, and so on.

In classical rhetoric, the canon of *invention* stood for a systematic search for arguments. Classical rhetoricians developed techniques and strategies for discovering and generating their primary claims and supporting details. Among these techniques were the topics, or checklists of argument types, and the concept of "stasis," in which the speaker would pose a systematic series of questions to clarify the main issues for a discussion. (Corbett and Connors 1998).

Similarly, to construct arguments, contemporary legal advocates choose from among a number of argument types. In this cluster of chapters, we focus on the argument types that are most useful for the legal advocate who sets out to establish a roadmap where none currently exists or to change the directions on existing routes. Through the use of these argument types, the advocate proposes that the current case be viewed through the filter or the frame of a story, a metaphor, or an analogy. Rather than being based on statutory rules or case precedent, the argument frames discussed in Part III are structured around (1) newly invented factual analogies that suggest a useful comparison of concepts (rather than cases); (2) novel and conventional metaphors and characterizations that seek to implicitly transfer inferences and results from one domain to another; and (3) master stories and everyday scripts that subtly predict the route of the journey and its ending.

Depending on the resources available and the purpose of your advocacy, there are many good reasons to rely on the syllogistic and analogical case argument structures discussed in Part IV, especially when the argument takes place within the context of controlling statutes or binding precedent. Effective use of syllogisms and case analogies also requires the advocate to use the skills of invention discussed in Part III. But rather than creating stories and images, the advocate is constructing logic chains and persuasive categories.

5

UNCOVER EMBEDDED PLOTS, CHARACTERS, AND IMAGES

Contemporary rhetorical theory and cognitive science agree that interpretive frameworks are always at work to filter, focus, and frame what we see and think. Within this universe of frameworks, this chapter uncovers some of the historical and cultural stories, metaphors, and images that are deeply embedded within the context of many legal problems. When "outmoded metaphors, simplistic images, and unexamined narratives" go unchallenged, they interfere with the judicial capacity to notice the current context and to understand individual lives and situations. (Berger 2009).

Stories are the frames that help us make sense out of a series of chronological events otherwise lacking in coherence and consistency: "We seem to have no other way of describing 'lived time' save in the form of a narrative." (Bruner 1987). Metaphor and analogy are the more familiar concepts that first help us understand how to view and interpret new information and then help us decide what to do with or about it.

Not only do stories, metaphors, and analogies make it easier for us to understand, explain, and communicate our experiences, they help us predict what will happen next. As a result, they unconsciously or consciously guide our decisions. When we see a young woman sleeping on a bench in the park, one stereotype (homeless person) may lead us to avoid the person and another (injured or unconscious person) may suggest that we should call 911. When we find ourselves entangled in a typical plight (jealousy, for example), we tend to turn to recognizable storylines (revenge) to help us understand and respond to the situation.

Why advocates need to uncover embedded stories and images

To construct the most persuasive case for their clients, lawyers must be able to uncover the embedded stories and images that affect how audience members interpret and react to their arguments. In many cases, these embedded concepts unconsciously influence the judge's intuitive understanding of the characters and the events in the case before her. And that understanding may in turn guide the decision maker's initial inclinations about the desired outcome of the case. Schema theory explains this kind of cognitive influence. Stories and images prevalent in history, culture, and personal experience constitute some of the many schemas we construct in our minds over time. All schemas are cognitively efficient: grouping things together and sorting them into categories helps us focus on what's important, and it helps us know where to fit new items of information into the apparently appropriate times and places. When we are able to fit new information into a long-familiar schema, we are able without conscious thought to make inferences that nevertheless lead us to decisions and actions.

Most schemas have a prototype at their center. Whether something new falls within or outside the schematic category is judged by how close or how far it is from the prototype. For example, if we consider Cinderella or Aladdin to be the prototypical character at the heart of the "rags to riches" story, a client who began his career busking on the streets and became the owner of Cirque du Soleil might be judged against his resemblance to Cinderella and her story. Only by examining this context can the advocate plan effectively. Is our Cirque du Soleil client like Cinderella, a heroine who works hard and is mistreated by jealous relatives? Or unlike Cinderella, is he callously ambitious, stepping on others on his way to the top? How well the client matches up with the identified prototype affects the assumptions and inferences that carry over from his classification within the Cinderella category.

As discussed in earlier chapters, effective advocates begin by understanding the context for decision making, including audience, timing, and location. Equally important, these advocates understand the historically shared and culturally embedded stories and images that affect the decision-making context. The best advocates look at existing judicial precedent as well as the opposing arguments and briefs to uncover such underlying stories and images.

Among those underlying stories and images, some narratives (such as the myth of the frontier) and some metaphors (for example, the wall of separation between church and state) are especially helpful for persuasive purposes because they are so deeply embedded within our history and culture. When an advocate uses these master stories and iconic images, he is able to convey expectations and assumptions without having to spell them out. When narratives and images like these settle into our minds, they seem to harden into seemingly universal and natural concepts. Once that occurs, the resulting concepts act as filters through which any new information or experience must pass. (Schank and Abelson 1995).

How to uncover master stories, archetypal characters, and iconic images

When we examine the context for decision making, we see more clearly not only the persuasive power of embedded stories and images but also the negative effects of schematic cognition or "chunking." Our reliance on often-unconscious cognitive filters and frames based on race, gender, ethnicity, and class has wide-ranging and discriminatory effects. These filters and frames are the source of implicit bias: not only do they fill in the gaps in the information we actually know, but they persuade us to overlook important details, and they reassure us that our often-unreliable understanding is consistent with what actually happened.

Through the widespread discussion of their 1980 book *Metaphors We Live By*, George Lakoff and Mark Johnson inspired metaphor hunters everywhere. (Lakoff and Johnson 1980). Legal scholars followed suit in uncovering many metaphorical concepts and images that underlie much of legal reasoning as well as those most prevalent in our history and culture. (Smith 2007; Oldfather 1994; Bosmajian 1992). All of these affect our potential for constructing effective legal arguments. As we will see in later chapters, one way to combat the negative effects of entrenched concepts is to activate alternative or multiple schemas, but doing so requires us first to become very familiar with the conventional terrain.

As starting techniques for exploration, we suggest that advocates consult Lakoff and Johnson's discussion of everyday and conventional metaphors, the most common and the most unconsciously effective. Once we become aware of the ways in which our thinking and conversation are dominated by metaphors – argument is war, up is good, life is a journey – we are better able to discover them everywhere.

For narrative excavation, we will discuss two approaches to uncovering, analyzing, and understanding embedded cultural and situational narratives. First, stories can be analyzed and understood by looking at an opinion or brief to discover whether it contains the steps in a typical storyline or plot. As described by Amsterdam and Bruner, the typical plot starts with a "steady state" that is disrupted by a "Trouble" or a conflict, which is eventually resolved by a return to either the original or a new steady state. (Amsterdam and Bruner 2002). Second, Kenneth Burke's narrative pentad can be used to assess – and then shift – the relationships among the narrative elements of characters, events, setting, means, and motives. (Burke 1969). In both narrative analysis frameworks, the fulcrum, and the starting point for analysis, is most often the conflict or the Trouble that drives the drama.

Existing plot structures can be revealed by looking for this Trouble, often depicted as the initial turning point in the story or identified as the problem that needs to be resolved. Plot structure analysis concentrates on the narrative arc from the current and ordinary state of things through the Trouble to the actions taken by the characters and completed with a resolution. For the advocate, plot analysis can be seen as useful in its own right and as the first step toward plot reconstruction.

Through the pentad, the reader looks first for the relevant events or actions in the story (that is, for any conscious or purposive action), and then identifies the characters who perform the actions as well as the means the characters used. The final elements in the pentad are the setting and the purpose. Pentadic analysis concentrates on the relationships among the elements in order to identify the predominant element. Again, for the lawyer, pentadic analysis is useful on its own and as a necessary step toward reorienting the emphasis to focus on another of the narrative elements.

∞ Case study: evaluating fact stories of political scandals using plot structure and Burke's pentad

As just discussed, plot structure analysis often begins by identifying the Trouble or the conflict that drives the plot by spurring the characters into action. Pentadic analysis allows the advocate to detect emphasis and imbalance in the underlying story structure. Examples of both are well illustrated in the stories told by leading U.S. political figures caught up in scandal. Contrast, for example, the internal drama portrayed in Senator Edward Kennedy's speech after a young woman who had been a passenger in his car drowned at Chappaquiddick with the story told in one of President Bill Clinton's speeches during the Monica Lewinsky investigation. In Kennedy's speech, he first explained that he had left a cookout for a "devoted group of Kennedy campaign secretaries" accompanied by one of the secretaries, Mary Jo Kopechne. The Trouble that drove the plot occurred "little over one mile away," when "the car that I was driving on an unlit road went off a narrow bridge which had no guard rails and was built on a left angle to the road." (Kennedy 1969). Similarly, a pentadic analysis of Kennedy's speech would find that the emphasis among the narrative elements was on the setting (an "unlit road," a "narrow bridge" built at an angle to the road, "no guard rails," a deep pond, cold waters, and a "strong and murky current"). (Kennedy 1969). The setting was so predominant in the drama recounted in the speech that it overcame and controlled the character and his actions.

In contrast, the Trouble in the Clinton speech about his relationship with Monica Lewinsky was that the situation distracted the country and jeopardized important family relationships. (Clinton 1998). Given this Trouble, the preferred resolution would be to keep private matters private and for the country to move on. A pentadic analysis of the speech shows that the predominant narrative emphasis is on the protagonist's (Clinton's) purpose of protecting his family. Clinton emphasized his family's privacy by noting that "this matter is between me, the two people I love most – my wife and our daughter – and our God. I must put it right, and I am prepared to do whatever it takes to do so. . . . Nothing is more important to me personally. But it is private, and I intend to reclaim my family life for my family." (Clinton 1998).

In both cases, the choice of the Trouble and the emphasis on a particular element in the drama (the setting, the purpose) took attention away from the main character and his harmful actions. The advocate can use similar narrative analysis to think about how to shift emphasis in a story to one dominant element, thereby deemphasizing other elements and changing the impression left by the story.

How schemas implicitly influence legal decision makers

Embedded schemas and stereotypes may exert powerful, and very harmful, influences on decision makers. Given what we know about thinking and decision making, it is not surprising that we make unconscious and unintended "associations based on gender, race, and ethnicity" and that these associations influence both our future decisions and our conduct. (Levinson 2009). Because these associations have influenced decision makers at every step in the legal process, it is important for advocates to be conscious of them.

∞ *Case studies: racial and ethnic characterizations in criminal law*

In recent years, historians and political scientists have studied the effects of the mobilization of the War on Crime as a successor to the War on Poverty. The shift in the object of the war – from poverty to crime – reflected assumptions by political leaders and lawmakers that young African-American men were deviant and deficient, and thus in need of repair and correction, rather than deserving of actions that would advance justice and equality. (Perry 2016).

These assumptions were often reinforced by academic studies. One specific example was the "superpredator" metaphor advanced by some psychologists in the 1990s. During the 20 years before the U.S. Supreme Court struck down mandatory life-without-parole sentences for juveniles in *Miller v. Alabama* (2012), the superpredator characterization of some juvenile criminals had been a driving force behind federal and state laws and policies governing juvenile crime. The metaphor, which referred to children raised in what some psychologists had characterized as dysfunctional homes without moral guidance, is infused with racial and class overtones. Still, the metaphor and the seemingly scientific story from which it emerged became an interpretive framework for making and enforcing the law.

In *Miller v. Alabama*, one of the amicus briefs set forth the many research findings demonstrating that the image of juvenile criminal superpredators was not only a metaphor, but a myth. In part, the brief argued that despite the superpredator image of antisocial youths who cannot change, "research has shown that most antisocial youths outgrow their deviant behavior through the support of specific environmental impacts such as marriage and employment. . . . Randomized controlled trials of systematic interventions for high-risk youths have also demonstrated conclusively that the trajectory of antisocial development can be interrupted." (Amicus Brief 2012). In striking down the mandatory laws, Justice Elena Kagan's opinion echoed these arguments, pointing out that juveniles' greater "proclivity for risk and [their] inability to assess consequences . . . lessened a child's 'moral culpability' and enhanced the prospect that, as the years go by and neurological development occurs," the juvenile will become a better adult. (*Miller* 2012).

The superpredator metaphor is only one of the many stereotypical characterizations of criminal defendants that influence every aspect of the law, from legislation to policing to prosecution to trial court decision making and beyond. Such stereotyping reflects societal views of criminality as a reflection of the inherent "badness" of the individual criminal rather than as a social problem. (Haney 2009). Another example of such stereotyping is the iconic drug kingpin. Pamela Wilkins confronted this deeply lodged image in her work seeking to identify narrative strategies that might help reduce the impact of implicit racial bias in death penalty cases. (Wilkins 2012). In her review of the arguments made in the trial of Alan Quinones, a Latino criminal defendant who had been convicted of racketeering, drug trafficking, and the murder of a confidential informant, Professor Wilkins surmised that the jury's view of Quinones must have been significantly affected by the prevailing stereotypical schemas of drug kingpins as ruthless and violent parasites. As discussed in a later chapter, Quinones's advocate countered these stereotypes by emphasizing that the jury could select from among several competing – and more favorable – role schemas. For example, the defendant might be viewed as a protective father figure and a first-generation immigrant as well as a violent criminal.

Similar embedded schemas were evident in prosecutorial comments made during the trial in *United States v. Calhoun* (2013). In *Calhoun*, the defendant was convicted of participating in a drug conspiracy; one issue was whether Calhoun knew the people he accompanied were going to engage in a drug transaction or whether he was merely along for the ride. The Supreme Court denied the defendant's petition, but in her dissenting opinion, Justice Sonia Sotomayor described the prosecutor's comments as an attempt to "substitute racial stereotype for evidence and racial prejudice for reason." During the prosecutor's cross-examination, after Calhoun testified that he didn't know what was going on at the time, the prosecutor said: "You've got African-Americans, you've got Hispanics, you've got a bag full of money. Does that tell you – a light bulb doesn't go off in your head and say, this is a drug deal?" (*Calhoun* 2013).

In a recent analysis of the legal standard requiring reasonable suspicion to justify an arrest, the author found that the use of race-neutral terms and so-called objective facts failed to minimize the impact of the defendant's race or ethnicity and the accompanying stereotypical characterizations and supporting stories. (Keene 2017). Instead, Professor Keene found that the "specific and articulable facts . . . taken together with rational inferences" that are deemed sufficient to justify reasonable suspicion are transformed by the very act of placing them into narrative form. Unconscious or conscious reliance on racially tinged stock stories fills in the gaps and assures the police officers, prosecutors, and reviewing judges that the facts support a reasonable suspicion.

∞ Case studies: gender- and family-based images

The metaphor evoking an image of men and women living out their lives in *separate spheres* has had long-lasting, tangible effects on the law and society. Although the concept has been around much longer, one of the most memorable expressions of the metaphor came in Justice Bradley's 1873 concurrence in *Bradwell v. Illinois*, the case in which the Supreme Court agreed that nothing in the Constitution precluded Illinois from denying a law license to Myra Bradwell. Justice Bradley's concurrence revealed the powerful metaphor at the root of the majority's apparently syllogistic legal reasoning about legal protections:

> [T]he civil law, as well as nature herself, has always recognized a wide difference in the respective spheres and destinies of man and woman. Man is, or should be, woman's protector and defender. The natural and proper timidity and delicacy which belongs to the female sex evidently unfits it for many of the occupations of civil life.
>
> *(Bradwell 1873)*

Related master narratives providing an ideal image of family life in American history and culture – and their accompanying characters – are seen at every level of judicial decision making. In Justice Scalia's words denying a biological father the right to visitation with his child:

> The family unit accorded traditional respect in our society, which we have referred to as the "unitary family," is typified, of course, by the marital family, but also includes the household of unmarried parents and their children. Perhaps the concept can be expanded even beyond this, but it will bear no resemblance to traditionally respected relationships – and will thus cease to have any constitutional significance – if it is stretched so far as to include the relationship established between a married woman, her lover, and their child, during a 3-month sojourn

in St. Thomas, or during a subsequent 8-month period when, if he happened to be in Los Angeles, he stayed with her and the child.

(Michael H. 1989)

Linked to these stories and images of natural families, the label of "single mother" isolates women based on their marital status and further supports the myth and model of a family as having two parents with the male as the primary breadwinner. The resulting frameworks influence decision making. For example, in a child custody dispute in *Young v. Hector* (1998), the mother and father married at a time when the father was an architectural designer and the mother was an attorney in New Mexico. After the children were born, and as the parties had agreed, the mother and father alternated childcare and housekeeping responsibilities. The family moved to Miami, where the mother became a very successful litigator, but the father was unemployed. The couple then separated, but continued to live together, and the father became more involved in the activities of his two daughters, now eight and five, primarily after school on weekdays. The father maintained that he was the "primary caretaker" in the three years before this proceeding. As the appellate court put it, "The trial court viewed this contention with some degree of skepticism as it was entitled [to do]."

[Father's attorney]:	Who picks the kids up?
[Father]:	Either Hattie [the housekeeper] or I. Typically, it's me. If I am tied up, whether it's a meeting or whatever, or if I go somewhere like your office, way up in North Miami Beach, and I don't get back in time and I thought I would, I can call Hattie and say, "Hattie, please pick up the children." She does. She picks them up frequently.
[The Court]:	Is Hattie there five days a week?
[Father]:	Yes sir. She comes at noon every day. She cleans the house in the afternoons. She prepares the dinners. The kids eat. We eat. I eat with the children every day typically at 6:30. She cleans up after that. She'll draw a bath for Avery and she leaves at eight o'clock in the evening five days a week.
[The Court]:	Maybe I'm missing something. Why don't you get a job. [sic]

Demonstrating the pervasiveness of the assumption that there was something unacceptable about the father's not working at a traditional job outside the home, the appellate court rejected the father's suggestion that the trial court's questions about the father's work and need for a nanny were evidence of gender bias or of an image of the father as breadwinner and the mother as caretaker (Young 1998).

∞ Case studies: the intersection of race-, gender-, and class-based characterizations

The pervasive effects of metaphors on public policy, popular perceptions, and legislative and judicial decision making as a whole have been documented by Ann Cammett in articles focusing on deadbeat dads and welfare queens. (Cammett 2014). These harmful metaphors evolved from the 1960s War on Poverty, designed in part to better integrate African-Americans into jobs, housing, and politics. As the Aid to Families with Dependent Children program provided broader access for African-American recipients and federal control overcame local discriminatory practices, the number of African-American welfare recipients increased. That brought a backlash, accompanied by a racialized and gendered image of the category of poverty as predominantly black and female. This in turn was followed by broad public support for new legislation and strict enforcement of laws punishing deadbeat dads as well as widespread public blaming and condemnation of welfare queen mothers. Both the narratives and the metaphorical stereotypes that grew out of those stories supported increasingly punitive enforcement of child support and increasingly restrictive support for mothers. (Cammett 2014).

Other myths and stereotypes affect policy making and decision making in similar ways. For example, in one study, sociologists found that married mothers were viewed as having the most positive personality traits: not only were they better parents, they were more forgiving, caring, warm, generous, and protective. (Berger 2009). In contrast, never-married mothers were characterized as poor parents and as having less positive personality traits: they were viewed as unpleasant, unhappy, deviant, and more likely to be irresponsible, unintelligent, or drug abusers. If a single mother is not single as a result of death (or an occasional well-justified divorce), she is a bad mother. If single women are poor, it is because immorality has made them poor. As for working mothers, a working mother is a good mother only if she would rather be at home raising her children, but instead is forced to work for financial reasons. These images influence judicial decision making in child custody disputes where working mothers are disadvantaged, especially when they seek financial security or independence by pursuing a demanding career. Single working mothers face special risks in disputes with fathers who have reconstituted the ideal family by remarrying a woman who stays home. Perhaps most unfair is the onus on poor mothers: although middle-class women are bad mothers if they work, poor single mothers are seen as bad mothers whether they work or not. (Berger 2009).

Summary

Inevitably, every advocate's version of the facts tells only part of the story. When there are two advocates, we try to reassure ourselves that together, they will present a sufficiently full and fair accounting for what happened. Even so, decision makers may be swayed by a panoply of influences beyond the four corners of the advocate's story: master stories, archetypes, prior experiences, and beliefs can cause judges to hear and interpret admittedly incomplete and partial stories in very different ways.

Because familiar concepts and common storylines become "recipes for structuring experience itself, for laying down routes into memory, for not only guiding the life narrative up to the present but directing it into the future" (Bruner 1987), we need to uncover the possible stock stories or stereotypes underlying judicial decision making. Judges may even subtly change a story as they read it and process it in order to make it "fit" with their sense of reality or experiences. Judges may alter stories to make them more "orderly" or more understandable, relatable or meaningful. (Zaltman 2003). In these chapters, we do not resolve these issues. We suggest only that lawyers approach them thoughtfully and deliberately.

Cases & briefs

Bradwell v. *Illinois*, 83 U.S. 130 (1873).
United States v. Calhoun, 133 S. Ct. 1136 (2013).
Michael H. v. Gerald D., 491 U.S. 110 (1989).
Miller v. Alabama, 132 S. Ct. 2455 (2012).
    Amicus Brief on Behalf of Jeffrey Fagan et al., 2012 WL 174240.
Young v. Hector, 740 So. 2d 1153 (Fla. Dist. Ct. App. 1998).

Bibliography

Amsterdam, A. and Bruner, J., 2002, *Minding the Law*, Harvard University Press, Cambridge, MA.

Berger, L.L., 2009, 'How Embedded Knowledge Structures Affect Judicial Decision Making: A Rhetorical Analysis of Metaphor, Narrative, and Imagination in Child Custody Disputes', *Southern California Interdisciplinary Law Journal*, 18, 259–308.

Bosmajian, H., 1992, *Metaphor and Reason in Judicial Opinions*, Southern Illinois University Press, Carbondale, IL.

Bruner, J., 1987, 'Life as Narrative', *Social Research*, 54, 11–32.

Burke, K., 1969, *A Rhetoric of Motives*, rev. edn., University of California Press, Los Angeles.

Cammett, A., 2014, 'Deadbeat Dads & Welfare Queens: How Metaphor Shapes Poverty Law', *Boston College Journal of Law & Social Justice*, 34, 233–265.

Clinton, B., 1998, 'Transcript of Speech to Nation', August 17, viewed from www.cnn.com/ ALLPOLITICS/1998/08/17/speech/transcript.html.

Corbett, E.P.J. and Connors, R.J., 1998, *Classical Rhetoric for the Modern Student*, 4th edn., Oxford University Press, Oxford.

Haney, C., 2009, 'On Mitigation as Counter-Narrative: A Case Study of the Hidden Context of Prison Violence', *UMKC Law Review*, 77, 911–946.

Keene, S., 2017, 'Telling Stories That Swim Upstream: Uncovering the Influence of Stereotypes and Stock Stories in Fourth Amendment Reasonable Suspicion Analysis', *Maryland Law Review*, 76, 747–69.

Kennedy, E.M., 1969, 'Address to the People of Massachusetts on Chappaquiddick', July 15, viewed from www.americanrhetoric.com/speeches/tedkennedychappaquiddick.htm

Lakoff, G. and Johnson, M., 1980, *Metaphors We Live By*, University of Chicago Press, Chicago.

Levinson, J., 2009, 'Race, Death, and the Complicitous Mind', *DePaul Law Review*, 58, 599–644.

Oldfather, C.M., 1994, 'The Hidden Ball: A Substantive Critique of Baseball Metaphors in Judicial Opinions', *Connecticut Law Review*, 27, 17–55.

Perry, I., 2016, '"From the War on Poverty to the War on Crime" by Elizabeth Hinton, Book Review', *The New York Times*, 27 May 2016.

Schank, R.C. and Abelson, R.P., 1995, 'Knowledge and Memory: The Real Story', *Advances in Social Cognition*, 8, 1–85.

Smith, M.R., 2007, 'Levels of Metaphor in Persuasive Legal Writing', *Mercer Law Review*, 58, 919–947.

Wilkins, P.A., 2012, 'Confronting the Invisible Witness: The Use of Narrative to Neutralize Capital Jurors' Implicit Racial Biases', *West Virginia Law Review*, 115, 305–362.

Zaltman, G., 2003, *How Customers Think: Essential Insights Into the Mind of the Markets*, Harvard Business School Press, Boston, MA.

6

INTRODUCTION TO STORYTELLING

What do we mean when we say "story"? A story may be identified by its elements (plot, setting, characters) or by its functions. For legal advocates, function comes first: that is, storytelling allows lawyers to carve out their client's individual situation from the midst of general rules, to imply causation by placing events into a sequence, to build characters through telling details, to evoke emotions, and to guide decision makers to naturally occurring outcomes. Though these functions are paramount, persuasion depends upon the lawyer's thoughtful and deliberate use of the story's elements.

Novelist E.M. Forster famously said that stories are "a series of events arranged in their time sequence." Distinguishing story from plot, Forster wrote that a "plot is also a narrative of events, the emphasis falling on causality: 'The king died and then the queen died' is a story. But 'the king died and then the queen died of grief' is a plot. The time-sequence is preserved, but the sense of causality overshadows it." (Forster 1961). Combined with John Berger's claim that "[a]ll stories are about battles, of one kind or another, which end in victory and defeat," Forster's definition is a helpful starting point for lawyers. (Berger 1984).

There are many possible uses for storytelling techniques in the course of investigating, theorizing, and litigating a case. (Alper et al. 2005). In this cluster of chapters, we concentrate primarily on the end-use of stories as argument elements or argument frameworks in trial and appellate briefs. In those situations, by weaving together events, characters, and causation, the lawyer tells a story that carries meaning. Most often, the story's meaning is most effectively conveyed to the reader or the listener when the story resonates emotionally with its audience.

When stories are put to work as elements within a brief or as frameworks for structuring the facts or the legal argument, they are no longer merely stories, but instead they offer the decision maker reasons for doing one thing or the other, whether those reasons are explicit or implicit. These reasons most often emerge from the plot, the narrative element that reveals "the design and intention of narrative, what shapes a story and gives it a certain direction or intent of meaning." (Brooks 1992).

Plot is central to legal storytelling. In Amsterdam and Bruner's commonly used definition, the typical story plot begins within (1) "an initial steady state grounded in the legitimate ordinariness of things." So, at the beginning of the story, the timing and the setting establish a sense of stability. The plot is kicked into action and driven by a problem or conflict that disrupts the calmness of the opening. This problem often is labeled as (2) the Trouble, and it consists of circumstances brought on by human characters or "susceptible to change by human intervention." Because the Trouble is created by or can be solved by the characters, the characters are then set to work on (3) efforts and actions aimed at bringing about either "redress or transformation." Here, the story is at a turning point. The characters' efforts and actions may succeed or they may fail, but (4) we will always return to a stable and ordinary state, either because the original conditions are restored or because a new and transformed situation is created. Finally, (5) the plot concludes by spelling out a characteristic moral of the story. (Amsterdam and Bruner 2002).

In addition to an individual storyline or plot, stories often have themes, and many stories belong to genres. The story's theme is the timeless aspect – or in Philip Meyer's term, the melody (Meyer 2014) – the overarching, seemingly universal "plight that a story is about: human jealousy, authority and obedience, thwarted ambition." (Bruner 1987). The plot carries out the more universal theme by conjuring it out of a particular time, place, character, and events. The genres of story plots, on the other hand, include "[r]omance, farce, tragedy, Bildungsroman, black comedy, adventure story, fairytale, [and] wonder tale." (Bruner 1987).

An example of the interaction of these concepts is the well-known plot of the original *Star Wars* movie. But what about its theme and genre? Among the themes that audiences have found in the movie are the victory of good over evil, the power of unseen forces, and the battle of father and son. As for the genre to which its plot belongs, *Star Wars* is both an adventure story and a fairy tale. When an advocate turns to a timeless theme or evokes a particular genre, he is calling up prior master stories that convey, for better or for worse, much more cultural and historical information than just the individual story itself.

What makes stories effective

Researchers have suggested a theory called *narrative transportation* to describe what happens when listeners or readers are transported into the world of a story. (Green and Brock 2000). And follow-up studies have shown that "identifiable story characters, an imaginable story plot, and [story] verisimilitude" have small positive effects on the extent to which narrative transportation occurs. (van Laer et al. 2014). Moreover, when audience members are transported into a narrative world, or "lose themselves in a story, their attitudes and intentions [may] change to reflect that story." (van Laer et al. 2014).

For legal advocates, the important finding from these studies is that immersion in the world of a story has been shown to result in narrative persuasion, or the kinds of changes in attitudes and conduct that the advocate hopes to bring about. The process is described as occurring in two steps: first, narrative transportation can effect changes in emotions, cognitive processing, and beliefs, and second, those changes may eventually affect the audience member's attitudes, intentions, and conduct. (van Laer et al. 2014).

Narrative persuasion is thought to differ from the more familiar version of analytical persuasion (or the intuitive-reflective or elaboration likelihood models discussed in earlier chapters) because of a difference in the effects of audience involvement – the listener's personal stake in the message. Audience involvement can affect whether the decision-making process is deliberative, System 2, or automatic, System 1. In analytical persuasion, the level of audience involvement depends on the extent to which the audience member recognizes personally relevant consequences, and the extent of personally relevant consequences increases the chances that the audience member will deliberate carefully on the problem or decision. In narrative persuasion, audience members listening to or reading literary or entertainment narratives – even without any personally relevant consequences – appear to be "far more engrossed in the message" (van Laer et al. 2014) than those attending to analytical persuasion. And while narrative transportation may produce long-lasting persuasive effects, all of this happens without the audience member's engaging in careful deliberation or evaluation.

In other words, immersion in a text or narrative transportation works differently, and perhaps more like the intuitive decision making associated with the use of conventional metaphors and familiar analogies. Audience members who are immersed in a text may be less likely to disbelieve or counter-argue the claims being made and less likely to access other schemas and experiences. (Green and Brock 2000). Researchers describe narrative transportation as a "convergent" process in which the audience member focuses completely on the events recounted in the story and is temporarily removed from his or her original situation.

The wide range of stories in law

Lawyers know that their real task when they set out to recount the facts of a client's problem, lawsuit, or transaction is to tell a coherent and plausible story. By imposing the narrative logic of a storyline on the facts of a client's situation, the "logic of the story becomes the logic of reality." (Bruner 1987). But lawyers' stories do much more than fit the client's facts into an appealing or persuasive story-imposed reality. They also guide the reader or listener to make the desired connections between those facts and the more abstract legal rules governing the situation. In other words, lawyers use storytelling to construct two kinds of reality: the world in which the legal issue arose (the facts) and the world into which the client's story has ventured for a solution (the governing law).

Storytelling to construct the world of the governing law occurs when, for example, the advocate develops an overarching theme for the legal argument and develops that theme through the narrative arc of prior precedents. Drawing on the universal theme of justice dispensed with mercy in *Callins v. Collins* (1994), Justice Harry Blackmun developed the narrative struggle of the Supreme Court's engaging for more than 20 years with death penalty cases in order "to develop procedural and substantive rules that would lend more than the mere appearance of fairness to the death penalty endeavor." As a fitting ending to the unresolved struggle, Justice Blackmun declared that "[f]rom this day forward, I no longer shall tinker with the machinery of death." (*Callins* 1994).

The legal setting complicates the seemingly simple task of telling a story. While recounting the facts of a case seems straightforward, every lawyer knows that the everyday telling of stories is impossible to fully script, whether inside or outside the courtroom. This is so because legal storytelling is open-ended; it involves many voices; and the lawyer has control over only some of them. Moreover, legal problems bring together many diverging stories – tales that belong to the client, the opposing party, the witnesses, the lawyers, and the judge and jury members. To an unusual extent among storytelling contexts, legal problems call on different narrators and a larger cast of characters as well as multiple questions of timing and setting. (Nixon and Landman 2003).

As a result, whether in the course of a lawsuit or a personal dispute or business transaction that has not yet reached the courtroom, competing storylines are always being created. In an appellate brief, the advocate can control his client's statement of facts, but the other side will always have an opposing narrative. Courtroom storytelling is more complicated; even as one story is being presented, it is already being interrupted, disrupted, and contested. Throughout the process, the lawyers, the witnesses, the parties, the judge, and the jury continue to create and tell additional stories, including some that are secret or unshared. Rather than the clear and controlled narrative many lawyers would like to present, courtroom storytelling is "more like postmodern narrative, characterized by gaps, fissures, unresolved conflicts and chance." (Nixon and Landman 2003).

Storytelling is involved as well in recounting each individual authority in a brief or judicial opinion. These case descriptions often contain short historical narratives as well as "miniature stories about how institutions such as the legal profession, the trial court, and the legislature are supposed to function." (Papke and McManus 1999). Even the case holding itself is a narrative. (Jackson 1988). Both the major premise (an abstract rule) and the minor premise (the summary of facts in the case being decided) comprise mini-narratives. "The resulting syllogism [is] a matter of perceived resonance between the rule and the fact." (Jackson 1988).

Stories involving case precedents can be used in a variety of ways. Consider Justice Sonia Sotomayor's dissent in *Utah v. Strieff* (2016), in which she used miniature stories to expand the audience's understanding of the legal concept of "search." In *Strieff*, which will be discussed further in the next chapter, the Supreme Court found that a police officer's search of the defendant was constitutional once the police found an outstanding warrant even though the initial search occurred without reasonable suspicion. In her dissent, Justice Sotomayor recounted a sequence of story details derived from prior opinions to support her disagreement. By helping the reader imagine what might happen after a police stop, she made the abstract and somewhat flat concept of a "search" into something vivid, real, and three-dimensional: First, "the officer may . . . ask for your 'consent' to inspect your bag or purse without telling you that you can decline." Next, no matter what you said in response to the request for consent, "he may order you to stand 'helpless, perhaps facing a wall with [your] hands raised.'" And "[i]f the officer thinks you might be dangerous, he may then 'frisk' you for weapons. This involves more than just a pat down. As onlookers pass by, the officer may 'feel with sensitive fingers every portion of [your] body. A thorough search [may] be made of [your] arms and armpits, waistline and back, the groin and area about the testicles, and entire surface of the legs down to the feet.'" (*Strieff* 2016).

Judging stories

Storytelling's primary gift to lawyers is that it humanizes the law and their legal arguments. It makes room for the particular, for individuals and situations not covered by general or abstract rules or concepts. The best stories approximate the way we view the events of our everyday lives; when stories appear to us to be lifelike, they "ring true." This lifelike quality, sometimes called narrative fidelity, is the reason stories arouse and appeal to human emotions. Because this quality is the product of the elements of the story, the elements must also "hang together." That is, we must try to impose a fairly coherent storyline on the specific, concrete, individual, and telling details about the characters, events, settings, timing, motives, and causes that make up the problem situation. This quality, sometimes referred to as narrative probability, helps satisfy humans' need for consistency. (Fisher 1985).

Decision makers judge stories the same way all of us do – by asking some version of the questions: does it hold together? And does it ring true? As Janet Malcolm pointed out, the lawyer persuades when the story "fits" or matches our views of how things are (or should be), regardless of whether that story is the "truth": "Trials are won by attorneys whose stories fit, and lost by those whose stories are like the shapeless housecoat that truth . . . has chosen for her uniform." (Malcolm 1999).

Judges evaluate the "fit" of lawyers' stories at multiple stages of litigation, from motions to dismiss to post-trial decisions and appeals. For example, when confronted by a motion to dismiss a complaint, according to the U.S. Supreme Court, the federal courts must make "plausibility" determinations. The Court pointed out that "[d]etermining whether a complaint states a *plausible* claim for relief will . . . be a context-specific task that requires the reviewing court to draw on its judicial experience and common sense." (*Bell Atlantic Corp. v. Twombly* (2007) and *Ashcroft v. Iqbal* (2009)). But in this context, and in any circumstance in which judges determine whether a story "fits," legal advocates should remember that judges, like the rest of us, will do so by referencing their conception of reality – their "judicial experience and common sense." And when they turn to experience and common sense, they will often draw on stock stories, master stories, stereotypes, and various forms of unconscious bias. (Kang et al. 2012).

Take, for example, the differing stories that match up with the decisions of two judges of the District of Columbia Court of Appeals in *Dixon v. United States* (1989), a manslaughter prosecution of a woman who had been menaced with a steel pole by her husband. (Resnik and Heilbrun 1990). Claiming prosecutorial misconduct, Evelyn Dixon appealed her conviction to the Court of Appeals. In rejecting the appeal, the majority, two male judges, focused on the harms of drug abuse on families, characterizing the husband sympathetically as a "young father" and writing that "[t]his case presents a particularly poignant illustration of the consequences of drug abuse on citizens of this community. As a result of irrational and assaultive conduct following his ingestion of PCP and alcohol, a young father is dead at the hands of his pregnant wife."

In contrast, the dissenting judge, the first African-American woman to serve on the District of Columbia Court of Appeals, focused on domestic violence. She characterized the victim as "crazed" and "destructive," and she concluded that "the government's evidence, taken alone, establishes one of the strongest circumstantial settings for a reasonable claim of self-defense that an accused could hope to establish – a wife and her mother fending off injury from the hands of a husband, crazed by alcohol and PCP, and destructively swinging a steel pole as a bat." (*Dixon* 1989).

Summary

Legal storytelling is persuasive when judges and juries become immersed in the narrative world to the extent that their attitudes and intentions change to reflect the story's plot, moral, or outcome. According to rhetoricians, audience members are more willing to join the author in mentally playing out the story when, as a whole, the narrative elements hold together, ring true, and resonate emotionally. Persuasion science reaches similar results; those studies show that identifiable characters, an imaginable plot, and a story that seems like real life increase the odds that listeners will enter the world of the story and change their attitudes as a result.

Cases and briefs

Ashcroft v. Iqbal, 556 U.S. 662 (2009).
Bell Atlantic Corp. v. Twombly, 550 U.S. 544 (2007).
Dixon v. United States, 565 A.2d 72 (D.C. 1989).
Callins v. Collins, 510 U.S. 1141 (1994).
Utah v. Strieff, 136 S. Ct. 2056 (2016).

Bibliography

Alper, T., Amsterdam, A.G., Edelman, T.E., Hertz, R., Janger, R.S., McAllister-Nevins, J., Rudenstine, S. and Walker-Sterling, R., 2005, 'Stories Told and Untold: Lawyering Theory Analyses of the First Rodney King Assault', *Clinical Law Review*, 12, 1–202.
Amsterdam, A. and Bruner, J., 2002, *Minding the Law*, Harvard University Press, Cambridge, MA.
Berger, J., 1984, *And Our Faces, My Heart, Brief as Photos*, Pantheon Books, New York.
Brooks, P., 1992, *Reading for the Plot: Design and Intention in Narrative*, Harvard University Press, Cambridge, MA.
Bruner, J., 1987, 'Life as Narrative', *Social Research*, 54, 11–32.
Fisher, W.R., 1985, 'The Narrative Paradigm: An Elaboration', *Communication Monographs*, 52, 347–355.
Forster, E.M., 1961 (reprint), *Aspects of the Novel*, Houghton Mifflin Harcourt, New York.
Green, M.C. and Brock, T.C., 2000, 'The Role of Transportation in the Persuasiveness of Public Narratives', *Journal of Personality and Social Psychology*, 79, 701–721.
Jackson, B., 1988, *Law, Fact and Narrative Coherence*, Deborah Charles Publications, Liverpool.
Kang, J., Bennett, M., Carbado, D., Casey, P., Dasgupta, N., Faigman, D., Godsil, R., Greenwald, A., Levinson, J. and Mnookin, J., 2012, 'Implicit Bias in the Courtroom', *UCLA Law Review*, 59, 1124–1186.
Malcolm, J., 1999, *The Crime of Sheila McGough*, Knopf, New York.
Meyer, P.N., 2014, *Storytelling for Lawyers*, Oxford University Press, New York.
Nixon, C.L. and Landman, J., 2003, 'Turning Our Minds to Minding the Law', *Social Justice Research*, 16, 169–195.

Papke, D.R. and McManus, K.H., 1999, 'Narrative and the Appellate Opinion', *Legal Studies Forum*, 23, 449–475.

Resnik, J. and Heilbrun, C., 1990, 'Convergences: Law, Literature, and Feminism', *Yale Law Journal*, 99, 1913–1953.

van Laer, T., Ruyter, K.D., Visconti, L.M., Wetzels, M. 2014, 'The Extended Transportation-Imagery Model: A Meta-Analysis of the Antecedents and Consequences of Consumers' Narrative Transportation', *Journal of Consumer Research*, 40(5), 797–817.

7

TELLING FACT STORIES DIFFERENTLY

The law often makes very conservative use of stories. Whether they are characterized as master stories (because they are so enmeshed in American history and culture) or stock stories (because they are familiar tales of ordinary life), well-established narratives may reinforce the status quo and invisibly persuade the listener of fitting endings. When the lawyer in a will contest implicitly compares his client to the young Jane Eyre, we recognize without being told his unstated argument that her relatives have treated her unjustly. Even when the circumstances appear to be much different, the use of a familiar story or a story that triggers recognition of a genre or master story (rags to riches, slaying the monster) will reinforce the outcomes that match the traditional plot.

As an example, recall the conventional child custody dispute. It has long been framed by pre-existing stories of nurturing mothers and wage-earning fathers. This idea of the mother as caregiver and the father as wage earner is so embedded in our culture that it appears to many decision makers as the preferred option in the natural and ordinary course of things. This conclusion is illustrated in the case of *J.A.L. v. E.P.H.* (1996), a custody battle in which one partner in a lesbian relationship who had given birth to the couple's child sought to deprive the other partner of any visitation with the child. Even though the court was dealing with a very non-traditional family structure, it still framed the rationale of the outcome in terms of "primary caregiver" versus "breadwinner." Thus, despite facts unlike those in conventional child custody disputes, the court apparently could not resist typecasting the party seeking visitation in the traditional paternal role and the partners as a traditional nuclear family. (*J.A.L.* 1996).

In such contexts, storytelling effectively persuades when it travels well-worn paths that lead to the advocate's hoped-for conclusion. Indeed, in *J.A.L.*, the court held that the "breadwinner" parent had standing to petition for visitation, even though she had no biological or legal relationship to the child. But it is the surprising use of old stories in new contexts and the lawyer's ability to re-configure storylines and re-arrange characterizations that can influence an audience to broaden its understanding or to follow an unfamiliar trajectory. If, for example, the advocate for Edward Snowden (who leaked classified information from the National Security Administration about global surveillance efforts) invokes the master story of freedom-loving rebels rising up against tyrants, we know that the story is being told to upend ordinary expectations of what constitutes patriotic action.

In addition to this example of the unexpected use of an old story in a new context, lawyers often use a series of stories to broaden audience understanding over time. Thus, advocates representing those harmed by domestic or intimate partner violence worked for years to counter the well-entrenched narrative that the partner who was threatened with violence could leave at any time. This story was bolstered by the embedded metaphor that home and work, like men and women, occupied separate spheres. If that was correct, then what happened at home was private and none of the public's business. Over several decades, domestic violence advocates widened the decision makers' perspective through storytelling. They countered the entrenched story about women choosing to stay with violent partners by telling and retelling the individual stories of victims who could not leave for any number of understandable reasons – the danger of more violence, their economic dependency, the responsibility to protect their children. They countered the public-private spheres metaphor with empirical research about the effect of domestic violence on worker productivity, health care, and medical costs – showing that what happened in one sphere was felt in the other.

Similarly, lawyers use stories to prompt an audience to consider a novel or competing schema. And, once a novel or competing schema has been prompted, the lawyer may use storytelling to help the audience visualize how the corresponding argument will play out. One example is found in the brief in *Cohen v. California* (1971), the First Amendment case in which a young man wore a jacket emblazoned with the words "Fuck the Draft" into a California courtroom in the 1960s. The conventional framework for the Supreme Court's analysis might have been that wearing a jacket was conduct rather than speech and so Cohen's action was not protected by the First Amendment. Cohen's brief prompted the competing schema that wearing a jacket with a message on it was "speech" – and that in fact it was the kind of political speech historically given the highest First Amendment protection. Rather than arguing the distinction between speech and conduct, the brief writer simply stated that wearing the jacket was speech and then walked the Court through the narrative that would follow if that metaphor governed the case. (Brief for Appellant 1970).

Recognizing that storytelling is persuasive both when it travels well-worn paths and when it crosses borders (or eases a reader's border crossing), the following sections further explore how to use storytelling in tandem with embedded frames or schemas when they are favorable to your client and how to use storytelling to undercut them when they are not.

Make and break connections through storytelling

We have suggested that the advocate has an initial choice when using stories for persuasion. She may choose to take advantage of the connections between her client's current situation and familiar narratives that would naturally lead to a favorable outcome, or she may choose to try to disrupt those connections when the familiar narrative path leads in unfavorable directions. Just as narrative connections make it easy for an audience to follow the plot of a master story or a stock story, the lawyer can use story elements to differentiate this situation (the individual and the particular) from the general course of things.

As discussed in the last chapter, through her use of storytelling elements, the advocate builds the world of facts and law within which audience members perceive, interpret, and decide. In the remainder of the chapter, we consider these story elements: (1) the plot linking the events that occurred, (2) the characters involved in those events, both of which are placed within (3) a particular time and setting, and all of which is portrayed from a particular (4) point of view. In addition to these elements, legal story crafters should remember that the purpose of telling stories is to convey meaning to the audience, that storytelling is a subtly suggestive way of doing so, and that meaning is most effectively conveyed when the story hits the right emotional notes for the audience. (Foley and Robbins 2001).

Connect with the audience

Erwin Chemerinsky once wrote that "the best predictor of whether the U.S. Supreme Court finds a violation of the Fourth Amendment is whether the justices could imagine it happening to them." (Chemerinsky 2012). When we imagine that something could happen to us, we move from what psychologists would call value involvement, in which our connection to the case is only in terms of our values and beliefs, toward outcome involvement, where we feel a more personal stake in the outcome of the case. (Stanchi 2006). The more deeply involved the audience members are in the outcome, the more connection they have to the outcome, and the stronger they will feel about which is the "right" decision.

When we choose our characters, our setting, our plots – and perhaps especially when we choose "the right moment" to tell a particular story – we are thinking of an implied audience whose members can imagine the story happening to them. To bridge the gap between teller and listener, our stories must coincide with, or at least not conflict with, the conceptions the audience members have of themselves. This is so because the primary modes of narrative persuasion are suggestion and identification.

For example, Justice Stephen Breyer's dissent in *District of Columbia v. Heller* (2008) seemed written for a very specific audience: the lower court judges who would soon be faced with a concrete problem. The dissent provided an implicit guidebook for those judges who Justice Breyer predicted would find little to help them in the majority's decision, but who would nonetheless be required to make decisions in the real world. Justice Breyer gave a narrative response to a question not asked or answered by the majority: How should the trial court judge approach the next lawsuit challenging a gun regulation on Second Amendment grounds after *Heller*? This question – not the question of how the Second Amendment should be interpreted – preoccupied Justice Breyer, both explicitly and implicitly. And it is the question that would most easily connect with trial court judges.

Similarly, the author of the plaintiffs' brief in *Kerrigan v. Commissioner of Public Health* (2000), the Connecticut Supreme Court case legalizing gay marriage, sought to connect the plaintiffs with the judicial audience by describing the plaintiffs as every-day citizens of Connecticut:

> The Plaintiffs are sixteen individuals – Connecticut residents, citizens and taxpay-ers. They are in their 30's, 40's, 50's and 60's. Most of them are parents, and sev-eral have cared or are caring for aging relatives. Each also participates in the larger community where they reside – in West Hartford, Colchester, Middletown, Wil-ton, Derby, Woodbridge, New Haven and West Haven. Three have dedicated their professional lives to public school students: two as teachers (in Hartford and Woodbridge) and one as a school principal. Three work in the insurance field. One has spent her career at General Electric while another operates her own database company. Five work in medical care: as an assistant to disabled adults; as a therapist and marriage counselor; as an AIDS educator; as an acupuncturist; and as an HIV and AIDS case manager for a non-profit agency. One is a librarian at a private university while another is an administrative law judge.
>
> *(Kerrigan 2008)*

To connect with the audience, the advocate depicted the plaintiffs and their stories as sharing much in common with the judges making the decision: the plaintiffs were no longer "different." The plaintiffs were neighbors, workers, parents, and community members just like the judges. This brief illustrated recognition of one of the major functions of category systems, to promote cohesiveness within cultural groups by giv-ing the group a cognitive solidarity and a powerful bond. This technique in effect puts the reader in the plaintiffs' shoes for the rest of the opinion, and the reader can more easily empathize with the plaintiffs' injury.

Disrupt first impressions

In this section of the chapter, we focus on how to reconfigure story elements to shift emphases and perspectives. This reconfiguration involves not only the plot and the characters but also the overarching themes that have emerged from established cultural stories.

For example, the theme of the traditional family was critical to the outcome in *Michael H. v. Gerald D.* (1989). In that case, a biological father sought visitation rights with his child, who was conceived when the father had an affair with the child's mar-ried mother. Because the child was born during the mother's marriage to another man, the mother's husband became the child's "legal" father under California law. The child therefore had two fathers, a biological one and a "legal" one. Staying within the traditional family paradigm, the plaintiff's brief argued that the biological father was the "real" father, noting that he had supported the child financially and that the child called him "Daddy." (Brief for Appellant 1987). The plaintiff's argument accepted the underlying premise of the opposing side: there can be only one real father. This tactic of attempting to substitute the biological father for the legal father within the tradi-tional "baby makes three" nuclear family failed. Denying the claim and writing for the plurality, Justice Antonin Scalia turned the underlying premise that there can be only one real father against the plaintiff, stating that "California law, like nature itself, makes no provision for dual fatherhood." (*Michael H.* 1989). Justice Scalia's image of the ideal nuclear family as a traditional "baby makes three" marital family allowed him to depict the biological father as an outsider without rights.

Instead of accepting the limits of the "baby makes (only) three" marital family, the plaintiff might have used another storyline to expand the picture. Rather than arguing about which father was the one "real" father, the plaintiff might have argued that this child's family fit into the well-known plot (*The Brady Bunch*, the Kardashians) of blended and step-families who live happily together though the children have more than one mother and father. Instead of a "broken" family, the child's family would have "grown" to give her a wider love and support system.

Plot

Advocates can adjust the plot in a number of ways to make the resulting story more persuasive. First, and probably most common, advocates can shift their identification of the conflict or the "Trouble" that sets the story's characters into action. As we saw in the last chapter with *Dixon v. United States* (1989), the case about the wife who killed her abusive PCP-taking husband, the Trouble can be characterized in radically different ways: from one point of view, the Trouble was the prevailing drug culture and what it does to families, but from another, the Trouble was the abusive husband. In addition to shifting perspectives on the Trouble, advocates also can adjust the starting point of the story. These two shifts often go hand in hand. For example, in *Brown v. Board of Education* (1954), the briefs advocating for the schoolchildren identified the Trouble that necessitated the Supreme Court's action as the ruling in *Plessy v. Ferguson* (1896) that separate but equal schools satisfied the Equal Protection Clause. Given *Plessy* as the Trouble, the briefs called upon the Supreme Court to resolve the problem by overturning *Plessy* and ruling that separate but equal schools were inherently unequal. Had the advocates chosen to start the story earlier – with slavery or with the adoption of the Constitution recognizing slavery – the Trouble might have been characterized as decades of Supreme Court inaction, and the plot would have unfolded in a different way.

∞ Case study: exchanging stories of the "Trouble" affecting women's reproductive rights

The power of stories, especially master stories involving motherhood, is evident in many of the cases relating to abortion and reproductive rights. Those cases also provide examples of how to counter a master story.

Competing stories marked the evolution of Justice Anthony Kennedy's view of abortion from *Gonzales v. Carhart* (2007) to *Whole Woman's Health v. Hellerstedt* (2016). Justice Kennedy wrote the opinion for the 5–4 majority in *Gonzales*. There, the Supreme Court ruled that Congress's ban on partial-birth abortion did not impose an undue burden on the right to an abortion. In the majority opinion, Justice Kennedy explicitly referred to a story contained in an amicus brief and said that maternal regret was among the reasons supporting his decision. Justice Kennedy's opinion and the amicus brief echoed one of our culture's oldest and most embedded narratives, the story of maternal sacrifice contained within the biblical narrative of King Solomon's adjudication of the dispute between two women who each claimed a baby as their child. The worthy mother was the woman who would sacrifice everything, even to the point of giving up her own child to a stranger, to save the child's life. We can see the echoes of this master story in Justice Kennedy's opinion:

> Respect for human life finds an ultimate expression in the bond of love the mother has for her child. . . . While we find no reliable data to measure the phenomenon, it seems unexceptionable to conclude some women come to regret their choice to abort the infant life they once created and sustained. Severe depression and loss of esteem can follow.
>
> *(Carhart 2007)*

Years later, the "regret" story was reconfigured in an amicus brief filed in *Whole Woman's Health*. In that lawsuit challenging regulatory obstacles imposed on Texas abortion providers in the name of protecting women's health, one of the amicus briefs countered the earlier story. This brief made a connection between women who had had abortions and the Supreme Court justices. The connection was not "people who have had abortions" (which would not work very well given the makeup of the Court), but rather "you know people who have had abortions." Similar to the brief described earlier in the Connecticut gay marriage case, the *Whole Woman's Health* brief shifted the focus away from the individual and toward shared experiences. The message it seemed to convey was this: "We are lawyers just like you, and you know young woman lawyers just like us. You have practiced with these lawyers, you have heard them argue, you have hired them as clerks, you know them as family members, as friends. We could be your daughter."

The reconfigured plot explored what abortions meant in the life stories of these woman lawyers:

> Amici are lawyers who have obtained abortions and who have participated in a wide variety of different aspects of the legal profession, including at private law firms, corporations, multinational governmental organizations, nonprofit organizations, and law schools. And Amici believe that, like themselves, the next generation of lawyers should have the ability to control their reproductive lives and thus the opportunity to fully participate in the "economic and social life of the Nation,". . . .
>
> . . . Amici are partners, counsel, and associates at private law firms; they are government attorneys, a former state legislator, and public defenders; they are members of legal service organizations and law school professors; they are counsel to corporations, universities, and foundations; and they include several attorneys who have argued before this Court or authored briefs submitted to it. Many Amici are former federal and state judicial clerks, and two Amici were judges themselves. Amici have achieved considerable professional success; among them are a MacArthur Fellow, published authors, former editors-in-chief of leading law journals, and former academic deans. Many are mothers, and some are grandmothers.
>
> *(Brief for Amicus Curiae 2016)*

Although the arguments made by the state of Texas in support of its abortion regulations in *Whole Woman's Health* were very similar to those made in *Gonzales*, Justice Kennedy joined the majority striking down the Texas regulations. The relationship between this second "stories" brief and Justice Kennedy's decision in *Whole Woman's Health* is unknown. Still, the advocates successfully re-characterized the Trouble established in *Gonzales* (regret) and replaced it with the Trouble of denying women reproductive choice and full participation in American life.

∞ Case study: shifting the Trouble and the resolution in the story of a police search

Another example of advocates shifting their characterizations of the Trouble – and thus changing the entire plot of the narrative – appeared in the Supreme Court's divided decision in *Utah v. Strieff* (2016). In *Strieff*, the Supreme Court decided that a police officer's originally unconstitutional stop of the defendant was "cured" by the discovery of a valid, preexisting arrest warrant.

In its opinion, the majority of the Supreme Court evoked a very conventional underlying story, one we've seen many times in the news, in movies, and on television:

> This case began with an anonymous tip. In December 2006, someone called the South Salt Lake City police's drug-tip line to report "narcotics activity" at a particular residence. Narcotics detective Douglas Fackrell investigated the tip. Over the course of about a week, Officer Fackrell conducted intermittent surveillance of the home. He observed visitors who left a few minutes after arriving at the house. These visits were sufficiently frequent to raise his suspicion that the occupants were dealing drugs. One of those visitors was respondent Edward Strieff. Officer Fackrell observed Strieff exit the house and walk toward a nearby convenience store. In the store's parking lot, Officer Fackrell detained Strieff, identified himself, and asked Strieff what he was doing at the residence.
>
> *(Strieff 2016)*

The Trouble for the majority of the Court was that the house Streiff visited was being used for drug dealing and that Streiff, a likely drug customer and witness to illegal activity, was walking away and might elude questioning. Most of us recognize the familiar storyline: a suspicious house has frequent visitors who stay only a short time, and police officers responsibly investigate tips they receive about drug activity. This familiarity helps us easily accept the opinion's conclusion as a foregone one: this looks like a "bona fide investigation of a suspected drug house" because we have seen the same scene many times before.

In contrast, a different, but still-conventional, plot is called up by the brief filed by Strieff's lawyers:

> Detective Doug Fackrell detained respondent Edward Strieff after Strieff left a house that Fackrell was watching. Fackrell knew nothing about Strieff. He had never seen Strieff before. He did not know who Strieff was. He had not seen Strieff enter the house. He did not know how long Strieff had been inside. He

did not know whether Strieff lived in the house. As the court below found, Fack-rell "knew nothing of him other than that he left the house."

(Brief for Respondent 2016)

As characterized in Strieff's brief, the Trouble was that a police officer with only an anonymous tip as evidence had searched someone who had done nothing more than enter and leave a house. In Strieff's version, we hear another familiar story: the police officer who has only a vague suspicion of wrongdoing but manipulates the situation in order to find incriminating evidence. Once this connection is made, the audience is led to a very different ending: that the police acted unreasonably and unconstitutionally. In her dissent, Justice Sotomayor picked up on Strieff's arguments, agreeing that the Trouble was that these unlawful stops were part of a pattern of "systemic [and] recur-rent police misconduct." (*Strieff* 2016).

Character

Like recognizable plots, familiar characters can make advocacy stories more persuasive, often unconsciously and automatically. Narrative theorists have identified a range of archetypal characters (the Hero, the Mentor, the Threshold Guardian, the Herald, the Shadow, the Trickster, and the Shapeshifter) whose appearance in a story will be sub-tly persuasive merely because they are identifiable and their actions need not be fully explained. (Robbins 2006). For example, Threshold Guardians mark the boundaries of challenges to the Hero's quest. Professor Snape in the Harry Potter books is a Thresh-old Guardian, as is Fluffy the Three-Headed Dog, whom the Hero had to hypnotize to get to the Philosopher's Stone. Tricksters like Jack Sparrow in *Pirates of the Carib-bean* or Bart Simpson use mischief and cunning to deceive. Advocates can influence the audience's view of the real-life characters involved in a legal conflict (and perhaps the desired outcome of the case) by broadening the narrative context or by suggesting alternative or multiple characterizations, including through use of these archetypes.

An alternative characterization in a child custody case involving domestic violence might, for example, depict the domestic violence survivor not as a battered woman (with a corresponding image of being weak and passive) but instead as a person engaged in a struggle for power and control (with a corresponding image of being able to protect and care for children). (Sheppard 2009). In the immigration context, the advocate may decide to expand an immigrant client's narrative beyond the stereotypical characters of good and bad immigrants by placing the client in another broader category familiar to all Americans. Thus, an advocate might frame the case of a young immigrant convicted of shoplifting as an instance of a typical teenager who makes bad choices rather than a "bad" immigrant or even a "good immigrant" who makes a mistake. The alternative schema of the typical teenager may be able to move the decision maker beyond the "bad immigrant" stereotype and stock story toward the widely available narrative that most teenagers who make mistakes grow up to be responsible adults. (Keyes 2012).

In yet another example, a common trope in our jurisprudence is the depiction of the female rape complainant as Eve, the woman who lures a man into trouble. This archetype is entrenched in our psyches and affects our emotional response. When con-fronted by this archetype, many of us, however enlightened and modern, cannot help but feel angry and eager to punish the woman. Advocates for the woman may try to re-categorize her as the opposite character or archetype, for example, the "good woman" or Madonna. But because this response focuses continued attention on the character of the woman – attention that may be harmful to the client's case – the better strategy might be to re-script the story so that the emphasis is placed on another element. For example, adapting the client's story to the recognized plot of "overcoming the monster" moves the decision maker away from a focus on whether the woman is good or bad and toward an examination of the characteristics of the assailant. The woman becomes an ordinary person, perhaps imperfect, who simply wants to walk home unmolested.

∞ Case study: characterizing the young female student who was assaulted in Gebser v. Lago Vista Independent School District

Alternative characterizations affect audience member's impressions of how the story should end. This effect is illustrated by contrasting the characterizations of the plaintiff in the fact statements submitted in the two parties' Supreme Court briefs in *Gebser v. Lago Vista Independent School District* (1998). In that case, Alida Gebser sued the school district under Title IX because her 50-year-old teacher, Frank Waldrop, had repeatedly committed statutory rape against her starting when she was 14. The Court held that students who are sexually assaulted by their teachers cannot sue school districts for money damages unless a district official actually knows of the abuse and does nothing about it. In *Gebser*, the Court concluded that the school district did not actually know of the teacher's abuse.

In the school district's brief, Alida Gebser, who was 13 years old when she met Frank Waldrop and 14 when he began raping her, was portrayed as if she were a mature adult who had chosen to engage in a secret relationship with Waldrop. The brief implied that Waldrop and Gebser were adults engaged in a forbidden love affair, and Gebser was implicitly pictured as a Lolita character who reveled in the attention she received from her teacher. The brief depicted Gebser as conspiring with Waldrop to hide the affair and protect Waldrop. This characterization was essential to the school district's argument that district officials could not have known about the abuse.

Characterizing Alida as someone of unusual maturity and savvy, and thus someone who was capable of having a consensual relationship with an adult, the brief began:

> Gebser first entered the district as a seventh grade student. She was quickly integrated into classes reserved for the gifted and talented. By the time she reached the eighth grade, she began participating in high-school level academic activities. It was in that context that she first met Frank Waldrop, who led a "great books" discussion group for high school students. Gebser joined that discussion group while still in the eighth grade because Waldrop and his wife (also a teacher in the district) believed she would advance faster at a higher grade level.
>
> *(Brief for Respondent 1998)*

The brief emphasized that Gebser liked the special attention she received from Waldrop, noting that "she appreciated being treated as his 'peer.'" When Waldrop's behavior escalated, although "Gebser had no doubt at the time that Waldrop's conduct was wrong," she did not report it to anyone. The brief concluded by noting that "Gebser knew Waldrop's advance was inappropriate. . . . She also knew that if she reported the relationship to school officials, it would end immediately. She did not report the relationship." (Brief for Respondent 1998).

In Gebser's brief, the characterizations of both Gebser and Waldrop are very different. While that brief acknowledged Gebser's initial welcoming of the attention, it portrayed her less as a knowing Lolita and more as an innocent naïf lured into abuse by a manipulative, sophisticated adult. She could be seen as Abel, naively agreeing to go "into the fields" with Cain, only to realize too late that she had agreed to her own victimization. The brief noted: "Initially flattered by her teacher's attentions, unable to recognize the inappropriateness of his behavior until it was too late, unaware of any person to whom she could turn for help, and convinced by Waldrop to keep his actions a secret, Gebser submitted to Waldrop in order to retain her position as his student." (Brief for Petitioner 1998).

The brief hammered home the point by describing Gebser's reaction when Waldrop revealed his true nature. He contrived a way to see Gebser alone, and then took the opportunity to kiss and touch her sexually. The brief quoted Gebser's testimony, which showed her to be a confused, scared child: "I was terrified. I had no idea what I was supposed to do. I had trusted him. I had believed him. I – you know, he was basically my mentor. And it was terrifying. He was the main teacher at the school with whom I had discussions, and I didn't know what to do." (Brief for Petitioner 1998).

In Gebser's brief, she kept Waldrop's secret because she was innocent and easily fooled by a Shapeshifter who at first appeared to care for her and her education, but soon revealed his own selfish interests. But the real villain in Gebser's story was the school district, the entity that gave the Shapeshifter the power and authority that he abused. These characterizations led to an inevitable end that the brief clearly articulated: "Waldrop capitalized upon his professional position as a teacher, and the authority that [the school district] granted to him, to prey on Gebser's vulnerabilities." (Brief for Petitioner 1998).

Echoes of both briefs' characterizations appeared in the opinions. In the majority opinion in favor of the school district, we see the impact of the school district's Lolita characterization of Gebser in the Court's repeated reference to Gebser and Waldrop's "relationship." The opinion never used the words "rape" or "abuse." (Bartow 2016). In the dissent, however, the influence of the very different characterizations in Gebser's brief was apparent. Justice John Paul Stevens's dissent characterized Gebser as "repeatedly sexually abused" by Waldrop. He concluded that the case presented a "paradigmatic example of a tort that was made possible, that was effected, and that was repeated over a prolonged period because of the powerful influence that Waldrop had over Gebser by reason of the authority that his employer, the school district, had delegated to him." (*Gebser* 1998).

Setting

In some contexts, setting can be as important as plot and character. Think, for example, of the hotel that played a starring role in *The Shining* or of the *perfect storm* as evoking any setting that diminishes the characters' responsibility for their actions. (Parker 2012). In addition to playing a starring role, the setting may govern the timing and the pacing of the plot.

Case study: government displays of the Ten Commandments

Setting was critical in two cases involving the display of the Ten Commandments on government property. In *Van Orden v. Perry* (2005), the U.S. Supreme Court decided that a Ten Commandments plaque on the grounds of the Texas State Capitol did not violate the Establishment Clause of the First Amendment. The Court's analysis centered on the use of the Capitol grounds to inform and educate visitors about Texas state history. This characterization of the setting as a kind of history museum led to the characterization of the Ten Commandments as a "monument," a word that divorced the commandments from their religious significance. The Court wrote that the inquiry of whether the "monument" violated the First Amendment required it "to consider the context of the display." The majority reasoned:

> In certain contexts, a display of the tablets of the Ten Commandments can convey not simply a religious message but also a secular moral message (about proper standards of social conduct). And in certain contexts, a display of the tablets can also convey a historical message (about a historic relation between those standards and the law) – a fact that helps to explain the display of those tablets in dozens of courthouses throughout the Nation, including the Supreme Court of the United States. . . . Texas has treated her Capitol grounds monuments as representing the several strands in the State's political and legal history. The inclusion of the Ten Commandments monument in this group has a dual significance, partaking of both religion and government.
>
> *(Van Orden 2005)*

By contrast, in an opinion issued the same day, the Court found the displays of the Ten Commandments at county courthouses in Kentucky to be unconstitutional. In *McCreary County v. American Civil Liberties Union of Kentucky* (2005), the Court again examined the setting of the placement of the Commandments. In the Kentucky courthouses, the Commandments had originally been displayed alone, without the surrounding context of additional historical material in the Texas Capitol case. The Court noted that the placement of the Commandments mattered: "The point is simply that the original text viewed in its entirety is an unmistakably religious statement dealing with religious obligations and with morality subject to religious sanction. When the government initiates an effort to place this statement *alone in public view*, a religious object is unmistakable." (*McCreary County* 2005, emphasis added).

Point of view

The point of view – or the vantage point from which a story is told – affects its telling. For persuasive purposes, a story's point of view may very much influence the audience's response and interpretation. Point of view is most persuasively used when the advocate is able to connect the audience member with the narrator from whose point of view the story is portrayed. One example occurred in First Lady Michelle Obama's speech at the 2016 Democratic national convention. The story she recounted, and the emotions she evoked, depended on her unique ability to tell the story from a particular vantage point:

> That is the story of this country, the story that has brought me to this stage tonight, the story of generations of people who felt the lash of bondage, the shame of servitude, the sting of segregation, but who kept on striving and hoping and doing what needed to be done so that today I wake up every morning in a house that was built by slaves. . . . And I watch my daughters, two beautiful, intelligent, black young women playing with their dogs on the White House lawn.
>
> *(Obama 2016)*

As compelling as that image is, as some of the negative reactions by political opponents indicated, it would not resonate with the audience, nor would it persuade, unless the audience members can identify with the speaker.

∞ Case study: point of view in briefs detailing a middle-school strip search

The Statements of Facts in the Supreme Court briefs in *Redding v. Safford Unified School District* (2009) are a study in point of view. *Redding* involved the strip search of a 13-year-old middle-school student, Savana Redding. The briefs of the School District and Redding approached the same facts from wholly different points of view, and as a result, the briefs told very different stories.

The School District told the story from the point of view of Kerry Wilson, the school administrator most involved in the events that followed. In this brief, the reader followed Principal Wilson as he investigated a serious drug-dealing accusation. The reader accompanied Wilson as each piece of evidence unfolded, knowing what he knew, not knowing what he did not know:

> The 2003–2004 school year arrived with renewed concerns about drug abuse among students at Safford Middle School. . . . [S]chool administrators, including Assistant Principal Kerry Wilson, received a call from the mother of another student, Jordan Romero, requesting a meeting. At the meeting, Jordan's mother described how her son had become violent with her a few nights earlier, and then suddenly sick to his stomach. Jordan explained that his fit of rage occurred after he took some pills that a classmate had given to him. . . .
>
> Jordan identified students by name, including Marissa [Glines] and Redding, along with detailed accounts of their illicit activities. . . . Days after the meeting with Jordan and his mother, Wilson received hard evidence that drugs were again being distributed on campus. Jordan sought Wilson out as school was starting and handed him a white pill that Marissa had just given to him. He also told Wilson that there were more pills on campus and that a group of students was planning on taking them that day at lunch.

. . . At that point, Wilson had a decision to make. He confirmed that prescription pills were being distributed again on campus that morning, although he still was not sure who else had pills and in what amounts, or for that matter, whether there were also other kinds of pills on campus. Marissa [had] directly implicated Redding as the supplier of the prescription pills, plus another OTC pill. . . .

Overlaying all of this, Wilson could recall at least two occasions when a student was harmed by taking pills distributed on campus. The most recent case was Jordan's just days earlier when he became violent with his mother and sick to his stomach. And the most serious case nearly resulted in a student's death the year prior.

(Brief for Petitioners 2009)

Savana's brief, by comparison, was presented from Savana's point of view – the point of view of a scared child who is hauled out of math class and forced to strip off her clothes:

Thirteen-year-old Savana Redding was an eighth-grade student at Safford Middle School in the fall of 2003. . . . Savana was in math class . . . on October 8, 2003, when the school's Vice Principal, Kerry Wilson, entered her classroom. Wilson asked Savana to pack her belongings in her backpack and follow him to his office. He did not explain to Savana why he was removing her from class.

When they reached his office, Wilson . . . pointed to four white pills and one blue pill, which were sitting atop his desk, and which he by then knew to be 400 mg ibuprofen and the over-the-counter anti-inflammatory pill Naprosyn. He asked Savana if she had seen these pills before, and she truthfully told Wilson that she had not previously seen the pills. . . . Wilson asked if he could search Savana's belongings, and Savana agreed. He and an administrative assistant, Helen Romero, searched Savana's backpack. Consistent with Savana's assurances, they found nothing – no indicia of drug use, drug possession, or any other illegal or improper conduct.

Having turned up no evidence to suggest any misconduct by Savana, Wilson nonetheless immediately ordered Romero to take Savana to the nurse's office. Savana did not know why she was being marched into the nurse's office. As the door slammed and locked behind Savana, the school nurse, Peggy Schwallier, was in the bathroom washing her hands. At that point, Romero explained that they intended to search Savana for pills. The two school officials then directed Savana to undress.

(Brief for Respondent 2009)

Because of the point of view from which these narratives are presented, reading the briefs one by one will leave the reader with two very different first impressions. Reflecting another perspective on the influence of point of view, during oral argument on the case and in a later interview, Justice Ruth Bader Ginsburg questioned whether her colleagues, all male at the time, had been able to fully understand the point of view of a thirteen-year-old girl subjected to a strip search. (Biskupic 2009).

∞ *Case study: point of view in a death penalty opinion*

In a much-discussed dissent in *Brumfield v. Cain* (2015), Justice Clarence Thomas shifted the point of view from the criminal defendant to the victim's son. At the time of Kevan Brumfield's trial for the murder of Betty Smothers, the U.S. Supreme Court had not yet decided *Atkins v. Virginia* (2002), the case in which the Court found that the Eighth Amendment barred the execution of the mentally disabled. After *Atkins* came down, Brumfield filed for post-conviction relief based on his mental disability. The Court found sufficient evidence that he might fit within the category of defendants who should be excluded from the death penalty.

In dissent, Justice Thomas did not argue with the holding in *Atkins*. Instead, he contrasted the life of one of Commander Smothers's children with that of Brumfield. "Though he had turned 18 just two days before Brumfield murdered his mother, [her son, Warrick Dunn] quickly stepped into the role of father figure to his younger siblings. In his view, it 'was up to [him] to make sure that everybody grew up to be somebody.'" Thomas explained further: "Like Brumfield, Warrick's father was not a part of his life. But, unlike Brumfield, Warrick did not use the absence of a father figure as a justification for murder. Instead, he recognized that his mother had been 'the family patriarch' when she was alive, and that he had a responsibility to take on that role after her death at 37." (*Brumfield* 2015). After describing Dunn's stellar football career, Justice Thomas recounted Dunn's devotion to his family and the memory of his mother, and he cataloged Dunn's charity work. At the end of his opinion, he included a photograph of Smothers.

Although effective emotionally, whether Justice Thomas's use of point of view was persuasive in this case is debatable. Two of the justices with whom he agreed on the outcome specifically distanced themselves from this part of the dissent.

Summary

When it comes to storytelling for persuasion, lawyers have a checklist full of choices. First, when its outcome would be favorable to their client, they can choose to follow a familiar master story or everyday script. When, on the other hand, the familiar narrative arc leads to an unfavorable result, lawyers can choose to try to disrupt the connections between their client's case and the existing narratives by re-arranging and re-emphasizing various story elements. When reconfiguration is the goal, advocates can adjust plots by shifting what constitutes the Trouble or the conflict that sets the story's characters into action. Or they may decide to re-cast the main characters, focus on the setting, or shift the narrator's point of view.

Cases

Atkins v. Virginia, 536 U.S. 304 (2002).
Brown v. Board of Education, 347 U.S. 483 (1954).
Brumfield v. Cain, 135 S. Ct. 2269 (2015).
Cohen v. California, 403 U.S. 15 (1971).
    Brief for Appellant [Paul Cohen], 1970 Westlaw 136795.
District of Columbia v. Heller, 554 U.S. 570 (2008).

Gebser v. Lago Vista Independent School Dist., 524 U.S. 274 (1998).
  Brief for Petitioners [Alida Star Gebser et al.], 1998 WL 19745.
  Brief for Respondent [Lago Vista Independent School Dist.], 1998 WL 63153.
Gonzales v. Carhart, 550 U.S. 124 (2007).
  Amicus Brief on Behalf of Sandra Cano et al., 2006 WL 1436684.
Kerrigan v. Commissioner of Public Health, 957 A.2d 407 (Conn. 2008).
  Brief for Plaintiffs-Appellants [Elizabeth Kerrigan et al.], 2007 WL 4725470.
McCreary County v. ACLU of Ky., 545 U.S. 844 (2005).
Michael H. v. Gerald D., 491 U.S. 110 (1989).
  Brief for Appellant [Michael H.] 1987 WL 880072.
Plessy v. Ferguson, 163 U.S. 537 (1896).
Safford Unified School District v. Redding, 557 U.S. 364 (2009).
  Brief for Petitioners [Safford Unified School Dist. et al.], 2009 WL 507028.
  Brief for Respondent [April Redding, legal guardian of minor child], 2009 WL 852123.
Utah v. Strieff, 136 S. Ct. 2056 (2016).
  Brief for Respondent [Edward Joseph Strieff], 2016 WL 1254378.
Van Orden v. Perry, 545 U.S. 677 (2005).
Whole Woman's Health v. Hellerstedt, 136 S. Ct. 2292 (2016).
  Brief for Amicus Curiae [Janice Macavoy et al.], 2016 WL 74949.
J.A.L. v. E.P.H., 682 A.2d 214 (Pa. Super. 1996).

Bibliography

Bartow, A., 2016, '*Gebser v. Lago Vista School District* Rewritten Opinion', in K. Stanchi, L. Berger and B. Crawford (eds.), *United States Feminist Judgments: Rewritten Opinions of the United States Supreme Court*, Cambridge University Press, Cambridge.

Biskupic, J., 2009, 'Ginsburg: Court Needs Another Woman', *USA Today*, 5 October 2009.

Chemerinsky, E., 2012, 'The Supreme Court and the Fourth Amendment', *Texas Lawyer Online*, 14 May 2012.

Foley, B.J. and Robbins, R.A., 2001, 'Fiction 101: A Primer for Lawyers on How to Use Fiction Writing Techniques to Write Persuasive Facts Sections', *Rutgers Law Journal*, 32, 459–495.

Keyes, E., 2012, 'Beyond Saints and Sinners: Discretion and the Need for New Narratives in the U.S. Immigration System', *Georgetown Immigration Law Journal*, 26, 207–256.

Obama, M., 2016, 'Michelle Obama Lights Up the DNC: "When They Go Low, We Go High"', *The New York Times*, 26 July 2016.

Robbins, R.A., 2006, 'Harry Potter, Ruby Slippers and Merlin: Telling the Client's Story Using the Characters and Paradigm of the Archetypal Hero's Journey', *Seattle University Law Review*, 29, 767–793.

Sheppard, J., 2009, 'Once Upon a Time, Happily Ever After, and in a Galaxy Far, Far Away: Using Narrative to Fill the Cognitive Gap Left by Overreliance on Pure Logic in Appellate Briefs and Motion Memoranda', *Willamette Law Review*, 46, 255–301.

Stanchi, K.M., 2006, 'The Science of Persuasion: An Initial Exploration', *Michigan State Law Review*, 2, 411–456.

8

DEVELOPING LAW STORIES

When lawyers think of stories, they think first of how to arrange and recount the facts of their client's pre-lawsuit plight or they think about the unfolding facts of the litigation itself. But legal briefs and lawyer's arguments are filled with other kinds of stories and, in particular, with stories about the law itself. As mentioned earlier, advocates use storytelling to construct two kinds of reality: the world of the facts (within which the client's legal issue arose) and the world of the law (into which the client's story has ventured for a resolution).

Revealing that multiple stories often are in play in a judicial opinion (as they would be in the briefs as well), John Leubsdorf analyzed the different narrative accounts interwoven within the opinion in *New York Times v. Sullivan* (1964). (Leubsdorf 2001). In *Sullivan*, Alabama public officials sued the *New York Times* for its publication of an advertisement alleging that the arrest of the Rev. Dr. Martin Luther King in Montgomery, Alabama, was part of an effort to derail the civil rights movement. The Supreme Court held that the advertisement was protected by the First Amendment because the Constitution provided a higher level of protection for allegedly libelous speech about a public official. The opinion began with the two stories common to every appellate case – the story of the facts, or the history of Dr. King's campaign, and the story of the judicial process, or what had happened during the libel lawsuit itself. After those stories, Justice William Brennan introduced another story, the legal narrative of the evolution of the First Amendment. (Leubsdorf 2001).

Justice Brennan's story of the First Amendment began by describing the Framers' intent of protecting public discussion, and especially discussion of significant issues of public concern. He noted the lengthy controversy over the Sedition Act, which led to a national consensus about the "central meaning of the First Amendment": to protect "free public discussion of the stewardship of public officials." Justice Brennan then portrayed the evolution of the meaning of the First Amendment as the Supreme Court interpreted it in case after case. In Justice Brennan's story, the journey of "Jefferson and Madison [to pass the Amendment] parallels the story of Martin Luther King and the Montgomery protesters." (*Sullivan* 1964). Both Justice Brennan's story of the law and his comparison of how the development of the law echoed the story of the civil rights movement led inexorably to the conclusion that the Alabama officials could not recover for libel when the appropriate level of First Amendment protection was applied. (Leubsdorf 2001).

Plot in law stories

Just as an inspirational law story was essential to the decision in *Sullivan*, a similar foundational law story established the setting for the decision in *Brown v. Board of Education* (1954). This story of the evolution of the law was first recounted in an amicus brief filed on behalf of the United States in *Shelley v. Kraemer* (1948), a case involving the constitutionality of racial covenants on land. In its brief, the Government told an uplifting story about the law's evolution from de jure segregation to a racial equality ideal embodied in the Fifth and Fourteenth Amendments to the Constitution. The government's equality story in *Kraemer* laid a foundation that the Solicitor General's Office would later advance in its briefs in *Brown I*:

> This Nation was founded upon the declaration that all men are endowed by their Creator with certain inalienable rights, and that among these rights are Life, Liberty and the pursuit of Happiness. To that declaration was added the Fifth Amendment of the Bill of Rights, providing that no person shall be deprived of life, liberty or property without due process of law; and the Fourteenth Amendment, providing that no State shall deprive any person of life, liberty or property, without due process of law, nor deny to any person within its jurisdiction the equal protection of the laws. And Congress, exercising its power to enforce the provisions of the Fourteenth Amendment, has provided that all citizens of the United States shall have the same right, in every State and Territory, as is enjoyed by white citizens to inherit, purchase, lease, sell, hold, and convey real and personal property.
>
> *(Brief for Amicus Curiae 1947)*

As these opinions demonstrate, the law itself may become the leading character in a story, and the development of the law can be traced in a plot that leads the audience toward a desired outcome. Several experts in legal advocacy have explored the effectiveness of structuring arguments about how the law should be interpreted or understood around a storyline. (Edwards 2010; Chestek 2008). In this argument structure, the relevant body of law is presented as a story, with a typical plot, characters, conflict, and resolution. The development of the plot supplants the typical logical syllogism as the primary structure for the argument. While this structure deviates from the conventional organization expected by the legal audience, organizing around a familiar story often will feel natural and familiar to the decision maker.

∞ *Case studies: birth (Miranda) and rescue (Bowers)*

In her influential article on the narrative of law, Linda Edwards described how story archetypes can be adapted to the organization of legal arguments. (Edwards 2010). She focused mainly on birth and rescue stories, although she acknowledged other potentially useful genres or master stories, such as narratives of betrayal and journeys. Applying the birth story framework to the development of the law will be most useful when the advocate has no supporting precedent that is directly on point and a new rule is needed. The "birth" story allows the advocate to argue that the progression and history of the law leads to the necessary new rule. In a birth story, the advocate relies on a historical review of the precedent. She organizes and presents that history as a series of steps leading toward the new rule, which is the logical and natural final step (the end or dénouement of the story). This organization closely parallels the foot-in-the-door approach covered in Chapter 16 as well as the gradual approach covered in Chapter 17.

Professor Edwards used the petitioner's brief in *Miranda v. Arizona* (1966) as the paradigmatic example of a birth story. To prevail in *Miranda*, the petitioner was required to argue that the right to counsel did not begin at trial, but extended to interrogation by police well before trial. In the brief, the petitioner charted the historical progress of the right against forced confessions starting with the 15th century and the "third degree." The brief then charted the constitutional right to counsel, from *Johnson v. Zerbst* (1938) (defendants entitled to counsel at trial in federal courts) and *Gideon v. Wainwright* (1963) (defendants entitled to counsel at trial in all state courts) to *Hamilton v. Alabama* (1961) and *White v. Maryland* (1963) (defendants entitled to counsel in federal arraignments and in all arraignments or analogous proceedings under state law at which anything of consequence can happen). The *Miranda* rule that law-enforcement officers must warn a person taken into custody that he or she has the right to remain silent and is entitled to legal counsel, one of the best-known rules in American jurisprudential history, came about because of the argument that all of these precedents were steps toward the birth of a right, and the inevitable conclusion that the Constitution required counsel at the interrogation stage.

In a rescue story, by contrast, the advocate has relevant supporting precedent, often well established, but the precedent is under attack from the opposing side. In defending the precedent from attack, the advocate relies heavily on policy arguments to convince the decision makers of the importance of protecting the goals served by the law. Professor Edwards used the respondent's brief in *Bowers v. Hardwick*, the 1986 Supreme Court case upholding the constitutionality of sodomy statutes, to illustrate a typical rescue story. In that case, the brief portrayed the sodomy statute and the State of Georgia as attacking and undermining the cherished constitutional right to privacy. While the law is the main character in a birth story, rescue stories center on judicial characters who must rescue something precious, like a constitutional right, that is under attack.

∞ Case study: the birth of rape law reform

In the Interest of M.T.S. (1992), a decision of the New Jersey Supreme Court, changed the proof requirements of the state's rape law. The court decided that the "physical force" requirement of the New Jersey sexual assault statute required only the amount of force necessary to achieve penetration. Perhaps recognizing the controversial nature of its holding, the court organized the opinion very differently from the traditional judicial decision. In analyzing what the legislature likely intended by "physical force," the opinion provided a lengthy exposition on the evolution of rape law, casting the current sexual assault statute as the culmination of a long history of rape reform. From a narrative perspective, the opinion falls into the genre of a classic birth story.

The opinion began with the English common law and its requirement that the rape victim "resist" penetration "to the uttermost." It explored how the resistance requirement was a result of the law's explicitly expressed distrust of rape complainants and how this distrust influenced rape law well into the modern age. Among other things, the opinion described how the resistance requirement, long after it had been removed from the law, shaped the law of consent, the spousal exemption, and the law's treatment of a complainant's sexual history. It charted the history of rape law and then moved to the feminist critiques of the 1970s. The New Jersey rape statute was finally portrayed as the triumphant product of these efforts at reform. Thus, the interpretation of "physical force" to require no real force or resistance beyond that required to accomplish the act appeared to be the natural result of the law's history and development.

The *M.T.S.* opinion demonstrates the power of the birth story organization, but also its potential pitfalls. To portray the birth of a new legal requirement, the court was required to provide a historical summary, which has the potential to be plodding, lengthy, and sometimes boring. It has none of the familiar flow toward a conclusion provided by the syllogism. Done poorly, a historical summary can read like a description of the law with no real focus or purpose. To make the presentation of historical context persuasive, the legal advocate must be explicit about the goals and purpose of the argument.

The *M.T.S.* opinion, for example, started with the statement that the sexual assault statute is best examined in the context of "200 years of rape law." A similar rhetorical tactic was used in the *Miranda* brief, in which the petitioner announced at the beginning that "We deal here with growing law and look to where we are going by considering where we have been." *M.T.S.* also used thesis sentences to guide the reader, showing explicitly the purpose of recounting all this history. The court made such statements as "[t]he circumstances surrounding the actual passage of the current law reveal that it was conceived as a reform measure reconstituting the law to address a widely-sensed evil" and "[t]he history of traditional rape law sheds clearer light on the factors that became most influential in the enactment of current law." (*M.T.S.* 1992)

To structure a story about the development of the law as a birth story also requires that the advocate make a deliberate choice about when to start, how far back in history to go. Because context is so important to the birth story, it is not uncommon to see birth stories starting far back in history. The decision in *M.T.S.* to go back to the English common law and its presumption that rape complainants are not truthful was certainly a tactical choice designed to show how far the law had come.

Character in law stories

When law stories are structured as journeys of progress or as birth narratives, they present familiar, comfortable, and reassuring plots that revolve around "the law" itself as the main character. Stories about judges and their roles in the judicial process often support the brief writer's plot about the law's development and his characterization of a particular judge as a hero or villain. In some circumstances, these stories may persuade the judge to act accordingly. In one example, first in the brief supporting Cohen and then in the decision in *Cohen v. California* (1971), the plot required the

Supreme Court justices to act heroically to reveal the true nature of the law. Taking on the role of a searcher for truth, Justice John Marshall Harlan was the primary actor and the main character. He began the opinion that would determine whether wearing a jacket containing the phrase "Fuck the Draft" constituted speech protected by the First Amendment by moving immediately to generate anticipation and build credibility: "This case may seem at first blush too inconsequential to find its way into our books, but the issue it presents is of no small constitutional significance." (*Cohen* 1971).

After recounting the facts and concluding the procedural history by stating that the Court was reversing the judgment below, Justice Harlan moved summarily ahead: "The question of our jurisdiction need not detain us long." In order to "lay hands on the precise issue," Justice Harlan cleared out the matters "which this record does not present." Because wearing the jacket conveyed a message, Justice Harlan wrote, the conviction "rests squarely upon his exercise of the freedom of speech" and "can be justified, if at all, only as a valid regulation of the manner in which he exercised that freedom." The Court – through the actions of Justice Harlan – must thus protect Cohen because "the State certainly lacks power to punish Cohen for the underlying content of the message the inscription conveyed." (*Cohen* 1971). After defeating the remaining obstacles, Justice Harlan declared victory for the Court. (Berger and Sammons 2013).

∞ Case study: the story of Title VII, chronicle of a trickster or story of the birth of equality law

Most lawyers have heard the story of how Title VII of the Civil Rights Act of 1964 came to include discrimination based on sex. The story has been repeated many times, including by the Supreme Court in *Meritor Savings Bank v. Vinson* (1986). It is the story of a trickster. According to this narrative of the life of Title VII, Representative Howard Smith of Virginia, a notorious opponent of civil rights and integration, was said to have added the amendment on sex discrimination at the last minute to kill the bill. This narrative is often repeated in briefs arguing that sex should not be afforded the same treatment as race under the Act. Consider this brief by the County of Washington, in *Washington v. Gunther* (1981), which argued that sex-based wage discrimination should be subject to a different standard of proof under Title VII:

> The bill that was to become the Civil Rights Act of 1964 – H.R. 7152 – was proposed on June 20, 1963. That bill did not in any way refer to discrimination with respect to sex, either when proposed or during the several months it was considered by the House Judiciary Committee. As proposed to and considered by the Committee, H.R. 7152 was legislation designed to prohibit employment discrimination only with respect to race, color, religion and national origin. H.R. 7152 was debated in the House from January 31, 1964 to February 10, 1964.
>
> Near the end of the debate, on February 8, 1964, Representative Smith of Virginia offered an amendment to add sex as a protected classification under H.R. 7152. The supporters of H.R. 7152 opposed the hastily introduced amendment, seeing it as a ploy by the opponents of the bill to overburden, weaken and defeat the legislation. Congresswoman Green, a supporter of H.R. 7152 (and a

sponsor of an equal pay proposal in 1962), argued against the Smith amendment because the House Judiciary Committee had never considered – indeed, had not even been asked to consider – the advisability of including sex as a protected classification in the proposed legislation. Congressman Celler, the sponsor of H.R. 7152, characterized the Smith amendment as "illogical, ill timed, ill placed and improper." The Smith amendment was accepted by the House on the same afternoon it was proposed, without any hearings or committee deliberations, and with hardly any debate. Thus, at the time of adoption of the Smith "sex" amendment, the intent of Congress as to its general meaning and scope is unclear.

Another story could, however, be told about the same history. Rather than a plot that focused on Representative Smith as the main character, the alternative plot would be a birth story. This story of the birth of a statutory right would detail the history of a committed group of feminists who had long been working behind the scenes politically, including with Representative Smith, to secure equal rights for women. Consider this alternative narrative by Katherine Franke:

> While this belief that there was a lack of congressional thinking about the meaning of sex discrimination has become true by virtue of repetition, it ignores a rich congressional legislative history concerning the equal rights of women. . . . The first Equal Rights Amendment (ERA) was introduced into Congress in 1923. . . . [The article then describes the history of the suffrage movement.] In August of 1962, Senator Pauli Murray developed a strategy. . . . Rather than continuing a losing battle to pass an amendment to the Constitution, she suggested a shift to the courts. . . . In the end, Murray's litigation strategy garnered enough support from a broad spectrum of feminists and culminated in the Supreme Court's decisions in *Reed v. Reed, Frontiero v. Richardson, Schlesinger v. Ballard, and Craig v. Boren.* . . .
>
> While feminists pursued this novel litigation strategy, President Kennedy took the position that the federal government, as an employer, should take the moral high ground with regard to equal employment opportunity. . . . When the law that we now know as the Civil Rights Act of 1964 was introduced into the House in June of 1963, it did not include sex in the list of prohibited forms of discrimination. The National Women's Party and other supporters of the ERA began a campaign to have sex included in the bill. To this end, they sought support from their long-time congressional allies, including many conservative southerners. ERA supporters Martha Griffiths (D. Mich.) and Katherine St. George (R. N.Y.) decided to endorse the sex amendment to Title VII but thought the best strategy would be to have Howard Smith (D. Va.), a conservative pro-ERA southerner, make the motion. For Smith, it was a win/win strategy: either the sex amendment would defeat the Civil Rights Act – a regulation of private business which he opposed – or it would amount to the passage of the ERA – a measure that he had always supported.
>
> *(Franke 1995)*

In Franke's version, the story of the inclusion of sex into Title VII is less the story of a Trickster, and more a story of the birth of a statutory right that was the culmination of an inevitable march toward equality. (Franke 1995). This story is, of course, much more advantageous to the advocate wishing to argue that Title VII creates expansive rights for women. Notice how far back in time Franke's story starts – in 1923, with the first proposed ERA. This early start to the story, coupled with the detailed history, shows that debates and political machinations had swirled around sex equality for years before the eventual passage of Title VII. Perhaps the Smith Amendment was not debated when it was introduced, but the debate about sex equality had been actively roiling in and around Congress and the courts for decades.

Summary

Whether statutory or common law, regulatory or constitutional, all laws are the outcome of a series of events and actions taken by characters after a Trouble or conflict arose. So all laws provide the necessary conditions for storytelling. The advocate need only look to find them. And as with other decisions about argument frameworks, the advocate may have a choice among multiple stories, myths, characters, and archetypes. The challenge for the advocate is to research and understand the law's history and then decide what story of the law's development best fits the client's purpose. For example, the insertion of "sex" into Title VII might be a trickster story (of a Senator trying to kill the bill) or a journey or birth story (of a long push toward women's rights starting with the suffrage movement). The story of Megan's Law might be a rescue story (saving children from predators) or a betrayal story (the law's abandonment of civil rights in the face of political expediency). The advocate's storytelling goal is to create harmonious or complementary worlds of fact and law.

Cases & briefs

Bowers v. Hardwick, 478 U.S. 186 (1986).
Brown v. Board of Education, 347 U.S. 483 (1954).
Cohen v. California, 403 U.S. 15 (1971).
    Brief for Appellant [Paul Cohen], 1970 Westlaw 136795.
Gideon v. Wainwright, 372 U.S. 335 (1963).
Hamilton v. Alabama, 368 U.S. 52 (1961).
Johnson v. Zerbst, 304 U.S. 458 (1938).
Meritor Savings Bank v. Vinson, 477 U.S. 57 (1986).
Miranda v. Arizona, 384 U.S. 436 (1966)
    Brief for Petitioner [Ernesto Miranda], 1966 Westlaw 87732.
In the Interest of M.T.S., 609 A.2d 1266 (N.J. 1992).
New York Times v. Sullivan, 376 U.S. 254 (1964).
Shelley v. Kraemer, 334 U.S. 1 (1948).
    Brief for Amicus Curiae [United States] 1947 WL 30432.
Washington v. Gunther, 452 U.S. 161 (1981).
    Brief for Petitioner [County of Washington], 1980 WL 339719.
White v. Maryland, 373 U.S. 59 (1963).

Bibliography

Berger, L.L. and Sammons, J.L., 2013, 'The Law's Mystery', *British Journal of American Legal Studies*, 2, 1–26.

Chestek, K., 2008, 'The Plot Thickens: The Appellate Brief as Story', *Legal Writing: The Journal of the Legal Writing Institute*, 14, 127–169.

Edwards, L.H., 2010, 'Once Upon a Time in Law: Myth, Metaphor, and Authority', *Tennessee Law Review*, 77, 883–916.

Franke, K.M., 1995, 'The Central Mistake of Sex Discrimination Law: The Disaggregation of Sex and Gender', *University of Pennsylvania Law Review*, 144, 1–99.

Leubsdorf, J., 2001, 'The Structure of Judicial Opinions', *Minnesota Law Review*, 86, 447–496.

9

MAKING INTUITIVE CONNECTIONS

For the advocate, a hard case is one in which there is no statutory rule or mandatory precedent leading to a favorable conclusion for the client. Take the plaintiffs' lawyer who in the 1940s argued that low and frequent flights by U.S. military aircraft over the plaintiffs' property constituted a taking. The Fifth Amendment provides that "private property" shall not "be taken for public use, without just compensation," but airspace had been likened to public highways, not private property. In *United States v. Causby* (1946), the Supreme Court nonetheless held that depending upon the frequency of the flights, a taking might have occurred when the government repeatedly flew Army bombers "directly above respondents' land at a height of eighty-three feet where the light and noise from these planes caused respondents to lose sleep, and their chickens to be killed." Although the dissenters objected that the decision would limit Congress's future ability to "keep the air free," the majority accepted the familiar analogy to a trespass on land, agreeing that just as the farmers owned their land and could keep it free from trespass, they had an interest in at least a few feet of the air above their farm. (*Causby* 1946).

Persuasion scientists describe the persuasion appropriate in these situations as response shaping (when the reader's initial response is neutral or uninterested); response reinforcing (when the initial response is favorable); and response changing (when the initial response is unfavorable). Although no hard and fast rules apply, as Chapter 10 describes, response-shaping persuasion often takes advantage of very familiar or conventional analogies and metaphors. Looking ahead, Chapter 11 will focus on the more extensive arguments based on analogy that are a primary method for reinforcing favorable responses, and Chapter 12 will address the use of novel metaphors and characterizations to shift perspectives in order to re-align initially negative responses.

Choosing among analogy, metaphor, and characterization

Intuitive connections are made when the advocate invokes embedded knowledge frameworks (or schema) through analogy, metaphor, and characterization (a metaphor

that is used to stand for the main characters or protagonists). Metaphor and analogy have the power to make and break connections because they first invite and then
enable us to see one thing "as" another. Seeing one thing as another is how we come
to understand new information (here's a comparable example); how we determine
where something new likely fits (that looks like the right slot); and how we are able to
consider a different point of view (now I see what you mean).

Although the cognitive difference is more significant, the linguistic difference
between analogy and metaphor is very simply illustrated:

Analogy: A is like B (The computer screen is like your desktop.)
Metaphor: A is B (The computer screen is a desktop.)

In both, A is the target, and B is the source. When the purpose of using an analogy or a
metaphor is to explain, the target (the computer screen early in its existence) typically is the
"new" concept or the more abstract idea, and the source (the top of your physical desk) is
the more familiar or concrete thing. The analogy or the metaphor makes the target more
understandable for one of several reasons: because the physical desktop is similar, but more
familiar or more concrete; because "desktop" has become a more abstract category of
examples into which the computer screen seems to fit; or because viewing the computer
screen as a desktop helps the reader see the computer screen in a different way.

When the reader agrees that the source and the target are similar in some ways, the
reader infers that further similarities exist, transferring attributes, relationships, and
meaning from the source (the desktop) to the target (the screen). This mapping and
transference explains why, after accepting the analogy, the reader is not surprised to
find that his computer screen holds virtual files, folders, and a trashcan.

Here's a different kind of example:

Analogy: A is like B (Argument is like war.)
Metaphor: A is B (Argument is war.)
Characterization: A's protagonist is C (Putin is a gladiator.)

Because most of us are more familiar with arguments than we are with war, this example does not appear useful in explaining a new concept (argument) by relating it to a
more familiar one (war). Using war as a source for reference and inference may, however, enable the reader to see argument in a new light. By transferring both favorable
and unfavorable qualities from war to argument, argument may now be seen as more
critical and more deadly. Similarly, characterizing one of the protagonists in the argument as a gladiator (rather than as a tyrant or a defender) transfers a partial view, and
a specialized meaning, to a character whose fully rounded depiction would include a
number of possibilities.

Although it is helpful to the advocate to understand how these comparisons differ,
more important than distinguishing among analogy, metaphor, and characterization
is being able to take advantage of the difference between their novel and their conventional uses, most often described with reference to metaphor. This difference too
is fuzzy at best. For one thing, novel metaphors may become conventional over time.

In addition, novel metaphors are not necessarily unique or unusual. Instead, they are novel because they have not previously been used within a specific context or as a basis for comparison to a particular target. (Berger 2013a).

Each of these comparisons – analogy, metaphor, and characterization – helps the reader make connections between what she encounters in the world and what's in the reader's mind. Because the connections help the reader tap into a large body of pre-existing knowledge, they provide a large potential boost to persuasion.

To make a thoughtful and informed decision about which comparison to use in a particular case, the advocate should consider how they filter and frame our understanding of the problem before us. Upon hearing an analogy for the first time – for example, man is like a wolf – the reader will try to think of ways in which man is literally like a wolf: Are men and wolves hunters? Do both live in packs? If the reader decides that there are enough surface-level similarities to make the analogy superficially plausible, the reader will test whether there are structural-level similarities as well. That is, the reader will ask: Is the relationship between wolves and other animals similar to the relationship between men and other animals? For example, are both predators? Is the relationship between wolves and their offspring similar to the relationship between humans and their offspring? Would both endanger themselves to protect their children? If the reader is satisfied that there are enough surface and structural similarities, the reader will transfer other attributes and characteristics of wolves to reach a changed understanding of men – for example, inferring that they are ferocious and ill-suited to living in urban areas.

In comparison, researchers say a different process of understanding takes place when the reader hears what has become a conventional metaphor, *Man is a Wolf*. Instead of matching up similarities between her literal understandings of Wolf and Man, the reader will simply fit Man into the Wolf slot in the reader's head. The automatic and intuitive connections that accompany the conventional category of Wolf will be transferred to Man with little conscious thought, leaving invisible traces that are more difficult to dislodge. Finally, as a characterization, Samuel is a Wolf is processed differently depending on whether it appears in its novel or its conventional form. In both forms, a characterization is used to shape the facts to fit within a specific legal category: even though a particular plaintiff has many qualities, the plaintiff is characterized for the purposes of a particular argument as an employee or a spouse or a minor. The proponent of a novel characterization might, for example, first describe the details of Wolf by focusing on the wolf's behavior, appearance, ideas, beliefs, actions, and so on. In doing so, the author will emphasize certain parts of Wolf and de-emphasize others. If the novel characterization works, the reader will come to see Samuel – who might be characterized in myriad other ways – in the same way, with the same highlights and lowlights. (Berger 2013b).

In the next three chapters, we discuss the times when one or the other of these comparisons is more likely to persuade.

Cases & briefs

United States v. Causby, 328 U.S. 256 (1946).

Bibliography

Berger, L.L., 2013a, 'Metaphor and Analogy: The Sun and Moon of Legal Persuasion', *Journal of Law and Policy*, 22, 147–195.

Berger, L.L., 2013b, 'Metaphor in Law as Poetic and Propositional Language', *The European Legacy: Towards New Paradigms, Journal of the International Society for the Study of European Ideas* (ISSEI).

10

SHAPE CONNECTIONS

Familiar analogies and metaphors

Familiar analogies and metaphors are effective because they leverage the human tendency to be persuaded when things seem to fall into place as a matter of course – when, in other words, the reader is able to fill in the blanks for herself because the situation is like something she already knows. The response-shaping argument that prompts intuitive recognition or adoption of a favorable schema differs from a syllogism because it is not an explicit argument from premises to facts to conclusion. Instead, it is a more subtle approach. The advocate uses words or images to prompt the reader to intuitively recognize the potential parallel in a familiar analogy, metaphor, or story.

This chapter focuses on familiar analogies and metaphors, one kind of argument that might be made in hard cases in an effort to prompt intuitive recognition or adoption of a favorable schema. For lawyers and students of legal persuasion, the intuitive problem solving used by experts – and studied by psychologists – suggests various openings for persuasion. This is especially so when the decision maker's initial response to a problem is neutral or uncommitted. In this situation, the advocate may prompt the lawyer or the judge to imagine a parallel pattern or path that matches up with a favorable outcome. Intuition is involved both in the lawyer's recognition of the cues that might be suggested and in the judge's recognition of the patterns and paths that might be tested. In these situations, familiar analogies and metaphors work to persuade because they can be unthinkingly accepted.

For both lawyer and judge, intuition works in the same way that it does for expert problem solvers more generally: the situation provides a cue or a prompt. This allows the expert to tap into information stored in memory, and that information provides an initial answer. In other words, intuition begins when the observer recognizes a potentially parallel or alternative pattern or path. (Berger 2013a).

Depending on the persuasive context, the advocate may aim for an intuitive judgment that is also a final judgment. Or the advocate may hope to initiate a process in which the flash of recognition is only the first step. As discussed in Chapter 2, the process we call intuitive problem solving often blends both intuitive and reflective thinking. First, the process invokes an intuitive response prompted by cues that trigger recognition of parallels: these allow the decision maker to size up the problem situation quickly and identify a workable option. Second, the process may require the decision maker to think through a mental simulation, which helps her imagine how she might carry out the responsive course of action. Throughout this process, analogy and metaphor enable the decision maker to draw on experience by suggesting parallels between the current situation and something else encountered in the past. (Berger 2013b). After the initial recognition, visualization (or storytelling) guides the decision maker through the experimental simulation and testing of whether a responsive course of action will be workable and what changes will be needed.

Response-shaping theory in practice

The case studies that follow illustrate advantages and disadvantages of relying on familiar analogies and metaphors.

∞ *Case study: the reader's first response may be lasting*

As we have already discussed, in *Michael H. v. Gerald D.* (1989), Justice Scalia relied on a familiar metaphor, the "family," when he decided that no liberty interest was at stake in the relationship between a biological father and his daughter. California had refused to recognize this father-daughter relationship because of the statutorily recognized relationship between the mother's husband and the daughter. Confronted with a family consisting of a mother, her husband, her lover, and her lover's daughter, Justice Scalia made an immediate intuitive connection. Recognizing the tie between a biological father and his daughter when the mother was married to another man would be unnatural ("California law, like nature itself, makes no provision for dual fatherhood."). (*Michael H.* 1989). Moreover, the circumstances of the case were so far from his familiar image of family ("The facts of this case are, we must hope, extraordinary.") that the father and daughter could not be considered to have established a family-like relationship. (*Michael H.* 1989). Because Justice Scalia could not connect this father and his daughter with his image of the "natural family" (the unit consisting of mother, husband, and child), the father and child could not be considered to have a constitutionally protected liberty interest in their relationship.

∞ *Case study: familiar analogies provide short-term solutions*

A less-than-perfect analogy may be persuasive when it is necessary to solve a short-term problem. In *United States v. Jones* (2012), the Supreme Court adopted a familiar analogy that allowed it to decide that installing a GPS monitor on a vehicle constituted a Fourth Amendment violation. Faced with the one-time installation of a GPS monitor followed by weeks of constant surveillance, the Supreme Court had to choose between applying the "trespass" rule, which did not appear to cover the month-long monitoring, and reinterpreting the "reasonable expectation" rule, which prior cases had said did not encompass surveillance on public streets such as those on which Jones's car had traveled. Because Jones was in possession of the Jeep registered to his wife, it was possible for the Court to find that the government had physically trespassed without a warrant onto the defendant's property. Not surprisingly, the majority decision was criticized for relying on antiquated trespass law and therefore being of less value in guiding future decisions by lower courts.

∞ Case study: familiar metaphor may overcome unfavorable precedent

When *Cohen v. California* (1971) came before the Supreme Court, the Court had very recently distinguished between conduct unprotected by the First Amendment and speech eligible for constitutional protection. In *Cohen*, the Court was asked to decide whether the defendant could be punished for wearing a jacket bearing an offensive phrase. The brief for the jacket-wearer relied on a familiar metaphor of speech, claiming that by wearing the jacket inscribed with the words "Fuck the Draft," the defendant was expressing his feelings about the draft. The Court had recently held that burning a draft card was conduct, not speech, and thus not protected by the First Amendment, and the dissent in Cohen concluded that "Cohen's absurd and immature antic, in my view, was mainly conduct, and little speech." But the author of the Cohen brief suggested (without pausing to discuss the conduct-speech distinction) recognition of another familiar pattern: "We begin with the incontrovertible fact that Appellant was engaging in speech. Since his expression was formulated in words, and since he was arrested because of his words, there is presented in this case, at least prima facie, an abridgment of Appellant's freedom of speech." (Brief for Appellant 1970). Through the intuitive equation of wearing a jacket bearing words with speaking those words, the advocate was able to counter unfavorable precedent without addressing it directly.

∞ Case study: a familiar analogy can avoid an argument

Some commentators blame a metaphor (the corporation is a person) for the result in *Citizens United v. Federal Election Commission* (2010), where the U.S. Supreme Court held that corporations must be treated "as" individuals for purposes of campaign finance regulation. But in the Appellant's brief, attorney Ted Olson prompted the reader toward an initially favorable response with a familiar analogy. (Brief for Appellant 2009). In this brief, Citizens United was described as being "like" any other documentary film maker: Citizens United had made a critical, fact-filled 90-minute documentary about a political figure that an audience might want to watch. Because readers are familiar with the informative value and First Amendment protection generally granted to documentaries, it was not a stretch for the argument itself to begin with the text of the First Amendment: "Congress shall make no law . . . abridging the freedom of speech," and to immediately claim that "[t]his constitutional injunction evidently was not in the forefront of Congress's mind when it enacted BCRA, a statute that imposes sweeping restrictions on core political speech."

The brief supported its intuitive prompt – a documentary is valuable political speech – by discussing Citizens United's history of distributing its political views through documentary movies, including movies about illegal immigration, the War on Terror, and the United Nations. According to the brief, the current documentary was more of the same: *Hillary: The Movie* was a biographical documentary about Senator Hillary Clinton offering a "critical assessment of Senator Clinton's record as a U.S. Senator and as First Lady in order to educate viewers about her political back-ground." Like any other documentary, it was based on facts and interviews. Having prompted recognition of the familiar pattern, the brief helped the reader visualize the proper result. If the Court accepted the brief's assumption that this film was like any other documentary film, the Citizens United production would constitute political speech. As a result, the brief was able to avoid the argument that the First Amendment should apply differently to corporate speakers than it does to individuals expressing their opinions.

Summary

To sum up, when confronted with a hard case, the advocate may rely on a familiar and comfortable comparison to begin to influence a neutral or uncommitted deci-sion maker. Familiar analogies and metaphors are persuasive because the conclusions derived from these comparisons seem to fall into place naturally. And because the decision maker has put together the picture by drawing on her own past experiences, her responses may be longer lasting. So whenever they are an appropriate fit for the circumstances and the client's desired outcome, advocates should rely on the tried-and-true, most familiar comparison.

Cases & briefs

Citizens United v. Federal Election Commission, 558 U.S. 310 (2010).
    Brief for Appellant [Citizens United], 2009 Westlaw 61467.
Cohen v. California, 403 U.S. 15 (1971).
    Brief for Appellant [Paul Cohen], 1970 Westlaw 136795.
Michael H. v. Gerald D., 491 U.S. 110 (1989).
United States v. Jones, 565 U.S. 400 (2012).

Bibliography

Berger, L.L., 2013a, 'A Revised View of the Judicial Hunch', *Legal Communication & Rhetoric: JALWD*, 10, 1–45.
Berger, L.L., 2013b, 'Metaphor and Analogy: The Sun and Moon of Legal Persuasion', *Journal of Law and Policy*, 22, 147–195.

11

REINFORCE FAVORABLE CONNECTIONS

Arguing by analogy

According to Sigmund Freud, even if analogies prove nothing, they are helpful because they make us feel more at home. (Broda-Bahm 2010). Analogical reasoning that compares case precedents is an obvious example of lawyers' use of analogy to persuade. But analogy has many persuasive applications beyond the use of prior precedents "to predict, explain or justify the outcome of the currently undecided case." (Berger 2013).

Analogies (A is like B) suggest a useful comparison of concepts. Although not subject to formal proof, analogies are subject to testing by examining similarities of surface features, relationships, and purposes. (Gentner 1983). In addition, the multi-constraint theory of analogy affects the lawyer's use of analogies in legal persuasion. Dan Hunter describes these as constraints at the surface or feature level, constraints at the structural or relationship level, and constraints of purpose. (Hunter 2001). So first, there must be at least some surface-level similarity between the features of the source and the features of the target. In fact, simple fact-matching often appears to be the basis of legal arguments based on analogy. Still, surface-level similarity is only the first step in analogy: many things can be argued to be similar to one another at the level of surface features. The structural constraint requires a finding of consistent structural parallels between the target and the source. If the surface level describes objects, the structural level describes relationships between or among those objects. The final constraint is the purpose for using the analogy, which, as Hunter pointed out, may be particularly important in using analogies for legal persuasion. If a particular analogy helps one side's case more than another, the lawyers' purposes will influence others' perceptions of whether the analogy is good. (Hunter 2001).

Most lawyers are experts at arguing about comparisons. It is commonplace to structure legal arguments around such questions: When a steamboat passenger loses her belongings to a thief, should the owner of the steamboat be treated more like an innkeeper (responsible) or more like the operator of a train with open-berth sleeping cars (not responsible)? This kind of argument by analogy – analogizing to case precedent – appears central to the advocate, but it is only the periphery of a much larger category of arguing by analogy.

In this chapter, we discuss the broader category of arguments that depend on substantial "mapping" or transfers from one domain to another. For example, when the advocate argues that intellectual creations are like property, flag burning is like speech, or a sentence to life without parole is like a death sentence, the advocate is arguing not only that there are similarities but also that legal consequences follow. If an intellectual creation is "like" property, it may be divided, bought, and sold. If flag burning is like speech, it is individual expression protected by the First Amendment. If a sentence to life without parole is like a death sentence, similar requirements and safeguards must be built into the sentencing process.

In the last chapter, we considered how the use of intuitive prompts or cues helps the advocate take advantage of an automatic and unconscious response favorable to his client's position. In this chapter, we consider a related issue: how that intuitive response may be used to set off a chain reaction, resulting in a more reflective problem-solving process that ends with conscious adoption of the intuitive response.

Why and how analogies persuade

The persuasive value of analogy derives from its ability to help people understand experiences and think through problems by drawing on their reserves of knowledge. Much scientific advancement is, for example, attributed to analogy making. Considering problems through the lens of an analogy leads not only to further exploration of unfamiliar phenomena, but sometimes to problem solution: viewing the heart as a pump enabled productive study, while an approach to destroying a tumor without destroying the surrounding tissue emerged from an analogy to military forces surrounding and bombarding a fortress. When Niels Bohr offered a new theory of the atom in 1913, visualizing the atom as a miniature solar system, the analogy generated useful hypotheses for testing. (Bohr 1913). As is true of its use in persuasion, arguing by analogy does not prove the truth of an argument, but instead provides a structure for reflectively considering a problem or thinking through an issue.

According to analogy researchers, when we think through an analogy, we compare the source and the target on several levels before we accept the analogy as conveying useful information. Researchers explain that analogy falls somewhere in between a literal similarity and a category-like abstraction. For example, in the sentence stating a literal similarity – The X12 star system in the Andromeda galaxy is like our solar system – there are similarities both in the characteristics of the objects involved (the X12 star is yellow and mid-sized, as is our sun) and in the relationships among them (the planets revolve around the X12 star, as they do around our sun).

But instead of literal similarities, the analogy – The hydrogen atom is like our solar system – depends more on similarities in the structure of the relationships in the target and the source: an electron revolves around the nucleus like the planets revolve around the sun. Some characteristics of the objects may be literally similar, but it is irrelevant that others are not. Conversely, the abstraction – The hydrogen atom is a central force system – depends only on similarities in relationships. (Gentner 1983).

Leading analogy researchers have settled on a hybrid model of "on-line" or mentally active processing of analogy, the so-called "structural alignment" model. (Holyoak 2001). This model incorporates initial alignment of elements between the target and the source with later projection of inferences from the source to the target. Because it incorporates both, the model explains how analogies may begin in comparison but end with new understanding. According to the model, the first step in processing an analogy is to access one or more potentially relevant analogs (parallel patterns or paths) in the reader's long-term memory. The reader then begins comparing the source and the target to identify matches and to align the corresponding parts of the target and the source. Once satisfied that the two are similar, the reader maps some attributes from the source onto the target, so the reader now knows more about how to interpret and interact with the new situation. (Holyoak 2001; Gentner 1983, 1987).

When confronted with an unfamiliar analogy, readers often test whether it holds up not only because the elements of the target and the source are comparable and correspond to one another, but also because the comparison is consistent, helpful, and plausible. That is, we look for surface similarity as well as parallel connections and structural consistency, and we prefer systems connected by causal relationships over independent matches. When we are deciding whether to accept an analogy, we are in search of both coherence and deduction – that things fit together and follow from one another. (Gentner 1983, 1987).

As this description shows, creating a persuasive analogy is challenging. First, the advocate must make sure that there is at least some surface-level similarity between the features of the source and the target. If you were to argue that a sailing ship is like a train, you would have to point out that both are means of transportation even though one is powered by wind across water and the other is powered by diesel and electricity across land. Next, the reader expects consistent structural parallels between the target and the source, that is, consistency in the relationships between or among the objects in the target and the source. Finally, the reader examines your purpose in offering the analogy: if a particular analogy helps one side's case more than another, the purpose will influence others' perceptions of whether the analogy is fitting or not.

Response-reinforcing theory in practice

Analogy works to persuade if, after finding initial similarities, the reader is persuaded to infer additional similarities from the source to the target – and those similarities help the client's case. As Professor Bruce Ching advises, an effective analogy draws on a familiar context, avoids unintended associations, and resonates emotionally with the audience. (Ching 2010). In the examples that follow, we explore how analogy works in practice.

∞ *Case study: analogy supports examination and explanation*

The use of an analogy may encourage the decision maker to explore and explain the reasoning behind a comparison to prior cases. In *California v. Carney* (1985), the Supreme Court was asked to decide whether the Fourth Amendment warrant requirement applied to the search of a motor home that was not parked on a street. Previous cases had applied the warrant requirement to searches of houses but not to searches of cars. Arguing by analogy prompted the Court not only to compare the motor home to a house or a car, but also to more fully explore the reasoning behind the prior precedent. A warrant was not required to search a car because unlike a house, a car was readily moveable and police officers might not have time to obtain the warrant. In contrast with her expectations within her home, the occupant of a car has a diminished expectation of privacy because of widespread government regulation of public highways. As a result, the Court concluded that even though Carney's motor home was parked in a parking lot and not on the street, it was nonetheless easily moveable and no warrant was required for its search. (*Carney* 1985).

∞ Case study: analogy helps answer a question of first impression

In *Tinker v. Des Moines Independent School District* (1969), the Supreme Court found a First Amendment violation in a decision by school officials to forbid students from wearing armbands to protest the Vietnam War. Rather than comparing the wearing of an armband to the conduct that had been found unprotected by the First Amendment in prior cases, the Court analogized the restriction to a hypothetical school regulation "forbidding discussion of the Vietnam conflict, or the expression by any student of opposition to it anywhere on school property except as part of a prescribed classroom exercise." The analogous regulation would clearly violate students' rights of free expression, and so the Court concluded that the prohibition on armbands did as well. In the opinion, Justice Abe Fortas distinguished the prohibition on wearing armbands from acceptable public school regulation of clothing, hair style, and disruptive group demonstrations: "Our problem involves direct, primary First Amendment rights akin to 'pure speech.'" (Tinker 1969).

∞ Case study: analogy develops the more favorable mental connection

An advocate can use an analogy to build on the more favorable of two possible connections. An example can be found in *Utah v. Evans* (2002).[1] In that case, the Supreme Court decided that census takers had not been engaged in "sampling" in violation of federal law, but instead had been acting lawfully when they estimated the number of residents on a block. Illegal sampling occurs when those doing the counting use a small sample of the actual data to generalize about the larger community. If census takers actually count the residents of only five blocks in a particular area, and then assume that the other 100 blocks in that area have the same number of residents, that is improper sampling. In *Evans*, the census takers instead tried to count every house in the area, but then they filled in some gaps by assuming the same numbers of houses as those found in their actual data for the surrounding area.

Although Utah's attorney argued that filling in the gaps in this way was exactly like sampling, the federal government's advocate, Solicitor General Ted Olson, characterized the census taker as similar to a librarian taking inventory. (Brief of Appellants 2001; Oral Argument 2002). If the librarian counted the books on only one shelf, and then generalized about all the shelves, that would be sampling. But if the librarian attempted to count all the books, while inferring that the empty spaces between books would contain the same number of books as had been found on surrounding shelves, that would not be sampling. The purpose of the librarian's imputation of a number

---

1 We are grateful to Professor Robert Reinstein for pointing out this example.

based on partial data was not to generalize from a small sample, but instead to account for missing data. The new connection – between the census taker and the librarian – helped dislodge the connection between filling gaps and sampling.

∞ Case study: to be accepted, an analogy must coincide with the reader's understanding of the world

If a lawyer suggested an analogy between killing a human being and breaking a window "because both are nasty and because both can be done with a brick," the lawyer would lose the case "in a snap." (Hofstadter 1985). Before offering an analogy, the advocate should test it from the reader's point of view: there are good analogies, absurd analogies, and some that are in-between.

For example, a federal court refused to accept a proposed analogy suggesting that individual automatic vending machines should be treated as if they were independent retail stores to qualify for an exemption to federal fair labor standards. (*Bogash v. Baltimore Cigarette Service, Inc.* 1951). The court said the analogy was not helpful because it was not consistent with reality. Instead of being like independent retail stores, the machines were "silent and automatic salesmen offering at retail the goods of a single enterprise." Rather than being stand-alone entities, the machines were "the mechanical arm of the operator" who was still selling directly to the customer. (*Bogash* 1951).

Effective analogies rely on similarities at both the surface level and in underlying structural relationships. This distinction can be seen in the opinions of two federal district courts who faced the same question six years after the decision in *District of Columbia v. Heller* (2008): does the Second Amendment protect the rights of visitors to carry loaded firearms on recreational property administered by the Army Corps of Engineers? The answer in the Idaho federal court was yes, because the right of a law-abiding individual to possess a handgun in his home for self-defense applied as well to the analogous situation of possessing a handgun in a tent. (*Morris v. U.S. Army Corps of Engineers* 2014). The Idaho federal court judge concluded that "[w]hile often temporary, a tent is more importantly a place – just like a home – where a person withdraws from public view, and seeks privacy and security for himself and perhaps also for his family and/or his property." (*Morris* 2014).

Asked the identical question, and referring to the Idaho opinion, the federal court judge in Georgia found the analogy unpersuasive because the property where the plaintiffs' tents were pitched was not private property but "property owned and operated by the United States Military [including property containing] infrastructure products central to our national security and well being." (*GeorgiaCarry.Org v. United States Army Corps of Engineers* 2014). Although plaintiffs had a right to privacy and security in their own homes on their own property, plaintiffs in the case had "no constitutional or statutory right to pitch a tent in the first place." (*Georgia Carry.Org* 2014).

∞ Case study: an effective analogy transfers emotion appropriately

Professor Ching's example of an effective analogy that resonates emotionally with an audience is the one offered by the advocate defending Elvis Presley's physician against criminal charges that he had illegally provided drugs to his patients. The advocate analogized the physician to the good Samaritan, noting that the doctor testified that he prescribed drugs to help his patients battle their addictions. (*New York Times* 1981). This analogy carried with it a generally positive emotional message suited to the advocate's argument on behalf of the physician. On the other hand, analogizing the Social Security system to a Ponzi scheme, though carrying a negative emotional message, might be effective when used by an opponent of Social Security. (Ching 2010).

∞ *Case study: an inappropriate transfer of emotions may mean an ineffective analogy*

Analogies whose emotional tone connects with the response the advocate expects are more likely to be accepted, but the emotions transferred by some analogies may undermine their effectiveness. Consider this analogy offered at trial by a defense attorney trying to undermine the prosecutor's closing argument:

> If you went to a nice restaurant, and you ordered soup, and your soup came with a cockroach in it, what would you do? Would you eat that soup? Probably not. No matter how good the soup looked or smelled, right? How about if the waiter fished out the roach and wanted you to eat the soup? Not then, either, right? Well, the prosecutor's story is like that soup. It has a big roach in it. You know it. And he tried to make it better, just like the waiter, but you know it is really still the same soup. And he wants you to eat that soup.[2]

In this analogy, a flaw in the prosecutor's argument – whether a witness's credibility or a logical gap – was analogized to the roach in the soup. The advocate wanted the jurors to map certain meanings onto the prosecutor's argument: concepts like "tainted" and "ruined" and "contaminated." The advocate hoped the jurors would associate the flaw in the story with something disgusting in their food. Although this analogy might have worked either to associate different meanings with the prosecutor's argument or to connect the emotion of disgust to the prosecutor's story, analogies raising such negative emotional connections run the risk of inadvertently transferring the audience's disgust to the person who pointed out the problem.

Another attention-grabbing metaphor that conveyed negative emotions came during the oral argument before the U.S. Supreme Court in *Zubik v. Burwell* (2016), one of a series of challenges to provisions of the Affordable Care Act. After the argument, some observers raised ethical objections to the metaphor employed by advocate Paul Clement. Clement told the Court that the government's plan through the Act was to "hijack" the health plans provided by organizations affiliated with religious groups so that the government could make sure female employees received contraceptives. (Greenhouse 2016). During oral argument, several justices picked up on and seemingly agreed with Clement's metaphor. Later, some observers objected that the metaphor was used not to explain or illuminate the argument but instead to evoke an emotional

---

2 This tactic was shared with Kathy Stanchi by Professor Paul Zwier, the director of Advocacy Training at Emory Law School, and a distinguished scholar of legal advocacy.

and unreasonable reaction against anything connected with the illegal and dangerous action of hijacking. The Court eventually ordered the parties to seek a compromise.

Other observers objected on similar ethical grounds to Justice Sonia Sotomayor's use of several analogies in *Glossip v. Gross* (2015), a death penalty opinion. There, she characterized the defendant's argument as contending that "Oklahoma's current protocol is a barbarous method of punishment – the chemical equivalent of being burned alive." Under the Court's decision, Justice Sotomayor wrote, the state could use any means it wished to carry out the death penalty, including having "petitioners drawn and quartered, slowly tortured to death, or actually burned at the stake." (*Glossip* 2015). Again, the objection was that the metaphors and analogies were offered not to illuminate but to overcome reflective judgment.

Summary

To sum up, carefully crafted factual analogies can provide the more extensive arguments needed to build upon a decision maker's initially favorable response. Once the reader agrees that the source and the target of an analogy are similar in some ways, the reader may infer that further similarities exist. Given those inferences, he may be persuaded to carry over from the source to the target additional helpful characteristics, relationships, and results. Constructing analogies is challenging, and readers will closely examine them to see whether the essential similarities hold up. In addition to testing for similar surface features, relationships, and purposes, audiences are more receptive to analogies that draw on a familiar context, avoid unintended associations, and prompt complementary emotions.

Cases & briefs

Bogash v. Baltimore Cigarette Service, Inc., 193 F.2d 291 (4th Cir. 1951).
California v. Carney, 471 U.S. 386 (1985).
GeorgiaCarry.Org v. United States Army Corps of Eng'rs, 38 F. Supp. 3d 1365 (N.D. Ga. 2014).
Glossip v. Gross, 135 S. Ct. 2726 (2015).
District of Columbia v. Heller, 554 U.S. 570 (2008).
Morris v. U.S. Army Corps of Eng'rs, 994 F. Supp. 2d 1082 (D. Idaho 2014).
Tinker v. Des Moines Independent Community School District, 393 U.S. 503 (1969).
Utah v. Evans, 536 U.S. 452 (2002).
  Brief of Appellants, 2002 Westlaw 237369.
  Oral Argument, 2002 Westlaw 521347.

Bibliography

Berger, L.L., 2013, 'Metaphor and Analogy: The Sun and Moon of Legal Persuasion', *Journal of Law and Policy*, 22, 147–195.
Bohr, N., 1913, 'On the Constitution of Atoms and Molecules', *Philosophy Magazine*, 26, 1–25.
Broda-Bahm, K., 2010, 'Stop Searching for the Perfect Analogy (but Don't Surrender a Communication Lifesaver)', *Persuasive Litigator*, 1 February 2010 (quoting Freud, S., 1933, 'New Introductory Lectures on Psycho-Analysis', in James Strachey (ed.), 1964, *The Standard Edition of the Complete Psychological Works of Sigmund Freud*, Vol. 22, 72).

Ching, B., 2010, 'Argument, Analogy, and Audience: Using Persuasive Comparisons While Avoiding Unintended Effects', *Journal of the Association of Legal Writing Directors*, 7, 311–315.

Gentner, D., 1983, 'Structure-Mapping: A Theoretical Framework for Analogy', *Cognitive Science*, 7, 155–170.

Gentner, D. and Wolff, P., 1997, 'Alignment in the Processing of Metaphor', *Journal of Memory and Language*, 37, 331–355.

Greenhouse, L., 2016, 'A Supreme Court Hijacking', *The New York Times*, 30 March 2016.

Hofstadter, D., 1985, 'Analogies and Roles in Human and Machine Thinking', in D. Hofstadter (ed.), *Metamagical Themas: Questing for the Essence of Mind and Pattern*, Basic Books, New York.

Holyoak, K.J., 2001, 'Introduction: The Place of Analogy in Cognition', in D. Gentner, K.J. Holyoak and B.N. Kokinov (eds.), *The Analogical Mind: Perspectives From Cognitive Science*, MIT Press, Cambridge, MA.

Hunter, D., 2001, 'Reason Is Too Large: Analogy and Precedent in Law', *Emory Law Journal*, 50, 1197–1264.

'Presley's Doctor Acquitted on All Prescription Charges', *The New York Times*, 5 November 1981.

12

BREAK UNFAVORABLE CONNECTIONS

Novel metaphors

If you learned today that the police had installed a GPS monitoring device in your car or that a government agency had hacked into your computer files, it's likely that you would assume these actions invaded your personal privacy. Common sense tells you that personal privacy should protect your right to travel undetected as well as your ability to keep your thoughts and documents to yourself. But because these methods of monitoring and snooping are new, you might wonder whether they are explicitly barred by law. And if you found that they were not, you would start to think about parallel patterns, that is, about how these methods were like other intrusions that you had experienced or heard or read about before.

In the case of GPS monitoring, you might think about an old-fashioned plainclothes detective following you around. In the case of hacking into your computer files, you might think of a government agent physically breaking into your home or office and going through your papers and other belongings. Once you made the connection to old-fashioned surveillance and to physical breaking and entering, you would "see" and think about GPS monitoring and computer hacking the same way – the only difference being that they are virtual rather than physical invasions of your personal privacy. And you would argue that a judge should interpret them the same way as well. That would be the easy case, where the initial mental impression and the reader's intuitive response support your argument.

What about the advocate for the government? He must persuade the decision maker to disassociate GPS monitoring from an invasion of privacy by severing the initial mental connections and forging others. In contexts like this one, where the first mental connection is unfavorable, recent cognitive research supports the use of novel metaphors and characterizations as a way to unsettle the intuitive link and prompt more reflective thought. As this chapter illustrates, the use of novel characterizations and metaphors may effectively suggest to the decision maker that the individuals and circumstances currently before him could fit into more than one framework, prompting new perspective and re-evaluation of an intuitive response.

Why and how novel metaphors and characterizations persuade

When we think through the filter of a metaphor or a characterization, cognitive researchers believe that we are sometimes guided by the more reflective process of comparison and at other times by the more automatic process of categorization. Thus, if we hear the relatively novel metaphor that *the brain is a muscle*, we try to come up with similarities between the two (both need exercise or they will wither away), and we consciously test the plausibility of the metaphor, but when we hear the now-conventional metaphor that *the brain is a computer*, we automatically and unconsciously assume that it is appropriate to view our brains as information-processing machines.

The brain is a muscle is the kind of novel metaphor studied by researchers who concluded that such metaphors are understandable only by actively comparing the target and the source. More conventional metaphors and more extended metaphor systems – a status reached over time by some metaphors that once were novel – are understood more automatically, by reference to prior concepts kept in memory and by transferring features from those prior concepts to the new one. Noting that a process of comparison remains at the core, analogy researchers point out that the prior concepts that we access were also created by past comparisons.

After studying how we process complex metaphors – for example, when we view *argument as a container* or *love as a journey* – Dedre Gentner and her colleagues concluded that the online-construction, structure-mapping theory that explains the processing of analogy also explains the processing of novel metaphors. (Gentner 2001). When a reader encounters a novel metaphor, the reader recognizes parallel features and structures shared by the target and the source, and then the reader creates new understanding by projecting inferences from the source to the target. As a result, when the reader is interpreting a novel metaphor, she is engaged in creating meaning. On the other hand, when the reader is interpreting a conventional metaphor, she is not creating meaning but is instead retrieving meaning from a mental storeroom.

The evolution of metaphorical processing from comparison to categorization can be seen in the career of the just-mentioned and now-conventional metaphor that *the mind is a computer*. When computers were new, some scientists suggested the mirror-image metaphor – *the computer is a brain* – as a way to describe and explain a machine that was capable of processing symbols, something that previously had been done only by human beings. Later, when scientists began studying the mind as an information-processing mechanism, it was in part because the mind had become the target of the metaphor (the more abstract concept to be explained), and the computer now served as the more concrete or familiar source for transferring understanding. When this later metaphor – *the mind is a computer* – was first used, it was novel, that is, the source domain (the computer) had not previously been applied to the target domain (the mind). To understand the metaphor, the reader had to try to align the characteristics and relationships existing within a computer with those existing within a mind: for example, both appear to take in data and to process it before producing some kind of report. In the beginning of its career as a novel image, *the mind is a computer* metaphor generated not only a new way of seeing but also a new way of studying the mind. Now that the metaphor has become conventional, saying that *the mind is a computer* appears to state the obvious – that the mind fits into the category of an information-processing mechanism.

Response-shifting theory in practice

As just discussed, when the advocate hopes to encourage an active and reflective comparison – rather than the automatic process of categorization – cognitive research supports the use of novel metaphors and characterizations. By encouraging the decision maker to look beyond the most immediately accessible framework to knowledge that might be derived from alternative schemas, the novel metaphor or characterization is designed to shift or broaden the decision maker's view of the same information.

Among the most famous novel metaphors is the one used by now-Supreme Court Justice Ruth Bader Ginsburg in the brief she submitted to the Supreme Court on behalf of the female spouse in *Reed v. Reed*, a 1971 case in which the Court ruled that an Idaho statute preferring males as the administrators of estates was unconstitutional. (*Reed* 1971). Ginsburg wrote that the "pedestal upon which women have been placed has all too often, upon closer inspection, been revealed as a cage" (Brief of Appellant 1971), a phrase repeated two years later in the majority opinion in *Frontiero v. Richardson* (1973). In *Frontiero*, the Court held that women who were members of the military could claim their spouses as dependents to receive increased benefits "on an equal footing" with male members of the military. Echoing Ginsburg, Justice William Brennan wrote that "[t]raditionally, such discrimination was rationalized by an attitude of 'romantic paternalism' which, in practical effect, put women, not on a pedestal, but in a cage." (*Frontiero* 1973).

∞ *Case study: the novel metaphor may counter an entrenched category*

To prompt more careful evaluation of a conventional metaphor that "goes without saying," the advocate may advance a novel alternative. In the following example, drawn from the briefs filed in *Nike, Inc. v. Kasky* (2003), the conventional metaphor is *the corporation is a person*, a metaphor so conventional that it often goes unnoticed. For example, Justice John Paul Stevens automatically referred to the corporation being sued as having human qualities: *Nike was besieged* with allegations; *Nike was participating* in a public debate about *Nike as a good corporate citizen*. These references indicate that the metaphor was automatically and unconsciously processed and that the entity of the corporation was simply fit into the category of persons, with all the ensuing implications. Here, a novel metaphor (*Nike's representations are manufactured products*) might have been used to prompt more reflective thinking in an effort to counter the automatic process of categorization that viewed Nike as a person.

In the lawsuit originally filed as *Kasky v. Nike*, a critic of Nike's labor practices in foreign countries sued the corporation under California statutes that allowed private lawsuits to enforce prohibitions against false advertising and unfair competition. Plaintiff Marc Kasky alleged that "Nike, for the purpose of inducing consumers to buy its products, made false representations of fact about the conditions under which they are made." Nike responded that the First Amendment protected Nike's communications because they were part of a debate about a public issue.

In the briefs they filed in the U.S. Supreme Court, both sides assumed that Nike was the kind of speaker whose representations might be protected by the First Amendment. Nike and its supporters used Nike's personhood to obscure any distinction between the corporation and any other speaker. At the same time, the attorneys representing Kasky did not try to displace the corporation-is-a-person metaphor. That acceptance seemingly made it more difficult to argue that Nike was distinguishable from other competitors in the marketplace of ideas or from other participants in a debate.

Through its use of a novel metaphor, the plaintiff's brief might have paved the way for an argument that the advertising and public relations products that Nike manufactures, distributes, and sells are not speech at all. For example, one amicus brief set out the novel characterization that Nike should be viewed as a manufacturer of products even when the product is speech. These amicus brief lawyers suggested that Nike's corporate public relations products should be seen "as" manufactured images, marketing tools, and cultivated commodities. Rather than Nike being engaged in speech, this brief described Nike as "engaged in a publicity campaign." The brief continued to use metaphors from activities other than speaking: "Nike Has Manufactured An Image Of Social Responsibility As A Means of Promoting Product Sales"; "Image Promotion Is An Essential Aspect Of Product Promotion"; and "Nike Has Cultivated A Corporate Image Of Social Progressivity As A Marketing Tool To Promote Product Sales."

If the audience is able to align the characteristics and relationships associated with manufacturers and products with those associated with Nike and its public relations campaign, the audience might also project inferences from manufacturing to public relations. Once Nike's representations are viewed as cars or shoes, the projected inferences suggest that they can be seen "as" part of a process that involves either a lesser or no First Amendment interest. From this perspective, the public relations products that Nike manufactures and disseminates are like any other product the corporation makes. And, like any other product, their manufacture, distribution, and sale should be subject to state regulation to protect the public.

∞ Case study: the novel metaphor may prompt second thoughts

Widely known for his barbed use of metaphor while dissenting, Justice Antonin Scalia's most influential dissent might have occurred in *Morrison v. Olson* (1988). With Justice Scalia as the only dissenter, the *Morrison* Court upheld the Independent Counsel Act against a separation of powers challenge. Justice Scalia characterized his position on the issue before the Court in the form of a novel twist on a conventional metaphor: "Frequently an issue of this sort will come before the Court clad, so to speak, in sheep's clothing: the potential of the asserted principle to effect important change in the equilibrium of power is not immediately evident, and must be discerned by a careful and perceptive analysis. But this *wolf comes as a wolf*." (*Morrison* 1988).

In *Morrison*, the majority determined that the independent counsel provision of the Ethics in Government Act did not violate the constitutional principle of separation of powers. But Justice Scalia wrote that the law should be struck down because criminal prosecution is an exercise of "purely executive power" as guaranteed in the Constitution and the law deprived the President of "exclusive control" of that power. After a number of investigations, including the one that led to the impeachment of President Bill Clinton, and much criticism that independent counsel investigations were being undermined by public and partisan political pressure, Congress let the Independent Counsel Act expire in 1999.

∞ Case study: a novel characterization may shift perspectives in situations where an analogy would be rejected

As discussed earlier, in *Michael H. v. Gerald D.* (1989), because Justice Scalia could not envision a biological father and his daughter as a family, he decided that no liberty interest was involved in their relationship. To combat Justice Scalia's immediate intuitive response that this father-daughter relationship was not like a "family" relationship, the advocate hoping to shift the decision maker's perspective might have suggested an analogy with some surface and structural similarities but a different result. For instance, the relationship between a "birth" or natural father and daughter could be characterized as similar to the relationship between a "birth" mother and daughter – and the state of California would not sever that relationship merely because the child's birth father was married to another woman. Despite the surface similarities – that both mother and father are birth parents – most readers would reject the analogy because they would immediately think of other important differences in the qualities and structure of a mother-child relationship and a father-child relationship.

In this case, a novel characterization might fare better than an analogy, as illustrated in the dissenting opinion. There, Justice William Brennan found a unifying theme in the prior cases: "although an unwed father's biological link to his child does not, in and of itself, guarantee him a constitutional stake in his relationship with that child, such a link combined with a substantial parent-child relationship will." Thus, when the natural father can be characterized as a fully responsible parent – even though not married to the mother – he may be seen in a different light. Again, in the words of the dissent,

> When an unwed father demonstrates a full commitment to the responsibilities of parenthood by 'com[ing] forward to participate in the rearing of his child,' . . . his interest in personal contact with his child acquires substantial protection under the Due Process Clause. At that point it may be said that he 'act[s] as a father toward his children.'
>
> *(Michael H. 1989)*

∞ Case study: when the advocate must counter a negative stereotype, a novel characterization suggests the decision maker can choose among schemas

By using a novel characterization or metaphor – one that already exists but has not previously been associated with this target – the advocate suggests alternatives for the decision maker. Within any decision-making context, a number of different schemas might be triggered. Which schema is selected depends on many variables, giving the advocate the opportunity to tilt the reader toward one or the other.

In criminal prosecutions, the defense attorney often has to counter the familiar narrative of the violent criminal as the primary cause of criminal behavior and societal breakdown. Criminal defense attorneys may encourage the decision maker to look at the defendant's life story beyond the defendant's criminal acts. But this approach often reinforces the preexisting narrative. Professor Pam Wilkins described a different approach taken by the attorney presenting opening and closing statements during the penalty phase of the trial of Alan Quinones, a cocaine and heroin dealer convicted of racketeering, drug trafficking, and murdering a confidential informant. (Wilkins 2012).

The defense attorney sought to counter the violent criminal schema otherwise associated with Quinones by putting forward competing role schemas depicting the defendant as a protective father figure and a first-generation immigrant. This use of the father-and-protector schema is an example of a novel characterization, one that already exists, but is not typically applied to violent criminals. The protective-father schema adds dimension to the juror's understanding of the defendant because protective fathers will use whatever methods they have available to look after and care for their families. Within this schema, even unlawful activity may be seen as understandable and deserving of respect. In other words, the novel characterization presents the decision maker with an opportunity to take on a new perspective. By encouraging the decision maker to look beyond the most immediately accessible framework to understanding that might be derived from alternative schemas, the novel characterization is designed to shift or broaden the decision maker's view of the same information.

∞ Case study: in addition to shifting perspective, a novel characterization may help the advocate forge a link to another favorable mental connection

When undocumented immigrant children are characterized as permanent residents, rather than as illegal, the advocate may be able to connect that image of resident children to the deeply embedded American belief in equal educational opportunity. In *Plyler v. Doe* (1982) and a companion case, *In re Alien Children Education Litigation*, the U.S. Supreme Court for the first time explicitly ruled that unauthorized immigrants were entitled to equal protection under the Fourteenth Amendment. In both cases, the plaintiffs challenged a Texas statute that allowed the state to withhold its funds for the education of children who were unauthorized immigrants.

In its briefs, Texas argued that the only justification the state needed for the statute was the characterization that the plaintiff children were themselves "illegal." According to the Texas briefs, all children of school age must fall into one of only two categories, legal or illegal, and the State had a responsibility to conserve its resources for the education of "legal" children.

The Supreme Court majority in *Plyler* turned to an alternative and novel (in this context) characterization: these children were neither legal nor illegal, but instead – because they were likely to remain in the U.S. indefinitely – they could be characterized as permanent residents. Allowing Texas to enforce a statute that refused permanent resident children access to free public education would lead to a "permanent caste of undocumented resident aliens." (*Plyler* 1982). By incorporating a novel characterization – that the plaintiff children, despite their lack of documents, are permanent residents – the majority was able to make a connection to an iconic American belief – that education allows all Americans to pursue equality and avoid a caste system.

This example illustrates how advocates and judges use novel characterizations and conventional metaphors to achieve different goals. The novel characterization (immigrant children as permanent residents) allowed the author to construct a bridge to a persuasive master story (equal access to education is necessary for equal opportunity to succeed) while the conventional metaphor (immigrant children as illegal) provided Texas with a category for automatic disposition without further reflection.

∞ *Case study: like familiar metaphors, novel metaphors may shortcut deliberation*

When a grand jury declined to bring criminal charges against the Cleveland police officer who fatally shot 12-year-old Tamir Rice, the prosecutor said that he had recommended to grand jurors that no charges should be brought. As justification, Prosecutor Timothy J. McGinty said the shooting had been the result of a "perfect storm of human errors, mistakes and miscommunications." (Homans 2016). In her article about the metaphor of the "perfect storm," Carol Parker pointed out that "the implicit message carried by the perfect storm metaphor is troubling . . . because it offers not only a way to avoid assigning blame but also a rationale for inaction and rough justice." If a particular situation can accurately be described as a perfect storm, nothing could have been done, and thus the "victims cannot be compensated, however deserving of compassion they may be." (Parker 2012).

Summary

To sum up, advocates should turn to novel metaphors and characterizations when they want to encourage the decision maker to look at various schemas beyond those that are immediately accessible. By using a metaphor or characterization not previously used within the context of the current problem, the lawyer may be able to shift the decision maker's perspective. The use of such novel characterizations and metaphors effectively suggests that there are alternatives to an audience member's first intuitive response. As a result, the advocate may prompt a more reflective decision-making process.

Cases & briefs

Frontiero v. Richardson, 411 U.S. 677 (1973).
Kasky v. Nike, Inc., 45 P. 3d 243 (Cal. 2002).
Michael H. v. Gerald D., 491 U.S. 110 (1989).
Morrison v. Olson, 487 U.S. 654 (1988).
Nike, Inc. v. Kasky, 539 U.S. 654 (2003).
    Brief Amici Curiae the States of California [*et al*], 2003 WL 1844750.
    Brief for Petitioners, 2003 WL 898993.
    Brief for Respondent [Kasky], 2003 WL 1844849.
Plyler v. Doe, 457 U.S. 202 (1982).
    Appellants' Reply Brief, 1981 WL 339678.
    Brief for the Appellants, 1981 WL 389967.
Reed v. Reed, 404 U.S. 71 (1971).
    Brief of Appellant, 1971 WL 133596.
United States v. Jones, 565 U.S. 400 (2012).

Bibliography

Berger, L.L., 2001, 'The Lady, or the Tiger? A Field Guide to Metaphor and Narrative', *Washburn Law Review*, 50, 275–318.

Berger, L.L., 2009, 'How Embedded Knowledge Structures Affect Judicial Decision Making: A Rhetorical Analysis of Metaphor, Narrative, and Imagination in Child Custody Disputes', *Southern California Interdisciplinary Law Journal*, 18, 259–308.

Berger, L.L., 2013, 'Metaphor and Analogy: The Sun and Moon of Legal Persuasion', *Journal of Law and Policy*, 22, 147–195.

Ching, B., 2010, 'Argument, Analogy, and Audience: Using Persuasive Comparisons While Avoiding Unintended Effects', *Journal of the Association of Legal Writing Directors*, 7, 311–315.

Gentner, D., 1983, 'Structure-Mapping: A Theoretical Framework for Analogy', *Cognitive Science*, 7, 155–170.

Gentner, D., Bowdle, B., Wolff, P. and Boronat, C., 2001, 'Metaphor Is Like Analogy', in D. Gentner, K.J. Holyoak and B.N. Kokinov (eds.), *The Analogical Mind: Perspectives From Cognitive Science*, pp. 199–255, MIT Press, Cambridge, MA.

Gentner, D. and Wolff, P., 1997, 'Alignment in the Processing of Metaphor', *Journal of Memory and Language*, 37, 331–355.

Homans, G., 2016, 'How the "Perfect Storm" Became the Perfect Cop-Out', *The New York Times*, 20 January 2016.

Hunter, D., 2001, 'Reason Is Too Large: Analogy and Precedent in Law', *Emory Law Journal*, 50, 1197–1264.

Parker, C.M., 2012, 'The Perfect Storm, the Perfect Culprit: How a Metaphor of Fate Figures in Judicial Opinions', *McGeorge Law Review*, 43, 323–360.

Smith, M.R., 2008, *Advanced Legal Writing: Theories and Strategies in Persuasive Writing*, 3rd edn., Wolters Kluwer, New York.

Wilkins, P.A., 2012, 'Confronting the Invisible Witness: The Use of Narrative to Neutralize Capital Jurors' Implicit Racial Biases', *West Virginia Law Review*, 115, 305–362.

PART IV

Arrangement

Organization and connection

While she is constructing or creating arguments, the advocate also has to make decisions about the arrangement of the arguments she invents. These decisions often fall into three categories: selection, emphasis, and phrasing. Selection and emphasis determine the order and placement of the arguments while phrasing is essential to framing issues and priming favorable interpretations and impressions in the listener's mind. Underlying all these concepts is the psychological concept of priming – that is, presenting information in a way that encourages the audience to connect one step or idea to another.

We know from cognitive science and contemporary rhetoric that the positions of emphasis and the words used in framing an issue can determine the answer. This is because framing foregrounds the most important favorable information and makes it both accessible and obvious to the audience. We need only look to modern polling to demonstrate the power of framing: in one survey, 62 percent of people said "no" when asked whether to *allow* "public condemnation of democracy," but only 46 percent of people said "yes" when asked the mirror image question, whether to *forbid* "public condemnation of democracy." (Plous 1993). Although the two questions are substantively the same, the answers differ depending on how the question is phrased.

Once the issue has been framed, the advocate may choose from among a number of argument structures – the less conventional narrative, metaphor, and factual analogies discussed in Part III or the more familiar organizational choices covered in this part. The syllogistic structure (the one that law students know as Issue-Rule-Application-Conclusion) is most comfortable for lawyers and judges, but it may not be the most persuasive in all contexts.

In classical rhetoric, the concept of arrangement focused on the order of the argument. Aristotelian arrangement reflected the syllogistic organization that lawyers know so well: introduction, thesis, proof, and conclusion. (Frost 1990). In the classical rhetoric model, the introduction was the beginning of the "weaving of the web" and the remainder of the arrangement was designed to mirror the thought process of the decision maker, making it the most persuasive organization for the advocate.

In this chapter, we give the classical view of arrangement its due, but build on it through the addition of both science and contemporary rhetoric. We start by explaining the concept of priming, which drives many other decisions about structure, order, and space. We then turn to the specifics of the most familiar modes of organizing legal arguments, starting with the syllogism, but giving some deeper treatment to the complexities of the syllogistic organization and delving into why the syllogistic framework is persuasive. Finally, we examine closely the many decisions that underlie how to construct a syllogistic argument, including its interwoven analogical case support.

13

INTRODUCTION TO PRIMING

Story and emotion

Imagine that you are walking quickly down the street to a friend's house. Someone is having a yard sale and has a table set up next to the sidewalk. Hundreds of random objects are crowded on the table – books, golf balls, paper, art supplies, a baseball, cups, bowls, children's toys, tools. Now imagine that you tell your friend about the yard sale, and she asks you what was on the table. Maybe you would remember some of the objects – perhaps things that had some special interest for you – but maybe you wouldn't remember any of them particularly.

But imagine instead that just prior to walking to your friend's house, someone told you a story about a classic baseball game, the 1986 World Series game where Boston Red Sox first baseman Bill Buckner committed an error that contributed to the Red Sox going on to lose the game and then the series. In that case, one of the items will jump out at you: the baseball. If you were discussing baseball prior to walking by the table, you are likely to notice the baseball out of all the objects on that table. And when your friend asks you what you saw, you will likely remember the baseball particularly. Subconsciously, that prior discussion about the baseball game made the baseball the most vivid object on the table to you among all the other random objects. You didn't realize it, but your brain was "looking" for the baseball.

This is an example of psychological priming. Put simply, priming is what happens when our interpretation of new information is influenced by what we saw, read, or heard just prior to receiving that new information. Our brains evaluate new information by, among other things, trying to fit it into familiar, known categories. But our brains have many known categories, and judgments about new information need to be made quickly and efficiently. One of the "shortcuts" our brains use to process new information quickly is to check the new information first against the most recently accessed categories. Priming is a way of influencing the categories that are at the forefront of our brains. When someone talks to us about a baseball game, the categories for "baseball" are at the forefront of our brains. Then, when we are confronted with new information, those most accessible categories will be used to interpret it.

In a typical litigation context, decision makers (judges and juries) are like the person looking at the yard sale table crowded with hundreds of objects. They are bombarded with volumes of information that they must sift through quickly to decide what is important.

The studies on priming suggest that how legal advocates introduce new information can influence how a decision maker sees and sifts through that information. Think of priming as performing like an efficient secretary who quietly places on the boss's desk the relevant files the boss needs to make a decision. Like that efficient secretary, the legal advocate can subtly influence what mental files or categories are at the front of the decision makers' minds when they read or interpret information.

Contemporary rhetoric and priming

In addition to what we know about priming from cognitive science, contemporary rhetoricians have reached similar conclusions through their study of real-life arguments. (Perelman and Olbrechts-Tyteca 1969). Chaim Perelman and Lucie Olbrechts-Tyteca suggested a theory of argumentation based on a metaphor of movement: an argument is designed to move the audience from agreement about premises to agreement about some conclusion. This theory, set forth in *The New Rhetoric: A Treatise on Argumentation*, grew out of their extensive study of the arguments made about values in legal settings, political discourse, philosophical discourse, and daily discussions.

While logic compels a conclusion based on deductive reasoning, Perelman and Olbrechts-Tyteca found that argumentation seeks audience adherence to a claim through persuasion. Beginning with premises the audience accepts, the aim of argumentation is a probable outcome, not a certain one. Some of the premises an audience member already accepts deal with reality while others address what is preferable. For example, starting points dealing with reality include facts that are already agreed to; truths that enjoy universal agreement (principles that connect facts to one another such as scientific theories or philosophical or religious conceptions); and presumptions about what is normal and likely. Starting points dealing with the preferable include values; hierarchies of values; and ways in which value hierarchies can be organized. Also akin to the priming studies, Perelman and Olbrechts-Tyteca suggested ways that speakers might focus attention on, or give presence to, the right elements in an argument.

Priming interpretation and emotion through story

Stories prime audience members to interpret information in particular ways, and stories prime audience members to feel a range of emotions. How might an advocacy story prime the reader to interpret a legal argument more favorably? For example, a story of government betrayal and prosecutorial misconduct in a habeas petition could lay the groundwork for an appeal in which the Supreme Court is cast as the hero who must rescue the betrayed defendant. (Meyer 2007). How might a story influence an audience member by priming a particular emotion? As Dan Kahneman explained, choosing between the statements "Italy won" or "France lost" to describe the results of the World Cup match between Italy and France poses an emotional framing problem. The statements are logically identical, but they have very different meanings depending on the emotional reaction of the listener. (Kahneman 2011).

We've all been emotionally affected by stories – we cry when we read heartbreaking stories in books or watch them at the movies; we feel fear and anxiety when we watch horror films or read thrillers. That emotional response is what we meant when we talked about stories "transporting" us – when a story is effective, we react as though we are *in* the story, as if the events in the story are really happening. That's why we cry when we watch *Schindler's List* or *Fruitvale Station*, even though we are safe in our seats, and why we want to yell "don't go in there!" to the ingénue in the horror film. Because we are in the story with the characters, we are invested in what happens and we react as if we can make a difference.

As Kahneman's World Cup example illustrates, even the simplest of stories can be told in different ways to elicit different emotions and convey different meanings. Akira Kurosawa's *Rashomon* tells the same story from four different perspectives, leaving the audience confused as to what happened and how to feel about it. As noted in the narrative chapters, almost all stories are or can be *Rashomon* stories: we change the story and its effect on listeners by changing themes, plots, characters, setting, and point of view. In this way, advocates can use story to influence listeners to interpret subsequent information in different ways.

Just as some lawyers and judges frown on the use of story, some believe that emotion has no place in legal decision making, which instead is dictated by cold, rational logic. But neuroscience confirms that we cannot make decisions without emotion. Without drawing on our emotions, we would often be paralyzed by indecision over the smallest tasks. (Damasio 1994). Even tangential emotions wholly unrelated to the immediate choice before us can significantly affect our judgment and choice. (Loewenstein and Lerner 2003). Emotions can affect not only perception (what people see and notice) but also cognition (how people think about what they perceive). (Keltner et al. 1993). Emotion's power has led one psychologist to refer to it as the "dog" that wags the "rational tail." (Haidt 2001).

Because emotions are always present in decision making, the critical questions are *which* emotions are influenced and what influence they have. One of the best ways to influence a decision maker's emotional response to an argument is through narrative priming. That means keeping the emotional dimensions in mind when picking a theme for the story that you will present to the decision maker and highlighting, through your structural choices, the most emotionally powerful and thus memorable facts.

Negative emotions

The influence of different emotions on decision making is complex and still being carefully studied by psychologists. But we know a few things. First, negative emotions like sadness or guilt tend to make people pessimistic, which in turn tends to make them look very closely at the details, particularly the negative details, of a story. This is a remnant of the oldest part of our brains – when things are going badly, we need to be more careful and look more closely. Negative emotions also make us feel as though we must do something to fix the situation. Plaintiffs' lawyers and prosecutors are more likely to want to take advantage of eliciting negative emotions in the decision maker. But they should do so cautiously – negative details and emotions are a powerful tool, and they should be employed judiciously. (Chestek 2014). Making people feel *too* bad about a situation may cause a kind of "kill the messenger" backlash. (Stanchi 2010). More discussion of the dangers of "going negative" will be found in the chapters on tone.

Negative emotions overall may have similar effects on decision makers, but different kinds of negative emotions can have different effects. An audience member who experiences sadness tends to attribute the events that occurred to the overall situation rather than to human actions. Stories evoking sadness make frequent use of the passive voice ("his leg just snapped") and highlight the outside forces that converged to cause the result (recall Ted Kennedy's Chappaquiddick speech and its focus on the setting – the murky water and the faulty guardrail – as well as the Tamir Rice prosecutor's "perfect storm").

When the audience member experiences anger, on the other hand, the emotion tends to reinforce the desire to blame someone, anyone, for what happened. A story of unresolved injustice is the surest way to evoke anger. Thus, for example, in scientific studies of anger's effect on decision making, researchers often evoke anger by telling stories about the abuse of powerless people. In one study, for example, a teacher bullied a student and humiliated him about his grade in front of the entire class. In most litigation scenarios, it is not difficult to evoke anger – someone has usually been hurt by someone else. But as with sadness, advocates must be careful when they encourage an angry reaction. We can never be sure who the target will be: the opposing party, the client, or even the advocate himself. (Stanchi 2010).

∞ Case study: anger and the underdog theme in Burlington Northern & Santa Fe R.R. v. White

Sheila White, the only woman working in her maintenance department in a railroad yard, sued under the retaliation provisions of Title VII. (*Burlington Northern & Santa Fe R.R. v. White* (2006)). She alleged that her supervisors at the railroad demoted and harassed her because she complained about a supervisor's sexual harassment. At the Supreme Court, the appeal was focused on the retaliation claim, not the original claim of sexual harassment. Nevertheless, in telling the story, White's counsel highlighted disturbing details from the harassment claim, including that White's supervisor forced her to shine a flashlight on him while he was urinating and made frequent references to menstruation and its effect on whether she was able to do her job. (As one lawyer said, only half-jokingly, if you have evidence that a supervisor forced his employee to watch him urinate, you win. Case over.) In describing the retaliation, White said that after she complained about her treatment, she was suspended for 30 days shortly before Christmas, and as a result, she was unable to provide a holiday dinner for her family.

This story is a classic example of a story priming anger in the decision maker: a powerless individual had been beset by cruel bullies. The bullies continued and even escalated their behavior when the victim tried to fight back, all while the authority figure (the railroad management) turned a blind eye to the behavior. The story worked. Not only did the Supreme Court find in favor of plaintiff, but its opinion highlighted the plaintiff's terrible Christmas:

> White and her family had to live for 37 days without income. They did not know during that time whether or when White could return to work. Many reasonable

employees would find a month without a paycheck to be a serious hardship. And White described to the jury the physical and emotional hardship that 37 days of having 'no income, no money' in fact caused. Brief for Respondent 4, n. 13 ("That was the worst Christmas I had out of my life. No income, no money, and that made all of us feel bad. . . . I got very depressed").

(Burlington Northern 2006)

Positive emotions

Priming decision makers to experience positive emotions also helps legal advocates, particularly those representing civil defendants. Positive emotions such as happiness, hope, and awe tend to make people feel optimistic, which in turn widens our lens for perception in favor of the big picture and away from the details. (Loewenstein and Lerner 2003). Because of this, especially if the other side is priming anger through an injustice story, telling a story of "justice served" can lessen the decision maker's desire to assign blame. Moreover, the emotions generated by such a story can counteract the feeling of needing to take action that was primed by negative emotions and even reinforce the cognitive bias that inclines people toward inaction.

The suggestion that defendants should consider telling a "justice served" story (when the facts make one possible) contradicts conventional wisdom. Defendants confronting unfavorable facts and thus having difficult stories to tell are often counseled to portray the facts in a bland, unemotional way. Indeed, this is what the railroad defendant did in the *White* case, in an otherwise fine brief. The facts were recounted in neutral, colorless prose. But the science suggests that this may be a mistake because it cedes all the emotional ground to the other side. Instead of that neutral story, the railroad might have told a story emphasizing that in the end, its own procedures provided justice to White: during its own internal grievance process, the railroad had suspended White's supervisor and sent him for sexual harassment training, and the railroad had reinstated White into her original position with full back pay (including for the 37 days of suspension). Even though in its legal argument, the railroad argued that White was made whole, it did not lay the groundwork for that argument in its facts. The story it told did not emphasize the "made whole" facts, and "justice served" did not appear to be a theme of the story. As a result, the audience (the Supreme Court) was not primed for the "justice served" arguments, which might have made all the difference.

Summary

Like the person hearing the story of a classic baseball game and then remembering only the baseball on the crowded table, priming in legal advocacy is a way of nudging the decision maker to focus on some points and not on others. Priming for emotional responses is important in legal advocacy, but it is something of a paradox for legal advocates. As we noted in the earlier chapters on decision making and the judicial audience, judges tend to disfavor direct appeals to emotion, but decisions are always the product of both emotional and cognitive components. This means that legal advocates must prime for emotions carefully and judiciously. Although the research on emotional priming is only in its infancy, it can provide legal advocates with some guidance.

Cases & briefs

Burlington Northern & Santa Fe R.R. v. White, 548 U.S. 53 (2006).
Brief for Respondent [White], 2006 WL 622126.

Bibliography

Chestek, K.D., 2014, 'Of Reptiles and Velcro: The Brain's Negativity Bias and Persuasion', *Nevada Law Journal*, 15, 606–630.
Damasio, A., 1994, *Descartes' Error: Emotion, Reason and the Human Brain*, Avon, New York.
Frost, M., 1990, 'Rhetoric – A Note on Classical and Modern Theories of Forensic Discourse', *Kansas Law Review*, 38, 411–431.
Haidt, J., 2001, 'The Emotional Dog and Its Rational Tail: A Social Intuitionist Approach to Moral Judgment', *Psychological Review*, 108(4), 814–834.
Kahneman, D., 2011, *Thinking Fast and Slow*, Farrar, Straus and Giroux, New York.
Keltner, D., Ellsworth, P.C. and Edwards, K., 1993, 'Beyond Simple Pessimism: Effects of Sadness and Anger on Social Perception', *Journal of Personality and Social Psychology*, 64(5), 740–752.
Loewenstein, G. and Lerner, J.S., 2003, 'The Role of Affect in Decision Making', in R.J. Davidson, K.R. Scherer and H.H. Goldsmith (eds.), *Handbook of Affective Sciences*, pp. 619–642, Oxford University Press, New York.
Meyer, P.N., 2007, 'Retelling the Darkest Story', *Mercer Law Review*, 58, 665–709.
Perelman, C. and Olbrechts-Tyteca, L., 1969, *The New Rhetoric: A Treatise on Argumentation*, John Wilkinson and Purcell Weaver, trans., Notre Dame Press, Notre Dame, IN.
Plous, S., 1993, *The Psychology of Judgment and Decision Making*, McGraw Hill, New York.
Stanchi, K.M., 2010, 'The Power of Priming in Legal Advocacy: Using the Science of First Impressions to Persuade the Reader', *Oregon Law Review*, 89, 305–350.

14

PRIMING INTERPRETATIONS AND IMPRESSIONS

In this chapter, we focus on lawyers' use of carefully selected words and phrases as primes. These language choices are designed to direct the reader's interpretive process. Priming to influence interpretation is particularly useful when the information presented can be interpreted in different ways. For example, how you interpret the sentence "Her apartment was filled with bugs" will likely change depending on whether you were previously discussing the National Security Agency (NSA) or cockroaches. (McNamara 2012). If you had previously been discussing the NSA, you would likely interpret "bugs" to mean spy devices, not insects. The discussion about the NSA is the prime. That prime leads the brain to search its memory stores for information connected to the NSA and spying. Within the memory stores are schema, or cognitive frameworks, that are used to interpret new information.

The NSA prime causes the brain to move its memory stores about spying to the forefront. So when the brain hears "Her apartment was filled with bugs," it checks the files at the front. As a result, it "knows" that "bugs" mean spy devices, not roaches. This cognitive process happens quickly and automatically. We may not even know why we "know" that bug means spy device and not cockroach in this instance; we just know it without really thinking about it.

Priming interpretation of ambiguous text

Priming allows legal advocates to focus a decision maker's attention on a particular word or concept, as with the baseball at the yard sale. It also allows legal advocates to influence the interpretation of that information, as with the bugs in the apartment. Statutory interpretation is an ideal example. Statutes are often dense and crammed with text, like that crowded yard sale table is crammed with items. Moreover, the text is frequently ambiguous and subject to a variety of plausible interpretations, like the "bugs" in the NSA example.

∞ *Case study: priming of statutory text in Title VII*

Title VII, the Civil Rights Act of 1964, is a good example of statutory text that can fluctuate in meaning. Title VII states that "[i]t shall be an unlawful employment practice for an employer . . . to fail or refuse to hire or to discharge any individual, or otherwise to discriminate against any individual with respect to his compensation, terms, conditions, or privileges of employment, because of such individual's race, color, religion, sex, or national origin." This critically important prohibition against discrimination has been the subject of countless cases interpreting virtually every word. Consider the examples below, which are two very differently primed formulations of Title VII's text. The priming here is both organizational and linguistic.

The citations have been omitted for this example:

Example 1	*Example 2*
Title VII seeks to balance the rights of employees and the rights of business owners to have freedom to run their businesses. The key word here is "unlawful." Title VII prohibits only "unlawful employment practice[s]" in which an employer "discriminate[s] . . . because of . . . sex." It does not prohibit all or even most adverse employment decisions. Indeed, the Supreme Court has noted that Title VII was never meant to "diminish traditional management prerogatives."	Title VII is a broad, remedial statute. With this act, Congress intended to "strike at the entire spectrum of disparate treatment of men and women in employment." This intention is evident in Title VII's text, which makes it unlawful to "discriminate . . . because of . . . sex." This language creates "a comprehensive statute proscribing all forms of sex discrimination, whether overt or subtle."

These two contrasting examples show how priming can lead to very different interpretations of identical statutory text. Example 1, written to favor the employer in a discrimination case, uses priming to focus the decision maker's attention on the word "unlawful." The prime is accomplished by word choice and quotation technique. If we think of the statute like that messy yard sale table, we can see the advocate's emphasis on a particular word as analogous to making that baseball the most vivid object on the table. As the decision maker's eyes pass over the statutory text, priming makes her focus on that one particular word. Even though the advocate hasn't explicitly told the decision maker how to interpret the word, just that small change affecting what word looms largest for the decision maker can make a difference in how she reacts to, and interprets, it.

Example 1 strengthens the decision maker's connection to the word "unlawful" by nudging the decision maker to see Title VII as covering only the most extreme, rare behavior. Unlawful is a word that conjures, for most people, behavior committed by "others." It is a distancing word. And, focusing the decision maker on "unlawful" has the collateral benefit of taking the decision maker's attention away from other words (such as "discriminate" and "sex"), thereby weakening the connection with words less favorable to the employer.

Once the decision maker is primed to focus on the word "unlawful," a chain reaction of connections may take place in the decision maker's mind. Think of what might happen when the yard sale customer sees the baseball – his mind may have a series of thoughts like "I remember tossing the ball with dad" or "I remember exactly where I was sitting when the Phillies won the World Series" and so on. These thoughts will trigger chain reactions of their own. A similar process will happen when a decision maker notices a particular word. The noticing of that word will trigger her "schema" or connections with that word. Those schemas can be other words, events, impressions, and emotions.

While the advocate can never be certain what connections or schema will be triggered by particular words, she can usually take an educated guess. Unlawful, for example, is a word freighted with negative connotations. It is connected in most people's minds to words like crime, criminal, wrongful, illegal, bad. When our brains take a word like "unlawful" and make automatic connections to other words like "crime" and "illegal," that is an example of what psychologists call "spreading activation." Spreading activation is one of the key persuasive advantages of lexical priming. Through spreading activation, our brains make rapid connections between words we read or hear and other, connected words. Figure 14.1 illustrates a possible way that priming the word "unlawful" might spread to other associations.

So, if we hear "bug," our brains might think of words like "cockroach" or "pest," and those words in turn might take us to things like "New York City" or "dirty" or "annoying." This spreading activation allows the use of a powerful word or phrase to evoke other words, as well as imagery and feelings, in the decision maker. "Bug," for example, might lead not only to other words ("pest") but can also lead to memories of events (that vacation in the bug-infested hotel) and feelings (disgust, annoyance). Most important, whatever word or phrase the writer has primed the decision maker to connect with "bug" will also be connected to "pest," the infested hotel, and the feeling of disgust.

In Example 1, the likely spread from "unlawful" to "crime" and "criminal" is a very powerful connection. Crime and criminal are words with particularly strong associations for most people. In other words, we have schema for "crime." When most of us think of "crime" or "criminal behavior," we do not immediately think of how employers treat their employees. We might not think of white-collar crimes at all. We will likely think of stereotypical crimes like murder or robbery. This may be particularly true of judges – the likely audience for this example of advocacy. By focusing the decision maker on the word "unlawful," the advocate made it more likely that the decision maker would connect what Title VII prohibits with aberrant, criminal behavior committed by "others." That will seriously diminish the scope of behavior that the decision maker is likely to see as violating Title VII, and that in turn will make it easier for the decision maker to reject the idea that the employer has violated the statute.

Simply by priming the decision maker to focus on one particular word, the advocate has reaped an interpretive advantage. Title VII is now potentially connected in the decision maker's mind to "crime" and "murder" and "other, bad people." This advantage is all the more powerful because the decision maker has done most of the work – the advocate has chosen the most advantageous word, but the decision maker's own mind has taken her to the other connections. Richard Perloff, a national expert

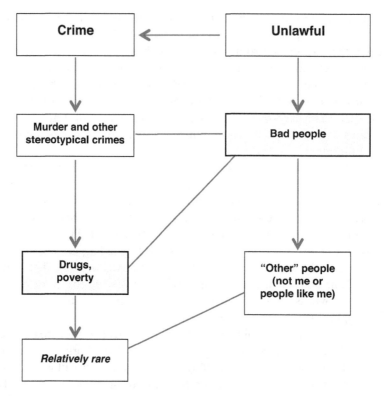

FIGURE 14.1

on persuasion, has noted that the most powerful persuasion takes place when the advocate simply "set[s] up the bait" and the decision maker essentially persuades herself. (Perloff 2010). This type of prime is a good example of that principle.

But Example 1 does more than prime the decision maker to pay attention to a particular word. It also makes the "bait" more attractive by using additional primes that direct the decision maker toward a narrow interpretation of prohibited "unlawful" behavior. Example 1 primes the decision maker to define "unlawful" by contrasting it with "freedom," a highly positive concept.

Note that Example 1 does not rely as wholly on the automatic response of spreading activation for its definition of "freedom" as it did for unlawful. Rather, Example 1 specifies that it is talking about the free market and business choices and prerogatives. This more expansive approach makes sense because a decision maker's mind might not automatically connect "freedom" with "business." The juxtaposition is meant to lead the decision maker to disconnect "unlawful" (bad, crime, other) from "business decision" (free, good, American, democratic). "Unlawful" action is bad and is what other (bad) people do; "freedom," which is connected to business decisions, is good (and is what the employer exercised in this case).

The combined result of the primes in Example 1 is that for a decision maker to interpret Title VII in a way that makes the employer liable, the decision maker has to connect the all-American concepts of freedom, free markets, and business with the negative concepts of "illegal," "criminal," and "wrongful." This is going to be cognitively difficult for most decision makers (perhaps particularly judges) who will not automatically connect those concepts. Even those decision makers who recognize that business decisions can often be illegal might not have the strong automatic connection between business and crime as they would have between, for example, murder and crime. Think of the example of an ostrich: most of us know that an ostrich is a bird, but studies have shown that people think of an ostrich as a "bad" example of a bird, whereas a robin is a more prototypical "good" example. The same type of categorical thinking is at work here. (Smith 2011; Rosch 1975). Employment discrimination is a "bad" example of a crime; murder is a more prototypical "good" example.

The primed contrast between "freedom" and "unlawful" will also likely have an emotional effect. Most decision makers (particularly judges) will resist an unpleasant connection condemning values that are so embedded in American culture (freedom, business choices) as "criminal" or "unlawful." Through the use of primes, the advocate has made it emotionally difficult to find against the employer.

While what we have done here is break the cognitive process potentially at work during priming down to its tiniest steps, keep in mind that these steps are not conscious to the decision maker. The journey from a focus on "unlawful" all the way to "the employer is probably not liable" is a largely subconscious one that happens quite quickly. The prime simply makes the decision maker feel like it doesn't make sense to find the employer liable. Having come to that first impression decision, the decision maker will then view the evidence and law through the prism of that first impression. Confirmation bias may also play a part here, leading the decision maker to pay more attention to evidence and law that supports her initial feeling and to ignore or discount contrary evidence and law.

Turning to Example 2, we can see a similar kind of lexical priming, but also a variation. Example 2 primes the decision maker to connect the language of Title VII with images and concepts of breadth by linking Title VII with words like "broad," "entire spectrum," and "comprehensive." Priming works not only on word associations, but on people's mindsets. In one experiment, for example, people who read the word "or" repeatedly were likely to view a box of tacks as two different things (a box, and some tacks), whereas people who read the word "and" were likely to see the box of tacks as one thing (a box of tacks). (Bargh and Chartrand 2000). In Example 2, a similar phenomenon is at play. Repeated use of words of breadth can encourage decision makers to see Title VII as something that covers a vast array of behavior. The prime fights against what might be a decision maker's stock schema about discrimination (something that happens to "other" people, rare behavior).

In addition to the words of breadth, Example 2 reminds the decision maker that the statute was meant to proscribe "all forms" of discrimination, "whether overt or subtle." So, to the extent a decision maker might think of discrimination in a narrow way, as obvious and apparent, the prime instead encourages the decision maker to connect "discrimination" with the word "subtle." Again, spreading activation will work here to connect discrimination with words associated with subtle – such as inconspicuous, hidden, complex. This prime might also lead the decision maker to look more closely at the actions in the case, because now he is looking for behavior that is "subtle" and might escape a casual scan. Again, confirmation bias may play a role here, as the judge will look for information that confirms the connection to "subtle."

Perhaps more interesting, however, is that some of Example 2's primes are meta-phorical. (Gibbs 1994; Allbritton 1992; Allbritton et al. 1995). In Example 2, Title VII is associated with active, aggressive verbs: it "outlaws," "strikes at," and "proscribes" evil acts. "Strikes at" creates a particularly strong, almost violent, metaphorical image – fists strike, lightning strikes, God strikes people down. Studies show that metaphorical primes like these can make the text more memorable. In one study, decision makers were more likely to remember sentences from a passage if the sentences were linked metaphorically. (Allbritton et al. 1995). The metaphorical primes at work in Example 2 – Title VII as avenging hero – are not only memorable but emotionally affecting. The decision maker deciding in favor of the employee has aligned himself with a righteous law that "strikes at" evil.

Priming impressions

In addition to influencing a decision maker's word associations and mindset, priming can also affect a decision maker's impressions, feelings, viewpoints, and value judg-ments. For example, people exposed to sentences depicting aggressive behavior (such as "break his arm") were more likely to behave aggressively in response to inconve-nience and more likely to see aggression in the behavior of those around them. In one famous study, subjects were asked to unscramble phrases that suggested hostile behavior, such as "leg break arm his." Others were asked to unscramble phrases that suggested kind behavior, such as "the boy hug kiss." (Srull and Wyer 1979).

After unscrambling these phrases, the subjects were given a passage about a person named Donald and were asked their impressions of him. The passage was purposefully ambiguous – it described a person whose behavior could be characterized in several ways. For example, the passage described Donald in his home with a friend and stated that "a salesman knocked at the door, but Donald refused to let him enter." Decision makers could see the act of refusal as solicitous of the friend or hostile to the salesman. Those subjects who were primed for hostility overwhelmingly saw Donald as "hostile" or "aggressive." Conversely, those primed for the trait of kindness characterized Don-ald's behavior, based on the exact same paragraph, as likable and pleasant. In the Donald study, the categories "aggressive" and "pleasant" were primed by words, but the effect on the subject was an overall impression, not a word or set of synonyms connected to the word. The prime influenced how the subjects saw the world around them.

The impressions created by primes tend to be strong and lasting. Once people have an impression or belief, they are inclined to pay less attention to subsequent informa-tion, particularly information that contradicts the impression. This is in part due to confirmation bias. Indeed, once primed, people will often remember primarily their impressions as opposed to the actual facts or information. They may even distort the facts to conform to their impressions. For example, once the subjects in the Donald study had decided Donald was hostile, they clung to this belief. When asked about their characterization, they tended to use their own impressions and memories, not the passage, to explain how they saw Donald. Those subjects quite literally remembered Donald as hostile, even though the vignette provided no real factual evidence for this "memory." If they looked back at the vignette, confirmation bias would likely lead them to interpret the facts in a way consistent with their own characterization.

Just like the Donald vignette, litigation often deals with facts, people, and events susceptible to multiple interpretations and value judgments. What the Donald study tells us is that certain word choices can prime a decision maker's impression of an ambiguous event or behavior. And, once the decision maker has that impression, she is likely to make future decisions based on that impression instead of going back to the facts.

We examine two case studies here. In the first, we look at the Questions Presented from the briefs in the U.S. Supreme Court case of *Safford v. Redding* (2009). The Question Presented in a brief is a key place for priming, because it generally comes at the very beginning, before the facts and argument, and is often the first "frame" of the argument that the court sees. In the second case study, we look at the use of a repeated, vivid word in the Argument section of the petitioner's brief in the U.S. Supreme Court case of *Lawrence v. Texas*. Through the use of that vivid word, and spreading activation, the advocates in *Lawrence* created an impression of the law that was evocative and indelible.

∞ Case study: priming impressions using the question presented

In *Safford v. Redding* (2009), school administrators strip-searched a 13-year-old girl who they suspected was selling drugs. The material facts were not in dispute. Here are the questions presented from the Supreme Court briefs of the school district and the 13-year-old student:

School District QP	*Student QP*
Whether the Fourth Amendment prohibits public school officials from conducting a search of a student suspected of possessing and distributing a prescription drug on campus in violation of school policy.	Whether it is reasonable to subject a thirteen-year-old girl to the indignity of a strip search based on an unreliable accusation that she previously possessed ibuprofen and no information that she possessed ibuprofen in her undergarments at the time of the search.

These two Questions Presented frame the issue in quite different ways and function as very different primes. First, the School District question asks not whether a school official can search, but whether the law will stop him from searching. Phrasing the issue this way suggests that the law, and the Court, might be an obstacle or obstruction to school policy. The facts make clear what the law would be obstructing: school safety and efforts to rid schools of crime. At its core, this question asks whether the Court should interpret the law to obstruct justice, which is a powerfully negative frame. That frame also takes advantage of omission bias, which leads decision makers to incline toward not acting. Here, the School District question strongly favors "getting out of the way" as opposed to doing something affirmative.

The main image called up by the School District question is the war on drugs in schools. Through use of language like "public school officials," "campus," "violation of school policy" and "possessing and distributing a prescription drug," the question calls up schema about drug-infested public schools and drug-dealing students who need to be stopped. The question notably does not mention the age of the student, her gender, the suspected drug, or the nature of the search. These gaps allow the decision maker to fill in the information with her own schema. What is the typical mental picture of a student drug dealer? Not a 13-year-old girl. The typical illegal prescription drug? Not ibuprofen. The question is phrased to allow the decision maker to feel a sense of urgency about the problem and a sense of the righteousness of the school officials before confronting the facts, including the adverse facts of the child's age and the relatively innocuous drug involved.

The student's question, by contrast, asks whether it is "reasonable" to strip search a child (a "girl") based on unreliable information about ibuprofen, which is something most people don't even consider a "drug." Like the ostrich, which is a bad example of a bird, ibuprofen is a bad example of a "drug." It is atypical. Moreover, asking whether something is "reasonable" creates a different feeling for the decision maker than asking whether something is "prohibited." The question of reasonableness invites the decision maker to probe her own experiences and values. The reasonableness query is then juxtaposed with facts that sound extraordinarily unreasonable because they are far outside the common experience of most people. The question emphasizes the child's age and gender at the beginning and repeats the atypical drug "ibuprofen" twice. It also specifies the nature of the search as a "strip search," which creates a vivid (and negative) image and feeling.

The main mental categories stimulated by this question are children and nudity/ strip searches. The juxtaposition of those two categories requires the decision maker to make the distasteful connection between "13-year-old girl" and "strip search." As a result, the question has an uncomfortable, somewhat repugnant feel to it. Even though sometimes adults and parents remove clothing from children for entirely innocuous reasons, we would rarely refer to it as "stripping" the child. Strip has both sexual (strip club, stripper) and coercive connotations – it even sounds forceful with its hard stop created by the plosive "p." We simply do not allow children to be "stripped" naked by adults. The question is designed for a decision maker to react to it with disgust. Add to that the reason for the search – "unreliable" information about "ibuprofen" – and the decision maker is left with the impression that something terribly wrong happened here. As the decision maker moves on to read the facts and the rest of the argument, he is mentally primed to condemn the despicable act that occurred.

These two questions also raise an important question about what happens when both sides prime effectively. Priming isn't a magic bullet that always works. And, in good legal advocacy, both sides will be or should be using priming strategies. But even though priming is not a guarantee, the likelihood that the other side will prime should make advocates more determined to prime in their own briefs, because if one side primes and the other doesn't, the risk of losing is that much greater.

∞ Case study: priming impressions using repetition of vivid words in Lawrence v. Texas *petitioner's brief*

In *Lawrence v. Texas* (2003), the petitioners, who argued before the U.S. Supreme Court that the Texas sodomy law was unconstitutional, peppered their brief with the word "brand." Specifically, they argued that the Texas sodomy law "brands" gays and lesbians as "second class citizens," as "lawbreakers," and as "criminals." The advocates used the word "brand" as a verb (as in the Texas law "brands") and as a noun (as in "suffer the brand of criminal").

The semantic connections conjured by the repeated use of the word "brand" as associated with "second class" status and criminality are powerful and negative. The word "brand" conjures images of cattle, livestock, and animals. But what human beings, historically, were branded? Criminals, as a way of stigmatizing them; and slaves, as a way of marking them as sub-human property and preventing their escape. Through spreading activation, the word "brand" conjures images of people treated as less than human, like animals, indelibly, unfairly, and permanently labeled. By connecting the Texas sodomy law to "branding," the advocates associated the law with a host of negative words and images. One of those words and images, slavery, is likely strongly connected with the concept "unconstitutional" for American judges. Simply by using the word "brand," therefore, the advocates created a potential connection for the decision makers between the Texas statute and the concept "unconstitutional."

The word "brand" and its associated words and concepts also likely evoked certain feelings in the Justices. Feelings of shame and guilt are strongly associated with historical instances in which human beings were treated like animals. By the repeated use of the word "brand," the advocates managed to connect the Texas law with strongly negative feelings of shame and guilt – an excellent emotional grounding for arguing that the law should be overturned.

Summary

Priming is a concept that can influence virtually every persuasive decision in law, from the big picture organizational and thematic decisions to the smallest word choice decisions. Think of priming as a way of shifting the audience's viewpoint – as you might shift your view of a statue as you walk around it. Your perspective shifts markedly if you look at the statue of Abraham Lincoln at the Lincoln Memorial from the side rather than the more familiar front view, and your understanding of the figure changes as your perspective shifts. Priming can help shift the reader's perspective through carefully chosen words with particular connotations or associations. When you choose your phrasing, think about what you want the audience to see when she considers the facts, the law, the analysis. Then, like a Freudian word association game, brainstorm about where certain words take you – what feelings, negative or positive, are related to those words? What other words do you associate with them? We often have a sense of what word seems "right" in a particular situation, but lawyers should explore and interrogate this feeling so that the choice is deliberate.

Cases & briefs

Lawrence v. Texas, 539 U.S. 558 (2003).
    Brief for Petitioners, 2003 WL 152352.
Safford Unified School District Number One v. Redding, 557 U.S. 364 (2009).
    Brief for Petitioners, 2009 Westlaw 507028.
    Brief for Respondent, 2009 Westlaw 852123.
Title VII, Civil Rights Act of 1964, 42 U.S.C. 2000e, et seq. (2012).

Bibliography

Allbritton, D.W., 1992, 'The Use of Metaphor to Structure Text Representations: Evidence From Metaphor-Based Schemas', Ph.D. Dissertation, Yale.

Allbritton, D.W., McKoon, G. and Gerrig, R.J., 1995, 'Metaphor-Based Schemas and Text Representations: Making Connections Through Conceptual Metaphors', *Journal of Experimental Psychology: Learning, Memory, and Cognition*, 21(3), 612–625.

Bargh, J.A. and Chartrand, T.L., 2000, 'The Mind in the Middle: A Practical Guide to Priming and Automaticity Research', in H.T. Reis and C.M. Judd (eds.), *Handbook of Research Methods in Social and Personality Psychology*, 253–285, Cambridge University Press, New York.

Gibbs, R.W., 1994, *The Poetics of Mind: Figurative Thought, Language, and Understanding*, Cambridge University Press, Cambridge.

McNamara, T.P., 2012, *Semantic Priming: Perspective From Memory and Word Recognition*, Psychology Press, New York.

Perloff, R.M., 2010, *The Dynamics of Persuasion: Communication and Attitudes in the 21st Century*, 4th edn., Routledge, New York.

Rosch, E., 1975, 'Cognitive Representations of Semantic Categories', *Journal of Experimental Psychology*, 104, 192–233.

Smith, M.R., 2011, 'Linguistic Hooks: Overcoming Adverse Cognitive Stock Structures in Statutory Interpretation', *Legal Communication and Rhetoric: JALWD*, 8, 1–36.

Srull, T.K. and Wyer, R.S., 1979, 'The Role of Category Accessibility in the Interpretation of Information About Persons: Some Determinants and Implications', *Journal of Personality and Social Psychology*, 37(10), 1660–1672.

Stanchi, K.M., 2010, 'The Power of Priming in Legal Advocacy: Using the Science of First Impressions to Persuade the Reader', *Oregon Law Review*, 89, 305–350.

15

INTRODUCTION TO SYLLOGISTIC FRAMEWORKS

Because many legal arguments take the syllogistic form (major premise-minor premise-conclusion), some advocates believe that deductive logic dictates the structure of all legal arguments. But this isn't so. While the organization of an argument is sometimes prescribed by the structure of the law or deductive logic, there are often many possible ways to organize an argument. Legal rules and issues rarely have a singular intrinsic "logic." Rather, the best argument structures are the result of careful tactical choices by the advocate that make the organization and conclusion of the argument *appear* to be mandated by logic.

Legal advocates generally make what Stephen Toulmin, "perhaps the pre-eminent modern figure in the field of argumentation theory," would call practical arguments. (Wangerin 1993). In a practical argument, the advocate asks the reader to make an inferential leap from data or evidence to reach a reasonable conclusion. Moreover, the advocate must justify the leap by making claims that fit the context of a specific situation. Toulmin distinguished these practical arguments from the comparatively rare theoretical arguments that are based on universal principles and require no inferences because the conclusion is certain. For our purposes, we focus on practical arguments, not only because theoretical arguments are rare, but also because practical arguments are more closely analogous with what lawyers actually do. (Toulmin 2003).

Toulmin noted that those who advance practical arguments – like lawyers – most often produce their reasoning *after* they arrive at their claims. That is, rather than inferring claims from evidence, they justify their claims retrospectively. Of course, that process might be attributed to the reality that a lawyer's advocacy position requires her to make a series of fairly certain claims that are known well in advance. But there is some scientific support for the proposition that most people make decisions this way as well; Jonathan Haidt has shown that people make moral judgments based largely on emotions and then work backward to construct "logical" rationales. (Haidt 2001). Given that the process for decision making and advocacy overlap in this way, the advocate must critically test and sift ideas so that her argument can survive criticism from experts in the field.

Syllogistic legal argumentation

Toulmin provided a basic layout of practical argument that metaphorically described legal argumentation: "An argument is movement from accepted data, through a warrant, to a claim." The claim is "the conclusion of the argument." It answers the question, "Where are we going?" The data are "the facts or other information on which the argument is based." The data answer the question, "What do we have to go on?" And the warrant "authorizes movement from the grounds to the claim." It answers the question, "How do you justify the move from these grounds to that claim?" (Toulmin 2003).

Toulmin differentiated practical argument from what he considered purely theoretical syllogisms. In the process, he recognized the form of syllogistic reasoning (the enthymeme) that occupies "most favored" status in legal advocacy and analysis. This syllogistic structure also serves as an organizational prime for the decision maker in that its structure prompts agreement with the conclusion or claim. As Martha Minow has noted, legal questions often ask "is this a that?" (Minow 1987). Concluding "this is (or is not) a that" is a form of deductive syllogistic reasoning asserting that what is true of the universal must be true for the particular. In other words, if we know that every member of a class has a certain characteristic, and that certain individuals are members of that class, then those individuals must have that characteristic. (Aldisert et al. 2007). In law, the common application of a general rule to a particular case is syllogistic reasoning.

As Toulmin pointed out, most legal arguments are not valid syllogisms in the formal sense. Instead, most legal arguments are presented in the rhetorical syllogistic form of enthymemes, that is, they are either missing premises or they contain premises that are only arguably true. Despite these differences from the formal syllogism, these arguments are effective because they appear to have the same airtight logic. Consider this syllogism from *United States v. Dionisio* (1973), in which the defendant was required to give a sample of his voice to a grand jury:

> [T]he Fourth Amendment provides no protection for what "a person knowingly exposes to the public, even in his own home or office. . . ." The physical characteristics of a person's voice, its tone and manner, as opposed to the content of a specific conversation, are constantly exposed to the public. . . . [Therefore,] . . . [the defendant] raised no valid Fourth Amendment claim [that his voice is protected].
>
> *(Dionosio 1973)*

The majority in *Dionisio* concluded that "this" (a voice sample) is not a "that" (protected by the Fourth Amendment). Notice how the simple transitive structure of the reasoning in *Dionisio* makes the conclusion seem indisputable, almost mathematical in its elegance and certainty. Because syllogistic reasoning draws from the mathematical principle of transitivity (if A equals B, and B equals C, then A must equal C), it has a unique persuasive force. If we assent to the truth of the premises (if we agree that A=B and B=C) then we must grant the conclusion. (Robbins 2002).

Dionisio, however, also demonstrates that legal arguments that appear to be ironclad and simple syllogisms are, upon closer inspection, eminently debatable. Does the Fourth Amendment really not cover anything that is public? Is a private figure's voice really something that is "public" in the sense of being known to everyone? These premises are probable but certainly open to argument. Yet the syllogistic form makes the argument seem indisputable. Why?

We start with the understanding that syllogistic reasoning has been around for a very long time – indeed, it was the only formal system of logic for millennia. (Tessler and Goodman 2014; Horn 1989). That suggests that there is something instinctive and primal about its appeal. That is consistent with what we know about decision making. Most of the reasons for the persuasive force of the syllogism circle back to our "System 1" thinking, our automatic, instinctive, emotional thinking process. The mental shortcuts we take with System 1 thinking are particularly common when we are reading quickly, or when we are tired or overworked, as many judges are when they are reading briefs. When we are using System 1 thinking, we are particularly prone to cognitive biases that might make us unlikely to recognize the faulty logic of a particular premise or series of premises. Hence, a syllogism like *Dionisio*'s looks more certain than it really is.

Moreover, when we process syllogisms, we make connections between the premises. To the extent that a syllogistic argument is crafted to ease the making of those connections, the argument makes the conclusion easier to agree with. As one example, look at the repetition of the key language "exposed to the public" in the *Dionisio* syllogism. The language closely mimics the form A-B, B-C, which makes the process of connecting the more complex premises in *Dionisio* almost as easy as connecting B to B and A to A.

The syllogistic form also feeds the brain's preference for simple, orderly thinking. That form feels good to our System 1 brain. Again, repetition helps here, as does the simplicity of the A-B, B-C, C-A form. The repetition in the *Dionisio* syllogism forms a neat, orderly, simple chain of logic. The form and language of the argument is emotionally appealing because it looks so easy and right. Of course the issues in *Dionisio* were not at all simple. But the Court makes them sound so straightforward and effortless that most of us are not even tempted to engage the deeper System 2 thinking that would expose the holes in the logic. Our lazy System 1 process loves for things to be easy, and unless something alerts us to think again, System 2 is content for System 1 to do most of the work.

Consider another example from *Personnel Administrator v. Feeney* (1979), in which the question was whether a hiring preference for veterans intentionally discriminated against women:

> Discriminatory intent is simply not amenable to calibration. It either is a factor that has influenced the legislative choice or it is not. The District Court's conclusion that the absolute veterans' preference was not originally enacted or subsequently reaffirmed for the purpose of giving an advantage to males as such necessarily compels the conclusion that the State intended nothing more than to prefer "veterans." Given this finding, simple logic suggests that an intent to exclude women from significant public jobs was not at work in this law.

Again, the question of whether a law was intended to discriminate is hardly simple (a point made by the dissent in *Feeney*). But here the Supreme Court disposes of a central and complex part of the case in just a few sentences. Something can be either this or that, not both. Because the something at issue here is "that," it cannot be "this." Simple logic.

Feeney and *Dionisio* illustrate the common use of syllogistic reasoning with arguable (as opposed to indisputably true) premises. But they also illustrate that what may appear on the surface to be the logical proof of a syllogism is instead the rhetorical argument of an enthymeme. In *Dionisio*, for example, one unstated premise is that stare decisis should be followed – prior Fourth Amendment law should dictate the resolution of the current case. In *Feeney*, one unstated premise is that legislative bodies have singular and identifiable intentions.

Legal argumentation almost always involves enthymemes, and there are good reasons for that. Enthymemes may be persuasive precisely because they leave out certain premises. Enthymemes keep syllogistic arguments simple and elegant, allowing the key points of the logic to stand out without additional clutter. This allows the decision maker to grasp the key points of the argument easily without having to wade through unimportant excess material. When constructed in the form of enthymemes, logical arguments "cut to the chase," which is appealing, particularly to the busy legal audience. Moreover, decision makers might become impatient with arguments in which all the small missing points were included. The argument might look like it was talking down to the decision maker by stating the obvious.

Well-crafted enthymemes also allow arguments to flow smoothly because the reader's journey through the argument is not interrupted by unnecessary premises. The reader may not even notice anything missing (did you notice anything missing in *Dionisio*?). That is System 1 at work again.

Even if the reader does notice the missing premise, if the unstated premise is something easily agreed upon (for example, "cases should be decided consistently with precedent"), decision makers are likely to supply the missing information automatically. Allowing the decision maker to supply missing premises may give enthymemes even more persuasive force because it engages the decision maker in the persuasive process. It transforms the decision maker's role in the persuasive process from objective outsider on whom an argument is being imposed to insider who is an active part of the persuasive process. By helping supply missing premises, the decision maker has essentially become the advocate's partner in the persuasive process. That greatly increases the chances of acquiescence with the message because the decision maker is now invested in the argument and has actively contributed to it by recognizing a shared, common understanding with the advocate. It has become, in part, the decision maker's argument and her desire for consistency will move her toward continuing agreement.

Often, though, premises are omitted from legal arguments because the premises are not easily agreed to and stating them will reveal the flaws in the argument. This is a common strategy, but riskier. The advocate is counting on the dominance of System 1 here, and hoping that the decision maker will not sense a problem that engages the more critical and probing System 2. You can see this at work in *Feeney* – the premise that legislatures have singular and identifiable intent is widely debated. This technique of avoiding risky premises has worked effectively in some of the major cases of our time, including *Brown v. Board of Education*. (Jamar 2008).

But when the tactic fails to work, it fails somewhat spectacularly. Consider the opinion of the Seventh Circuit Court of Appeals in *Parker v. Astrue* (2010), which found Judge Richard Posner admonishing an administrative law judge for relying on "contradictions and missing premises." The administrative law judge had concluded that because a social security claimant did not present "objective" proof of pain, she did not truly suffer from chronic pain. Judge Posner, an able rhetorician, exposed and denounced the faulty logic:

> It [is] a mistake to say "there is no objective medical confirmation of the claimant's pain; therefore, the claimant is not in pain." But it would be entirely sensible to say "there is no objective medical confirmation, and this reduces my estimate of the probability that the claim is true." The administrative law judge said the first, not the second.
>
> *(Parker 2010)*

Summary

The syllogistic framework is the most common organizational scheme in legal advocacy – and its popularity has a reason. The syllogism is a form of logic with a rich and long history. But it is important for legal advocates to recognize that legal arguments more often take the form of enthymemes that involve unstated or arguable premises. Most of the time, making legal arguments in the form of enthymemes strengthens the persuasiveness of the message, but not always. So, while enthymemes and syllogistic reasoning are the backbone of legal organization, the advocate must employ them carefully and wisely. A critical aspect of this reasoning is choosing the premises of the syllogism carefully, a topic addressed in the next chapter.

Cases & briefs

Brown v. Board of Education, 347 U.S. 483 (1954).
Parker v. Astrue, 597 F.3d 920 (7th Cir. 2010).
Personnel Administrator of Massachusetts v. Feeney, 442 U.S. 256 (1979).
United States v. Dionisio, 410 U.S. 1 (1973).

Bibliography

Aldisert, R.J., Clowney, S. and Peterson, J.D., 2007, 'Logic for Law Students: How to Think Like a Lawyer', *University of Pittsburg Law Review*, 69(1), 100–121.
Berger, L.L., 2010, 'Studying and Teaching "Law as Rhetoric": A Place to Stand', *The Journal of the Legal Writing Institute*, 16, 3–64.
Haidt, J., 2001, 'The Emotional Dog and Its Rational Tail: A Social Intuitionist Approach to Moral Judgment', *Psychological Review*, 108(4), 814–834.
Horn, L.R., 1989, *A Natural History of Negation*, University of Chicago Press, Chicago.
Minow, M., 1987, 'The Supreme Court, 1986 Term – Forward: Justice Engendered', *Harvard Law Review* 101, 10–95, in D.K. Weisberg (ed.), 1993, *Feminist Legal Theory: Foundations*, pp. 301–319, Temple University Press, Philadelphia.
Tessler, M. and Goodman, D., 2014, 'Some Arguments Are Probably Valid: Syllogistic Reasoning as Communication', in *Proceedings of the Thirty-Sixth Annual Conference of the Cognitive Science Society*, last viewed 8 December 2016, from https://web.stanford.edu/~ngoodman/papers/cogsci14-syllogisms_tessler.pdf
Toulmin, S., 2003 (updated), *The Uses of Argument*, Cambridge University Press, New York.
Wangerin, P., 1993, 'A Multidisciplinary Analysis of the Structure of Persuasive Arguments', *Harvard Journal of Law & Public Policy*, 16, 195–234.

16

SYLLOGISTIC AND ANALOGICAL CASE ARGUMENTS

To construct an effective syllogism, the advocate first creates the appropriate categories and frames the relevant questions. Here, *appropriate* and *relevant* mean the categories and questions that appear logically to lead to the advocate's preferred outcome. The syllogistic framework can be used for the more straightforward application of rules (major premises) to facts (minor premises) and the more complex process in which arguments are built both on the rules themselves and on comparisons with precedent cases from which the rules emerge.

As we have discussed throughout the book, schematic cognition, or categorical thinking, is a mainstay of decision making. For example, one subject in a psychological study of syllogistic reasoning reported that when he read the premise "all the artists are bee-keepers," he pictured in his mind a group of "artists in [a] room and imagined they all had beekeepers' hats on." (Johnson-Laird and Steedman 1978). This not only gives us information about one way in which we process syllogistic reasoning (through images), but also about how one kind of syllogistic fallacy can occur. In the hypothetical, all the artists are beekeepers but not all the beekeepers are artists. But if we process the categorical statement "all the artists are beekeepers" by imagining a room containing people who are wearing both berets (artists) and beekeepers' hats (beekeepers), it is easy to flip the premise. In our imagined room, it looks like all the beekeepers are also artists, which is not true. Our way of imagining the premise (visualizing a room of people) can lead easily to this fallacy. That's our System 1 thinking at work, and it is the same category error people make when they see primarily African-American men arrested on the nightly news and conclude that all or most African-American men are criminals.

The beekeeper-artist syllogism also shows how categories concretely influence our logical reasoning, and how mistaken our categorical thinking sometimes is. For legal advocates, constructing the categories that form the basis of their major and minor premises is critical. In judicial opinions, and in their descriptions of their own decision making, judges often suggest that syllogistic reasoning happens spontaneously and without human intervention. In other words, legal reasoning involves little more than "finding" the category or rule and then "applying" the category or rule to the facts.

When we use syllogistic reasoning to ask "is this [new thing] a that?" we assume that the category defined by "that" already exists. The only question is whether the new thing fits within the preexisting category. Judges reinforce this perspective on legal decision making when, like Justice Roberts, they characterize themselves as umpires whose only "job is to call balls or strikes."

Category construction

Despite this impression, the truth, as most advocates and many judges know, is that much more discretion goes into the construction and application of categories and rules than the "balls or strikes" analogy acknowledges. Within certain limits, different umpires establish different strike zones. Any individual factual scenario can fit into multiple categories and rules, and the law's categories and rules sometimes appear endlessly malleable. Contrary to earlier formalist views, categories are neither fixed nor automatic. As Amsterdam and Bruner wrote, categories are made and not found, and their construction is "rarely innocent." (Amsterdam and Bruner 2002).

People create categories, consciously and unconsciously, out of their own stories, theories, or experiences about how the world works. Categories can be helpful or invidious, and they can be more or less truthful or outright misleading. Good or bad, once entrenched, categories are remarkably resilient. Once the decision maker creates or accepts a category, that category often becomes the filter through which all new information or experience is processed. The decision maker will attribute all the features he sees in the existing category's prototypes to any new information he places into the category, and he will find it difficult to discern any significant differences.

Category construction and selection affect the syllogistic arguments that follow, but they also, and more immediately, affect the advocate's framing of the issue or question. Some rhetoricians refer to this as "frame-shifting," others as "characterization." (Little 1996). In frame-shifting or characterization, the lawyer begins with the same basic set of information and changes the lens or "frame" to provide a different perspective and to shift the meaning of what happened. For example, think of how different a mountain like El Capitan in Yosemite looks when we see it from the east and when we view it from the north. One view looks like a beginner's climb, another view appears to offer the climber certain death. In the same way, the same facts can lead to opposite impressions. Take, for example, the video in *Scott v. Harris* (2007), which showed a police chase of a speeding car that resulted in a crash. Some viewers saw extraordinarily reckless driving justifying the use of deadly force by police officers and others saw a life-threating overreaction by police officers involved in chasing a speeding car. (*Scott* 2007; Kahan et al. 2009).

Some researchers specifically attribute the influence of framing to the same cognitive processes as priming; that is, a frame, like the use of priming language, makes certain information more salient or accessible. Thus, a question about whether the Ku Klux Klan should be able to march can be framed to emphasize free speech concerns (should a disfavored group be allowed to march?) or as a public safety issue (should a racist organization be allowed to terrorize a neighborhood?). (Iyengar 1991).

As an example of frame-shifting, consider the history of the legal treatment of pregnancy. In *Geduldig v. Aiello* (1974), the Supreme Court (at the time, all male justices) upheld a statute that excluded pregnancy from the disabilities for which workers could receive benefits. Rejecting the equal protection challenge to the statute, the Court concluded that the statute did not discriminate against women, but rather differentiated between "pregnant persons," a category made up of women, and "non-pregnant persons," a category that included men and women. The Court framed the question as whether it was discriminatory to provide disability benefits to only non-pregnant men and women. The Court's framing of the question inevitably led to the answer that it cannot be sex discrimination if the statute benefits both men and women, and simply excludes a subset of women.

Some feminist commentators explicitly criticized the Court's framing and choice of categories, believing that it revealed the Court's blinkered male perspective. The categorical choice (pregnant vs. non-pregnant "persons") allowed the Court to simultaneously neutralize the gendered aspect of pregnancy and view pregnancy as outside the category of "normal" disability (normal being the kinds of disability that happen to men). Put in syllogistic form, the feminist argument was that *all* pregnant persons are female, and men are *always* non-pregnant persons, so when benefits are excluded for pregnancy, *all* the people excluded from benefits are *always* women. If we think about categories as rooms containing the designated persons, all the people in the "no benefits" room are women; all the people in the "full benefits" room are men.

Framing questions

Changing the category description changes the framing of the question. Compare these two questions. First the Supreme Court's question: does a law discriminate on the basis of sex if it provides disability benefits for non-pregnant persons, both men and women, but excludes "pregnant persons"? Then another question: does a law discriminate based on sex if it singles out for adverse treatment a disability that affects only women? Both questions have in common the ultimate question of sex discrimination, but they differ in their construction of the appropriate categories. (See Fig. 16.1). Laura Little might refer to this as "rival components" – the issue grows out of the same shared impetus, but its resolution depends on different characterizations of what components are important. (Little 1996).

Another option for re-framing the issue is to widen the lens. (See Fig. 16.2). Rather than focusing on pregnant persons, the advocate might broaden the category to cover all "people exercising reproductive capacity." (Littleton 1987). When the category is "people exercising reproductive capacity," the rooms look very different. The "no benefits" room includes all the people who reproduce and are treated adversely – and it contains all and only women; the "benefits" room includes all those who reproduce and suffer no adverse consequences – and that room is all men. Again, the new category definition changes the frame of the question. The question becomes whether a law is sexually discriminatory if it burdens women and not men who exercise reproductive capacity. The law looks much more biased and discriminatory through the lens of the new category and frame. Laura Little refers to this common frame-shifting approach as an "expanding universe" because the context was expanded from the narrow "pregnancy" to the more expansive "reproducing." Other advocates have adapted Sartori's term and refer to this kind of frame shifting as moving up on the "ladder of abstraction" from the more concrete concept (pregnancy) to the more abstract one (reproducing). (Beazley 2014).

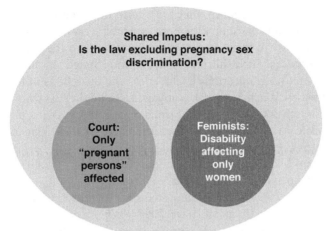

FIGURE 16.1 Rival Components

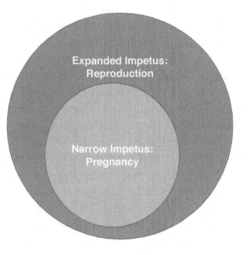

FIGURE 16.2 Expanding/Contracting Universe

Effects of shortcuts

As the *Geduldig* example shows, shifting categories and frames can mislead or illuminate: even some of the brightest legal minds were persuaded that it was meaningful to distinguish between pregnant and non-pregnant persons (*Geduldig* was decided 6–3). In part, this is because categories provide helpful mental shortcuts. Categories allow us to treat one thing as equivalent to or substitutable for another. They are "guardians against complexity," whose role often is to hasten and simplify our thinking so that we experience the world as less complex and more predictable than it actually is. (Krieger 1995). Indeed, this is the purpose of categorical thinking; without the ability to categorize, our brains would be forced to approach each experience and decision anew, which would be overwhelming and paralyzing. Framing effects are similar mental shortcuts. Even though framing effects are quite persuasive, they are a form of cognitive bias that induces our brains to answer the same question differently depending on how it is asked.

The shortcut quality of these cognitive processes leads to the kind of flawed thinking we saw in *Geduldig*. Such shortcuts make up our System 1 thinking process, and we know that System 1 is notoriously unable to recognize flaws in logic and is laden with cognitive biases. When System 1 is engaged, we might pass over category errors. We might find ourselves exaggerating the similarities of things or people that fall within the category while we overemphasize the differences of those outside the category. (Krieger 1995). As a result, it might seem simple logic to exclude pregnancy from other disabilities, perhaps because it seems "different" from other disabilities or because it is something that happens to "other people."

Moreover, because categorical thinking stems from "prototyping," it naturally leads to stereotyping. (Amsterdam and Bruner 2002). When constructing categories, and when placing new information into existing categories, we tend to rely on a mental prototype that is often visual (think of the artists with the beekeeper hats). What mental picture did you have of "artist"? Was it male or female? Beret? Holding a palette? Our System 1 brain does not care that most artists don't wear berets or use hand-held palettes. This process is more disturbing when the categories are legal. When we hear about crime, we call up a mental prototype of a criminal. And within that category we have sub-category prototypes of burglars, drug dealers, mob bosses, embezzlers. When we imagine these prototypes, they have races and genders, and that's where the process gets very problematic. While it is the advocate's task to craft a rule or category that is most advantageous to the client's position and that is plausible to the decision maker, the ethical advocate should avoid rhetorical techniques that reinforce the damaging stereotypes that emerge from classifying people into categories.

Framing effects create similar ethical dilemmas. The bias exerted by a clever or partial frame is one of the strongest cognitive biases (and, interestingly, our susceptibility to it increases with age). It can even corrupt our memories. In one example, study participants saw a film about a traffic accident. The participants who were asked about the cars "hitting" each other tended to remember correctly that the film showed no shattered glass. But those who were asked about the cars "smashing" each other *incorrectly* remembered seeing shattered glass in the film. (Loftus and Palmer 1974).

Though we might expect only the uninformed to be influenced by framing, studies have shown that even experts in a particular field are susceptible to framing effects. For example, the loss aversion bias was evident in studies of medical experts and judges. Medical experts were taken in by Daniel Kahneman's Asian disease hypothetical, which asked about an identical medical protocol in two different ways; one version was framed in terms of the number of potential lives saved, the other in terms of potential lives lost (many medical experts preferred the "lives saved" protocol, even though the two protocols were exactly the same). Similarly, judges were influenced by Jeff Rachlinski's settlement hypothetical, in which a proposed settlement was framed two different ways – in terms of amount gained versus amount lost. Many judges tended to prefer the choice framed in terms of gains, even though the settlement was exactly the same. (Kahneman 2011; Guthrie et al. 2001).

When the advocate highlights particular views of the facts through framing, her goal is to influence the audience member to be more receptive to the arguments that come next. Like the priming words discussed in previous chapters, different ways of framing the issue encourage the listener to focus on different subsets of information. The frames are designed to cause the audience to focus on a particular subset of the facts, often to the exclusion of other pieces of information. Remember the baseball on the yard sale table? If the mind is taken up with the baseball, the other objects are less likely to be remembered.

Syllogistic argument construction

As just discussed, because they drive the major and minor premises that follow, the construction of categories and the creation of framing questions are the critical first steps for the advocate working within the syllogistic framework. The right choice of category allows her to organize her argument around deductive logic and the familiar syllogistic structure that is both comfortable and looks convincing (if not irrefutable) to the decision maker.

∞ Case study: categories and framing in United States v. Jones

Consider Table 16.1, which outlines two very different categorizations in *United States v. Jones* (2012), the case about whether the warrantless attachment of a GPS device to a suspect's car violated the Fourth Amendment.

In this case, the advocates likely chose the categories labeled "1." in Table 16.1 (public information vs. private property) based on the available precedent. A long line of cases starting with *Katz v. United States* (1961) supported the government's argument (recall the syllogism about the voice samples above). The defendant's argument was based on a case called *United States v. Silverman* (1961) in which the Supreme Court had held that the government's use of a listening device pushed into the heating ducts of a private building violated the Fourth Amendment. The advocates likely evaluated the precedent, crafted a category/rule inductively, and then fit the case into the category/rule in syllogistic form.

TABLE 16.1

Government Argument	*Defendant Argument*
1. What is knowingly exposed to the public is not protected by the Fourth Amendment (category is "public information")	1. The Fourth Amendment protects our ability to exclude others (including the government) from private property (category is "private property")
2. Defendant's riding on public roads is public information (category is "driving route") 3. Defendant's driving routes are exposed to the public and therefore not protected by the Fourth Amendment	2. Defendant's car is private property (category is "car") 3. Because the defendant's car is private property, the government's installation of the GPS is a form of "trespass" that violates the Fourth Amendment

This process of inductive crafting of categories is a common method of legal reasoning and is one of the most important skills for the legal advocate. Here again we see a version of the "ladder of abstraction" or "expanding and contracting universe." (Beazley 2014; Little 1996). Using the ladder of abstraction, for example, *Silverman*'s holding is generalized from the more concrete "listening devices cannot be implanted into heating ducts" to the more general rule that the government cannot trespass, even with a tiny device, onto private property. This process of abstraction can make categories bigger and broader, enabling the advocate to fit her case more easily into the category.

Of course, in distinguishing cases, legal advocates are more likely to narrow the holdings to limit them to their particular facts, making it easier to distinguish. The defendant used this technique in *Jones*, arguing that precedent permitting the government to place beepers into suspects' vehicles was distinguishable because in those cases the government did not physically trespass into the vehicle to place the beeper within it. Moreover, the defendant argued that beepers reveal much more limited information as compared to the 24-hour surveillance allowed by GPS. Thus, the defendant contracted the precedent to apply only to cases involving use of a limited surveillance device requiring no physical trespass into a private vehicle.

There is some category work going on in the second premise as well, as illustrated in Fig. 16.3. The government is talking about driving around on public roads; the defendant is talking about the private property (car) that he owns. In terms of framing, Laura Little might call this tactic "rival components": while there is some overlap between a car and driving routes, they are really two different things, and which alternative the decision maker decides to focus on makes a significant difference in outcome.

FIGURE 16.3 Rival Components

Construction of the analogical case argument

The *Jones* case study illustrates not only the syllogistic structure and pliability of categories, but also another key component of legal reasoning: reasoning by analogy to the precedent case law. Analogy construction, like category creation, is fundamental to syllogistic reasoning. Edward Levi has written that the process of legal reasoning can be reduced to three steps: finding similarity between cases, deriving a rule of law from the precedent, and applying the rule to the new case. This description illuminates how analogy is embedded into the syllogistic structure. As Levi notes: the "finding of similarity or difference is the key step in the legal process." (Levi 1948).

In both arguments in *Jones*, analogies are embedded into the syllogistic structure to bolster the argument. So, instead of the argument "skeletons" in Table 16.1, the actual arguments have a bit more meat to them, and we start to see the structure in its complete and complex form in Table 16.2:

TABLE 16.2

Government Argument	*Defendant Argument*
What is knowingly exposed to the public is not protected by the Fourth Amendment (category is "public information").	The Fourth Amendment protects our ability to exclude others (including the government) from private property (category is "private property").
Defendant's riding on public roads is public information (category is "driving route").	Defendant's car is private property (category is "car"). Therefore, he has a reasonable expectation of privacy because of his ownership and right to exclude others.
Analogy to *United States v. Knotts*: the Court held that no Fourth Amendment search occurred when the government, without a warrant, installed an electronic beeper in a container that was subsequently transported in a vehicle.	Analogy to *United States v. Silverman*: *Silverman* held that the government violated the Fourth Amendment when it "usurped" the petitioner's private property by trespassing and inserting a "spike mike" into the heating duct.
Analogy to *United States v. Lee*: the Court held that the nighttime use of a searchlight to observe liquor on a ship's deck did not constitute a search.	
Analogy to *Smith v. Maryland*: the Court held that the use of a pen register to record the numbers dialed on the defendant's telephone was not a search.	
Defendant's driving routes are exposed to the public and therefore not protected by the Fourth Amendment.	Because the defendant's car is private property, the government's installation of the GPS is a form of "trespass" that violates the Fourth Amendment.
Analogy: driving route (both *Jones* and *Knotts*); driving route to ship's deck and numbers dialed on telephone (exposed to public); beeper, flashlight, and pen register to GPS (all involve enhancing senses).	Analogy: physical trespass onto private property (both); a spike mike to GPS (surveillance technology); house/office to car (private property).

Building on the traditional syllogistic form

The examples above illustrate that while syllogistic structure can form the foundation of many legal arguments, legal advocates often build on and supplement this foundation. Most legal syllogisms use categories derived from inductive reasoning and rely on analogies or policy arguments embedded in them. Thus, they are almost always a bit more complicated than the A-B, B-C, A-C form we see in simple logic. We talked earlier about the advantages of using the rhetorical syllogisms called enthymemes to simplify legal arguments. In this section, we talk about the advantages of including additional premises as links in the syllogistic argument chain. While this structure risks stating the obvious to the decision maker, it has other advantages that outweigh the risks.

With this structure, sometimes called "foot in the door" organization, the major or minor premises of the syllogism (A-B or B-C), or both, are preceded by a series of assertions that are linked to the premise. The key is that these preceding assertions are more certain and less debatable than the major or minor premise. This has the advantage of making an arguable premise (like "The Fourth Amendment does not protect people's voices") more likely to be accepted. Although this structure works well with conclusions or premises that are a bit controversial, it can work with any premise.

We also discuss the foot in the door approach in the chapters on tone, because it is a way of easing the reader into more controversial premises. Essentially, foot in the door takes the basic syllogistic form, but reinforces one or more of the premises by breaking them into component steps. Each of those component steps is a more easily accepted premise than the "major" premise, making the major premise more palatable to the decision maker. So, instead of A-B, B-C, A-C, the foot in the door approach can be modeled as: (A1+A2+A3)-A-B, B-C, A-C.

Foot in the door works because of our bias in favor of consistency. If A is a disputed premise that might prevent the decision maker's acceptance of the conclusion, the advocate can help the decision maker accept A by showing that A is simply composed of a number of smaller premises with which the decision maker agrees. In other words, "A" is simply the sum of a number of easily accepted parts. Once the decision maker agrees with these smaller premises, it is more difficult for the decision maker to disagree with A. The decision maker's desire for consistency will propel her toward agreement. Moreover, the advocate has connected those smaller premises to the major premise in the decision maker's mind, making it tougher for the decision maker to then see the major premise in terms other than those defined by the advocate.

Foot in the door influences the decision maker well before the conclusion, while the decision maker is interpreting and retrieving relevant data about the conclusion. By breaking A up into smaller premises with which the decision maker easily can agree, the advocate influences what data the decision maker retrieves to interpret and evaluate the major premise. The more controversial major premise "sneaks up" on the decision maker because the smaller premises influence "bit by bit the data upon which his decision is eventually based." (Krieger 1995).

∞ *Case study: foot-in-the-door organization in* Lawrence v. Texas

In *Lawrence v. Texas* (2003), the petitioners faced a significant legal and emotional hurdle in their argument that the Texas law criminalizing homosexual sodomy was unconstitutional. First of all, the Court had decided against petitioners' position relatively recently in *Bowers v. Hardwick* (1986). Second, the petitioners likely confronted a Court with views about homosexual sex that were outdated or biased. While many parts of the brief retain the familiar syllogistic form, the petitioners had to provide additional support for their premises, as illustrated in this excerpt.

> "It is a promise of the Constitution that there is a realm of personal liberty which the government may not enter." *Casey*, 505 U.S. at 847. It is well settled that the Due Process Clause of the Fourteenth Amendment guarantees the personal liberty of Americans against encroachment by the States, and that this protection of liberty encompasses substantive fundamental rights and interests that are unenumerated. [multiple Supreme Court citations omitted.] Giving substance to "liberty" is necessary to maintain the individual freedoms that are the essence of American democracy, while also allowing government action that is justified by the collective good. See *Casey*, 505 U.S. at 849–51.
>
> Among the liberties protected by the Constitution is the right of an adult to make choices about whether and in what manner to engage in private consensual sexual intimacy with another adult, including one of the same sex. This extremely personal sphere implicates three aspects of liberty that have long been recognized as fundamental: the interests in intimate associations, in bodily integrity, and in the privacy of the home. For the State to limit and dictate the intimate choices of American couples in this realm without any substantial justification is repugnant to ordered liberty. *Stare decisis* does not require continued adherence to the Court's contrary decision in *Bowers*.
>
> *(Brief for Petitioners 2003)*

The basic syllogism here is: the Constitution's liberty guarantee protects adult choices about sexual intimacy (A-B), any law that limits and dictates the intimate sexual choices of adults is unconstitutional (B-C), therefore *Bowers* (and the Texas law) are unconstitutional (A-C, that *Bowers* limits and dictates intimate adult choices is a missing premise meant to be easily supplied by the reader). But there is a lot more going on here with A-B, because at the time of the brief, the proposition in A-B was a controversial premise, at least as applied to homosexuals. Notice that the word or concept of homosexuality is not mentioned explicitly in the A-B premise (without doubt a category choice) except in a short adjunct clause. But the main structural point here is that A-B is led into with a series of easily agreed-to premises. If we break A-B down, it looks like this:

A1 – the Constitution protects a liberty interest that the government cannot violate (easily agreed with, multiple citations to Supreme Court law)

A2 – that liberty interest includes rights that are substantive and unenumerated (hard to argue with based on multiple Supreme Court case citations)

A3 – these freedoms are essential to American democracy (who could disagree?)

A-B – this freedom includes the right to make intimate choices including choice of partner (pretty easily agreed to), including a partner of the same sex (the controversial point)

This complex premise is then followed by a series of quick analogies that connect this new right to choose a same sex partner to other uncontroversial and connected liberty interests, including "intimate associations, . . . bodily integrity, and . . . the home." The result of this organization is that when the decision maker is beginning to engage in the decision-making process and is searching his memory for related information and decisions, the advocate has alerted him to – and made salient – those prior decisions that are most helpful to the advocate's cause. The organization ensures that the decision maker is thinking about un-enumerated liberty interests, particularly those involving intimate decisions. Instead of whatever data (perhaps unfavorable) might otherwise spring to the decision maker's mind when he thinks of "homosexual sex," the strategy is designed to make sure that what springs to mind is something along the lines of "can the government really tell me with whom I can associate? Whom I can choose as a wife? That can't be true."

The syllogistic organization worked well in *Lawrence* even though the legal advocates faced directly adverse precedent. This outcome provides a lesson in the significance of categorization. By categorizing the right at stake as the right of "adult intimate association" as opposed to the right to engage in "homosexual sex" (expanding the universe), the legal advocates in *Lawrence* were able to place the advocated right comfortably within the overwhelming majority of precedent, making *Bowers* look like the blip in an otherwise consistent history of constitutional protection. Thus, even in the most unconventional, controversial cases, the traditional organization can be effective and persuasive.

Deviating from the traditional syllogistic form

Although the traditional syllogistic form, give or take some minor variations, will be the most effective organization in most cases, a departure from conventional organization might sometimes be the legal advocate's best approach. The advocate should depart from syllogism with care, however. The legal audience is likely to expect and be comfortable with syllogistic organization. That comfort confers substantial advantage to the legal advocate. But sometimes, a jolt of discomfort can work for the advocate. The trick is to know when and in what kinds of cases. That requires knowing a bit about what audience discomfort means for processing and decision making.

Starting with a risky premise: door-in-the-face organization

The syllogism works in part because the early premises (A and B), even if debatable, are reasonable and often easily agreed to. The strength and logical power of the structure derives from this easy, agreeable aspect. It is also a form with which the legal audience has familiarity and comfort. But sometimes, it may be in the advocate's interest to upend the usual structure and arouse the decision maker from the comforting lull of the traditional logic. One way to do this is to start the logical chain with a premise that is controversial and then lead into a more agreeable premise. Sometimes called "door in the face," this common negotiating tactic is based on the social norm of reciprocity. We cover this tactic in Chapter 17 as part of tone, because it is a way of reaching compromise.

Simply put, we are more likely to get what we want when we overshoot in the original request – when we ask for something big, get rejected, and then ask for something smaller (ideally the smaller ask is what we really wanted all along). The psychology of door in the face stems from the human discomfort with saying "no" too often, which conflicts with our sense of ourselves as generous, just, and helpful. People tend toward decisions that affirm their views of themselves as good people – this is called "ego affirmation." Ego affirmation explains why door in the face tends to work best in contexts involving social justice or charity.

In legal advocacy, door in the face runs counter to the accepted conventional wisdom: ask only for what you need to win and begin your argument with your strongest point. Door-in-the-face organization starts with a risky premise and invites rejection. Nevertheless, certain advocacy situations lend themselves to this organization. Impact litigation, and especially amicus briefing, are common places to see door-in-the-face tactics. In these scenarios, the advocate faces no ethical problem with demanding more than needed because the individual client is either a stand-in for a policy goal or there is no individual client. Moreover, large-scale change is the purpose of the advocacy, so the risk of asking for the big thing first is minimal.

Similarly, door in the face may be useful in contexts in which the advocate has determined that the issue is worth litigating, but winning is unlikely. Much criminal defense work and plaintiff-side employment discrimination cases involve enough of an uphill battle that jolting the decision maker with an unusual argument structure can actually encourage the decision maker to think about the case in a different way.

In addition to understanding in what kinds of cases door in the face might be effective, the other very important aspect of this strategy is that the initial risky premise must be *reasonable*. It cannot be outrageous or the psychological effect will backfire. With door in the face, the decision maker must feel that she made a real choice in rejecting the premise – her autonomy in making that choice is essential to the psychological effect. If the premise is too extreme, the decision maker has not experienced the process involved in truly deciding and will likely not feel the dissonance required to prime her agreement to the next argument.

Summary

It is important for advocates to recognize that they have many organizational options. That means part of the persuasive process is choosing an organization carefully and deliberately. The first step is to determine what overall organization is most favorable to the client's position. Once the advocate has determined that she will focus on the syllogistic framework, the next question is whether to follow the traditional syllogism, some variation on the traditional syllogism, or a radical departure. In thinking about the syllogistic framework, carefully consider all the category possibilities. Perhaps the best arguments can fit within current precedent if the advocate chooses her category carefully. Advocates should play with the potential to choose among different categorizations by generating synonyms and associations for the issue and position and by thinking narrowly or broadly (this is a process that effective advocates engage in while researching the legal problem). They should consider analogies and distinctions while experimenting with the various categories. This process will open the door to many organizational options, and it will lead advocates to make the best, most effective decision about how to arrange the arguments.

Cases & briefs

Bowers v. Hardwick, 478 U.S. 186 (1986).
Geduldig v. Aiello, 417 U.S. 484 (1974).
Katz v. United States, 389 U.S. 347 (1967).
Lawrence v. Texas, 539 U.S. 558 (2003).
    Brief for Petitioners, 2003 WL 152352.
Planned Parenthood v. Casey, 505 U.S. 883 (1992).
Scott v. Harris, 550 U.S. 372 (2007).
Silverman v. U.S., 365 U.S. 505 (1961).
Smith v. Maryland, 442 U.S. 735 (1979).
United States v. Knotts, 460 U.S. 276 (1982).
United States v. Jones, 565 U.S. 400 (2012).
    Brief for Respondent, 2011 Westlaw 4479076.
    Brief for the United States, 2011 Westlaw 3561881.

Bibliography

Amsterdam, A. and Bruner, J., 2002, *Minding the Law*, Harvard University Press, Cambridge, MA.

Beazley, M.B., 2014, *A Practical Guide to Appellate Advocacy*, 4th edn., Wolters Kluwer, New York.

Guthrie, C., Rachlinski, J.J. and Wistrich, A.J., 2001, 'Inside the Judicial Mind', *Cornell Law Review*, 86, 777–830.

Iyengar, S., 1991, *Is Anyone Responsible? How Television Frames Political Issues*, University of Chicago Press, Chicago, IL.

Johnson-Laird, P.N., 1978, 'The Psychology of Syllogisms', *Cognitive Psychology*, 10, 64–99.

Kahan, D.M., Hoffman, D.A. and Braman, D., 2009, 'Whose Eyes Are You Going to Believe? *Scott v. Harris* and the Perils of Cognitive Illiberalism', *Harvard Law Review*, 122(3), 837–906.

Kahneman, D., 2011, *Thinking, Fast and Slow*, Farrar, Straus and Giroux, New York.

Krieger, L.H., 1995, 'The Content of Our Categories: A Cognitive Bias Approach to Discrimination and Equal Employment Opportunity', *Stanford Law Review*, 47, 1161–1248.

Levi, E.H., 1948, 'An Introduction to Legal Reasoning', *University of Chicago Law Review*, 15(3), 501–574.

Little, L.E., 1996, 'Characterization and Legal Discourse', *Journal of Legal Education*, 46(3), 372–406, also in *Journal of the Association of Legal Writing Directors*, 6, 121–159.

Littleton, C., 1987, 'Reconstructing Sexual Equality', *California Law Review*, 75, 1279–1337.

Loftus, E.F. and Palmer, J.C., 1974, 'Reconstruction of Auto-Mobile Destruction: An Example of the Interaction Between Language and Memory', *Journal of Verbal Learning and Verbal Behavior*, 13, 585–589.

PART V

Connecting through tone

Well-known trial lawyer Gerry Spence has been quoted as saying that he goes "to court to do battle, not dance the minuet." (Margolick 1988). He is not the only one who has likened lawyering to war – legal advocacy is replete with war and battle metaphors. But war-like advocacy can undermine persuasion by pushing the audience away. War is about winning through force, and force is divisive.

In previous chapters, we've talked about the importance of connection, both emotional and cognitive, to persuasion. Tone is an important part of this. Although lawyers disagree about how aggressively to push, the answer from the persuasion science is pretty clear on this question: an advocate who adopts a more tempered, reasonable tone is more likely to connect to her audience. In other words, an advocate may be fighting a war, but a frontal assault is probably not the best strategy. In the words of Richard Perloff, a national expert in persuasion science:

> Many . . . view persuasion in John Wayne, macho terms. Persuaders are seen as tough-talking sales people, strongly stating their position, hitting people over the head with arguments, and pushing the deal to a close. But this oversimplifies matters. It assumes that persuasion is a boxing match, won by the fiercest competitor. In fact, persuasion is different. It's more like teaching than boxing. Think of a persuader as a teacher, moving people step by step to a solution, helping them appreciate why the advocated position solves the problem best.
>
> *(Perloff 2010)*

Because tone encompasses different aspects of advocacy, we have divided the material on tone into three separate chapters. All of the chapters are bound together by the principle that a more moderate, tempered tone is more persuasive than a one-sided, aggressive tone. Chapter 17 begins with the organization of the arguments. The chapter encourages advocates to structure arguments so that they appear to be the product of measured, gradual deliberation or even compromise. Even if you think of advocacy as a battle you want to win, you do not want your decision maker to think of himself as doing battle with you (or, even worse, as being embattled by you). The difference between what Dr. Perloff calls "hitting people over the head" and "moving people step by step" is, in large part, a matter of organization. Chapter 17 discusses why an organizational strategy that moves people gradually toward a solution is more likely to succeed.

Chapter 18 then moves beyond structure into substance. An effective way to set a reasonable tone in advocacy is by forthrightly acknowledging flaws in your argument. Including information that undermines the message may seem counterintuitive to the goal of persuasion, but it really does make the message stronger. The Peace Corps' motto is "the toughest job you'll ever love" and not "you'll love this job" for a reason. The motto is stronger for its frank acknowledgment of the difficulties of the work.

Finally, Chapter 19 addresses a common advocacy mistake that can damage the connection between advocate and decision maker. Advocates who excessively disparage the other side not only fail to make their own case, but actually push decision makers away from their position. An employee cannot persuade an employer that she is a good worker by arguing that her colleagues are lazy and dishonest. By disparaging her coworkers, the employee has given her employer no evidence of her own positive value, and the disparagement may very well have led the employer to distrust her.

All three principles support Dr. Perloff's point that advocacy is most successful when it takes a reasonable rather than coercive tone. Litigation may resemble war, but the path to victory is through moderation, not aggression.

17

STRUCTURING ARGUMENTS TO APPEAR REASONABLE

If you wish to convince someone that the death penalty for juveniles is wrong, you could take a number of advocacy approaches. You could simply declare passionately: "It is barbaric and immoral to execute children! They are just kids!" This is what Dr. Perloff means when he refers to hitting people over the head with arguments. This approach is passionate but also abrupt and conclusory. It rarely persuades. Indeed, it can often have the paradoxical effect of making people push back against the advocated position.

A second possibility is to build a more gradual structure. You could break down the argument into small parts: children act impulsively; adults have better judgment than children; since adults have better judgment, the acts of adults should be judged by a different standard, because they are more conscious and more responsible. And so on. In this gradual organization, the persuader is a helpful guide to be followed, not a force to be opposed. This is Dr. Perloff's "step-by-step" approach and it can be quite effective.

A third approach depends on compromise. The compromise approach starts by overshooting the target result – in the juvenile death penalty argument, perhaps you might begin by arguing that the death penalty is wrong for everyone. If the decision maker rejects that argument, then you could retreat and offer a compromise position by contending that the death penalty should at the very least be abolished for children. This approach is riskier than the gradual approach but can also be quite effective.

Chapter 17 shows how and why the gradual and compromise approaches to advocacy are almost always more successful than hitting your decision maker "over the head." Both the gradual and the compromise tactics work, in part, because they make the message, and the advocate, look less aggressive and strident. And the tactics are not mutually exclusive. The structure of most legal briefs can take advantage of the psychological reactions that occur with both tactics.

Foot in the door: the gradual approach

Imagine you are trying to convince someone to dive off a high dive. If you start your argument by pointing out the diving board itself, some 30 feet in the air, you are likely to inspire fear and a "whoa" response. Starting with the 30-foot diving board is likely to lead the person to reject your suggestion to dive. It is overwhelming. But if you start by leading your audience first to the initial step, then the second step, and so on, until she is at the top, at some point it becomes easier and more comfortable psychologically for her to dive than to walk back down all those steps. Diving is consistent with having agreed to climb up all those steps; walking down is an acknowledgment that she was wrong to take the early steps. (Funkhouser 1986).

Legal arguments can work the same way. If advocates are too abrupt with their audience, the audience may be startled and uncomfortable and may reflexively resist the argument. On the other hand, arguments that are structured to appear more gradual and deliberate are more persuasive because they more closely track the decision-making process of the audience, one step at a time.

The gradual approach works because human beings like consistency. So, if an advocate presents an argument that allows the decision maker to feel as though he is behaving consistently with his beliefs and his prior decisions (such as the decision to take that first step up the high dive), the argument is more likely to be persuasive.

Even if an advocate does not know the decision maker's beliefs, and we often do not, the advocate can present an argument that makes the decision maker feel consistent. For example, a decision maker is more likely to accept our ultimate premise – the premise at the heart of our case and usually one with which the other side disagrees – if we structure that ultimate premise so that it appears to be related to other premises with which the decision maker agrees. In other words, the decision maker is more likely to dive off the high dive if the advocate has convinced her to take the first, second, and third steps up the high dive ladder. (Stanchi 2006).

The science behind this strategy involves what are called "sequential requests." In one study, for example, scientists tried to persuade homeowners to post a large sign on their lawns about safe driving. When, as a first step, scientists asked people to put up the large sign, most people declined. But the scientists were able to change this high rejection rate by first asking homeowners to do something easy – to sign a petition to "Keep California Beautiful." Most of the homeowners agreed to sign the petition. And once the homeowners agreed to sign the petition, they were much more likely to agree to post the large sign. The homeowners were much more likely to agree to the big request (one that they ordinarily would have rejected) if they first agreed to an easier request. (Freedman and Fraser 1966).

This phenomenon is sometimes called the "foot-in-the-door" strategy. It works because decision making grows out of our prior behavior and decisions. When we are asked to make a decision, our brains go through a fast, largely subconscious process in which we try to determine whether we have made a similar decision previously and what we decided. We tend to treat prior decisions as a kind of precedent and make current decisions that are consistent with past ones.

For legal advocates, the key is that arguments can be structured so that the premise we want the decision maker to adopt feeds the decision maker's desire for consistency.

Legal advocates can do this by breaking down the controversial premise into component premises that are easier to agree to – the legal version of the "Keep California Beautiful" petition. (Stanchi 2006).

By breaking down a controversial premise into components with which the decision maker is likely to agree, the advocate can build and influence the decision maker's relevant cache of prior decisions. And because the premises presented by the advocate are the most recent, they are the ones at the forefront of the decision maker's mind (psychologists would call them "salient") when the decision maker starts that lightning-fast search of prior decisions to gauge, and maintain, consistency

The component arguments or premises should have two qualities: they must be easy for the decision maker to accept, and they must be linked to the ultimate controversial premise. The more attractive the component premises, and the more closely linked to the ultimate premise, the harder it will be for the decision maker to reject the ultimate premise.

∞ *Case study: the gradual approach in* **Cruzan v. Missouri Department of Health**

The headings for the petitioner's brief in *Cruzan v. Missouri Department of Health* (1990) are an excellent example of the kind of gradual, step-by-step arguments discussed in this section. (Brief of Petitioner 1990). In the *Cruzan* case, the petitioners had to argue a highly controversial premise: that the parents of a woman in a persistent vegetative state should be permitted to discontinue life-saving medical treatment and, essentially, cause their daughter to die. Starting with that premise would have been akin to pointing to the 30-foot high dive. So instead, they started with a much smaller, easily-agreed-to set of points:

A. All Persons Have A Fundamental Liberty Interest To Stop Unwarranted Bodily Intrusions By The State
B. Incompetent Persons Retain Constitutional Rights Even Though They Cannot Now Voice Their Choices
C. The Concept Of Family Decision Making Is Deeply Rooted In The Traditions Of This Country
D. Missouri's General Interest In Prolonging Life Is Not Sufficient To Override Nancy Cruzan's Constitutional Rights To Withdrawal Of Unwanted Medical Treatment

Notice how this chain makes agreement with the last controversial premise ("D") seem more reasonable and objectively true. The advocate has done this by leading up to D with a series of easily accepted premises. Who could disagree that people have a right to avoid "bodily invasion" by the state? That incompetent people retain constitutional rights? That "family decision making" is deeply embedded in our culture?

The advocate has also structurally linked A, B, C, and D such that D feels like a natural next step in the decision-making process. This structure also has made A, B, and C part of the decision maker's "cache" of prior decisions that will be used to decide the current case. The structure means that the easiest path to the comfortable feeling of consistency is diving off the metaphorical high dive (accepting premise D). Now, like all persuasive techniques, this isn't a magic bullet. It may not work on someone who comes to the argument predisposed against the "right to die." But even in that case, the format makes disagreement more difficult because the decision maker has to work to disconnect A, B, and C from D. That work will engage cognitive processes and deliberation in an active way that might not have occurred without the structure. That active cognitive work is where attitude change can happen.

But the gradual approach is not the only way to convince a decision maker. An advocate can persuade by leading off with a big and bold request – as long as she follows up with a compromise request.

Door in the face: the compromise approach

Would you agree to take a bunch of juvenile offenders to the zoo? Most people would not. In one study, researchers asked people to volunteer to take a group from a local juvenile detention center to the zoo for just two hours. Almost no one (only 17% of people) said yes. But the zoo volunteer rate shot up to 50% when researchers first asked the subjects to volunteer two hours a week for two years at the detention center. When the subjects said no, then the researchers asked about the zoo trip. The first "big" request made the second request look like a compromise, and many more people accepted it. Scientists called this the "door-in-the-face" principle because the agreement to the second request was primed by the rejection to the first one. (Cialdini et al. 1975).

Negotiators use a version of the compromise or "door-in-the-face" tactic frequently. Despite the benefits of the compromise tactic, however, these arguments are less common in legal advocacy because many legal advocates see them as a sign of weakness. Far from being weak, compromise arguments actually can make an advocate's position more powerful because they change the tone of the persuasive situation.

The power of compromise arguments is that they appear cooperative and reciprocal – in other words, reasonable. If the advocate offers a compromise position, the persuasive interaction becomes more like a negotiation. Instead of the advocate "hitting [the decision maker] over the head" with her arguments, the advocate and decision maker are engaged together in trying to find a solution. Compromise arguments can change the tone of the advocacy situation from contentious to mutual, leading decision makers to be more open and accepting.

To make a compromise argument, an advocate must commit to making two arguments. The first argument is a "big" request, one that is tenable but above the advocate's "bottom line." The key is that this argument must be tenable. It should be a reach but not preposterous. If your initial argument is too aggressive, you risk a reactance response like those described in the next chapters. Calvin, of the cartoon Calvin and Hobbes, oversteps famously when he asks his mother whether he can ride his tricycle on the roof (she says no) and then asks for a cookie (she says no again). Don't make this mistake. Second, your next argument is your compromise position. The idea is that even if the decision maker rejects the lead argument, he will be more open to accepting the compromise.

∞ *Case study: the compromise approach in* Meritor Savings Bank v. Vinson

In *Meritor Savings Bank v. Vinson* (1986), the respondent began her merits brief before the U.S. Supreme Court with a big, bold argument. (Brief of Respondent 1986). She argued that the Court had improvidently granted *certiorari*. This unusual argument openly contended that the Supreme Court had made an error and asked that it reverse itself. The argument certainly overshot what the respondent needed to win her case. But after this first bold step, the respondent followed up with traditional arguments on the merits. The arguments were about cutting-edge legal issues, but in comparison with that first argument, the follow-up arguments looked less surprising and more conventional.

The respondent won her case in *Meritor*. Although the Court did not find that it had improvidently granted certiorari (indeed, the Court never even mentioned the respondent's certiorari argument in its opinion), the Court did agree with many of the respondent's compromise arguments. Even more interesting, aspects of the respondent's arguments about the grant of certiorari, particularly the abstract and ambiguous quality of key facts in the record, are echoed in the Court's discussion of the merits of the case.

Summary

To sum up, as noted in an earlier chapter, the gradual and compromise strategies discussed here certainly appeal to the decision maker's preference for logical arguments and therefore seem to function on a logos level. They lead decision makers to make cognitive connections between ideas, arguments, and points. But as Professor Melissa Weresh has pointed out, these strategies also work on a social and emotional level. These strategies "establish and reinforce a relationship" between advocate and decision maker. In other words, they establish a "relationship" connection with the decision maker. (Weresh 2012). That connection is just as important to the persuasive process as the cognitive connections discussed in earlier chapters.

Cases & briefs

Cruzan v. Missouri Department of Health, 497 U.S. 261 (1990).
   Brief of Petitioners, 1989 WL 1115261.
Meritor Savings Bank v. Vinson 477 U.S. 57 (1986).
   Brief of Respondent [Mechelle Vinson], 1986 WL 728234.

Bibliography

Cialdini, R.B., Vincent, J.E., Lewis, S.K., Catalan, J., Wheeler, D. and Darby, B.L., 1975, 'Reciprocal Concessions Procedure for Inducing Compliance: The Door-In-The-Face Technique', *Journal of Personality and Social Psychology*, 31(2), 206–215.
Freedman, J.L. and Fraser, S.C., 1966, 'Compliance Without Pressure: The Foot-In-The-Door Technique', *Journal of Personality and Social Psychology*, 4(2), 195–202.

Funkhouser, G. Ray, 1986, *The Power of Persuasion: A Guide to Moving Ahead in Business and Life*, Crown, New York, NY.

Margolick, D., 1988, 'At the Bar: Rambos Invade the Courtroom, and the Profession, Aghast, Fires Back With Etiquette', *New York Times*, B5.

Perloff, R.M., 2010, *The Dynamics of Persuasion: Communication and Attitudes in the 21st Century*, Routledge, New York.

Stanchi, K.M., 2006, 'The Science of Persuasion: An Initial Exploration', *Michigan State Law Review*, 2, 411–456.

Weresh, M.L., 2012, 'Morality, Trust, and Illusion: Ethos as Relationship', *Legal Communication & Rhetoric: JALWD*, 9, 229–270.

18

VOLUNTEERING ADVERSE INFORMATION

Defense counsel in *Roper v. Simmons* (2005) confronted one of the worst pieces of negative information about a client that any lawyer ever had to face. When he was just 17 years old, the defendant in *Roper* had duct-taped a woman's arms and legs together and pushed her over a bridge into a river while she was still alive and conscious. The defendant was found guilty of murder and sentenced to death. Before the U.S. Supreme Court, the only issue was whether the Eighth Amendment permitted execution of defendants who had committed murder while under the age of 18.

Although the defense attorneys certainly had every reason to ignore or downplay the details of the crime, they did not. Of course they devoted the bulk of the Statement of the Case to the defendant's immaturity and abusive home life, but the attorneys opened the Statement of the Case with details about the victim's death and the defendant's participation in it.

The brief was successful. The defendant in *Roper* is still alive, and it is now unconstitutional in the United States to execute juvenile offenders. Defense counsel's decision to begin the Statement of the Case with a description of the defendant's horrendous crime may or may not have made a difference in the case. But it is an excellent example of what this chapter recommends as good persuasive practice.

The science of disclosure: the persuasive power of two-sided messages

Scientific studies of persuasive messages consistently demonstrate that voluntarily disclosing harmful information makes the message more convincing. The key is in both the disclosure and an effective rebuttal. As Professor Geoffrey Hazard has argued, a message that confronts opposing arguments is stronger because "[t]he weight of an argumentative position can be properly gauged only by reference to what can be set against it." (Hazard 1982). In other words, you are better off acknowledging your flaws than ignoring them, and you should address why your message should be accepted despite those flaws. You should say not only why you are right, but also why you are not wrong.

Psychologists refer to messages that contain positive arguments but also confront opposing arguments as "two-sided messages" because they address two sides of an argument. And, in study after study, two-sided messages that openly acknowledge and consider opposing views and then rebut them were most successful. They tended to result in more decisions in favor of the message and those favorable decisions were longer lasting and less vulnerable to attack. (Stanchi 2008).

Scientists offer a number of reasons for the consistent results of studies that show two-sided messages are more persuasive than one-sided. First, most people strongly believe that nothing is perfect and all arguments have two sides. When an advocate's message appears to consider pros and cons, the advocate looks more knowledgeable. The advocate who employs a two-sided message also looks more honest. The audience then trusts the advocate as an intelligent, knowledgeable, credible source and is more amenable to accepting the advocate's message. (Allen 1991). Classical rhetoricians would call this a demonstration of the advocate's "ethos" – as Professor Michael Smith wrote, lawyers can display their "ethos" by showing their intelligence or their trustworthiness. (Smith 2008). Psychologists refer to this as "source credibility."

In the *Roper* case, for example, defense counsel undoubtedly demonstrated ethos by including the murder facts so openly. The murder was such a big fact, and so awful. Trying to bury it would have looked not only dishonest, but perhaps somewhat preposterous, like a child who believes no one can see her if she covers her eyes. Some bad facts can be downplayed by structurally "burying" them in the middle of the Statement of Facts, or minimizing their detail. The murder in *Roper* was not that kind of fact. The brief writer gained credibility and respect by including it, and that credibility and respect likely made the decision makers open to accepting the other arguments.

Second, if the decision maker decides in favor of a two-sided message, that decision is also stronger and less susceptible to being changed based on an attack from an opposing side. Psychologists believe that volunteering information harmful to one's own message can actually insulate the message from attack. The reason is that the decision maker has gone through a process of considering at least some pro and con points before rendering a decision. This strengthens the conviction of the decision maker that he has made a correct decision and makes him less likely to change his mind if confronted by counter-points. (Perloff 2010).

Third, when an advocate discloses negative information, the audience can sometimes even change the information to be more favorable to the advocate. Psychologists call this phenomenon "change of meaning." Because we find disclosure of adverse information by an advocate surprising, our minds subconsciously try to make sense of this surprising occurrence by making the information appear to be less negative. The subconscious thought process is something like "the advocate disclosed this information, so it must not be as bad as I think." The "change of meaning" phenomenon has been documented in the trial context in a quite famous study of a criminal trial involving vehicular homicide. (Dolnik et al. 2003).

∞ *Case study: change of meaning in a homicide trial*

In this study, mock jurors read a trial transcript in which the defendant was charged with vehicular homicide for his involvement in a car accident that killed another person. (Dolnik et al. 2003). Researchers tested mock juror reactions to two different trial strategies: one in which defense counsel voluntarily disclosed negative information about the defendant and one in which defense counsel waited for the prosecution to disclose it. Researchers tested several different pieces of negative information: evidence that the defendant had been drinking before the accident, evidence that the defendant was speeding, and forensic evidence that the defendant had veered into the other lane.

Across all of these variables of negative information, subjects who heard the defendant voluntarily disclose the negative information consistently discounted it. They quite literally remembered it as being weaker and less damaging when compared with the trial in which the prosecution disclosed the flaw. In other words, the subjects subconsciously changed the meaning of the bad information to be less harmful. The subjects also rated the defendant's credibility as higher when he voluntarily disclosed the negative information and attempted to explain it, so voluntary disclosure of harmful information helped the defendant's case in two distinct ways.

As important as it is to confront weakness, the advocate should avoid some common errors. First of all, while you should acknowledge weakness, do not let it overwhelm your argument. Psychologists refer to the persuasion tactic as "inoculation" because you are giving only a small, weak dose, not the full-blown disease. Your argument should still be predominantly positive (why you win). If you need to, count paragraphs or sentences. Positive should far outweigh negative. Second, you must rebut or otherwise "handle" the weakness. Do not raise it and let it hang there without answer. The science is clear that two-sided messages must be "refutational" to be effective. (Allen 1991). Finally, the *Roper* example notwithstanding, it is generally risky to lead with a weakness because of priming effects (discussed more fully in Chapters 13 and 14). There are, as *Roper* demonstrates, exceptions, but as a rule, you should tread very carefully in deciding to start with negative information.

The flip side: the weakness of one-sided messages

As powerful as two-sided messages are, one-sided messages that contain only positive, supporting information are correspondingly weak. Although they can look deceptively persuasive, one-sided messages can actually turn people against the message. In other words, "hitting people over the head" with how right you are can often lead them to think you are wrong.

Think of how you feel when politicians exhort you to "trust me" or "believe me" or "read my lips." In his 1988 presidential campaign, Gary Hart famously responded to reports of his extramarital affairs with a vigorous denial: "Follow me around. I don't care. I'm serious. If anybody wants to put a tail on me, go ahead. They'll be very bored." (Sheehy 1987). This vehement denial spurred journalists to do just that, and resulted in the publication of a photo of Hart snuggling with a young blonde woman on a boat called the *Monkey Business* that caused Hart's withdrawal from the race. Not boring at all.

Self-serving statements do not usually reassure; rather, paradoxically, they often arouse suspicion or skepticism in direct proportion to how vehement the statements are (the more vehement, they more skepticism they arouse). Of course, politicians may have a problem with credibility generally, but skepticism is a common reaction to all overly positive messages. When a message is too positive, people tend to look for the negative.

A classical rhetorician views this disconnect between the advocate and his audience as a problem of ethos. The decision maker does not trust the advocate because the message is too positive and appears to be biased. A too-positive message means that the advocate is either dishonest (hiding something) or incompetent (does not know the pros and cons).

The science demonstrates a similar effect. One-sided messages stimulate skepticism because most people strongly believe that nothing is perfect and that most cases have two sides. So, much like our response to self-serving politicians, when a decision maker confronts a one-sided persuasive message, he will be skeptical and search for the other side. And much like the journalists following Gary Hart, a decision maker in a litigation context is likely to find the negative information he is seeking. The other side will usually point it out.

When he finds the negative information that he is seeking, the decision maker will likely feel a surge of relief and satisfaction. People usually react to flaws with indifference, understanding, or empathy. Under some circumstances, as discussed above, we will even mentally discount or diminish the flaw. But to someone seeking a flaw in a one-sided argument, finding that flaw is validating and satisfying. It creates the feeling of "Aha! I knew it!" (which is how many people felt when Gary Hart got caught on the *Monkey Business*).

Think of how often people enjoy reading about the flaws or foibles of celebrities or others with seemingly "perfect" lives. Or when our belief that something is "too good to be true" is validated. Consider that Gwyneth Paltrow was voted the "Most Hated Celebrity" at a time when Chris Brown was famous for beating Rihanna and Mel Gibson's bigoted rantings had been all over the Internet. (Le Vine 2016). Why do we hate Paltrow so much? In part for the same reason that people do not like one-sided arguments. We like to see the perfect cut down to size. This feeling of validation can exaggerate the importance of the flaw for the decision maker. It can make that negative information bigger and more significant to the case than it might otherwise have been and much more difficult for the advocate to overcome.

Instead of looking for flaws, decision makers can also respond to one-sided messages by "over-correcting." As noted, decision makers tend to perceive one-sided messages as biased. Over-correction results when the decision makers attempt to correct for the perceived bias of the one-sided message. Human beings are generally very poor at correcting for perceived errors. We usually overshoot the target. Imagine a pendulum. If defense counsel makes a one-sided argument that a judge perceives as unduly biasing, the judge will think that the pendulum has swung too far in favor of the defense. The judge will then attempt to swing the pendulum toward fairness (the middle) by swinging it back toward the plaintiff's side. But the judge will likely swing the pendulum too far toward the plaintiff because he is susceptible to the over-correction bias. So, by making a one-sided argument, defense counsel has actually pushed the judge toward a decision for the plaintiff. (Stanchi 2014).

Finally, one-sided arguments also risk that the decision maker will reject the message outright. If a decision maker feels that an advocate is deliberately withholding information in an effort to manipulate or bias her, she is likely to reject the message entirely. This response, referred to as "reactance" by psychologists, is a kind of "throw the baby out with the bathwater" reaction. It is a backlash against a persuasive message in which decision makers reject the message, not because of the merits of that message, but because they react negatively to the feeling of being controlled. (Brehm and Brehm 1981).

∞ Case study: reactance to one-sided argument

In *Gonzalez-Servin v. Ford Motor Co.* (2011), the Seventh Circuit Court of Appeals exhibited a paradigmatic reactance response. In that case, the plaintiff's lawyer took a classic one-sided approach to advocacy. He devoted his briefs to positive precedent only and did not mention potentially controlling adverse precedent. The Seventh Circuit not only ruled against the plaintiff, but also criticized the plaintiff's lawyer in the opinion. Obviously angry with the lawyer, the court compared him to an ostrich with its head in the sand and said his advocacy "left much to be desired." This unusual public criticism of a lawyer in a judicial opinion signals a reactance response. The court was no longer fully focused on the merits of the case, but was instead distracted by what it perceived as the lawyer's deceptive behavior.

There is one final drawback to one-sided messages. In addition to being unpersuasive, they are also highly susceptible to attack. That is, even in the unlikely event that the decision maker makes a decision in favor of the one-sided message, that decision is likely to last only as long as it takes for the other side to attack the message with counter-arguments. This susceptibility to attack is, of course, a significant weakness in legal advocacy, as there is always an opposing side whose job it is to generate counter-arguments. In *Gonzalez-Servin*, for example, the opposing authority was cited extensively in defense counsel's brief. So, even if plaintiff's counsel had temporarily convinced the court with its one-sided argument, that success would have been short lived.

Summary

To sum up, showing flaws in an argument can strengthen it, and putting forward a "perfect" argument can weaken it. At the heart of these two seeming paradoxes is the advocate's connection with the decision maker. That connection is weakened by arguments that appear biased or manipulative and strengthened by arguments that appear to be objective and reasonable. This doesn't mean that advocacy should be even-handed – if advocacy is truly objective, then it is no longer advocacy. But the more effective advocacy looks even-handed as it persuades; it is subtle and not the "hard sell." As Dr. Perloff says, it is "more like teaching than boxing." (Perloff 2010).

Cases & briefs

Gonzalez-Servin v. Ford Motor Co., 662 F.2d 931 (2011).
Roper v. Simmons, 543 U.S. 551 (2005).
   Brief for Respondent, 2004 WL 1947812.

Bibliography

Allen, M., 1991, 'Meta-Analysis Comparing the Persuasiveness of One-Sided and Two-Sided Messages', *Western Journal of Speech Communication*, 55, 390–404.

Brehm, J.W. and Brehm, S.S., 1981, *Psychological Reactance: A Theory of Freedom and Control*, Academic Press, New York.

Dolnik, L. et al., 2003, 'Stealing Thunder as a Courtroom Tactic Revisited: Processes and Boundaries', *Law and Human Behavior*, 27, 267–287.

Hazard, Jr., C.G., 1982, 'Arguing the Law: The Advocate's Duty and Opportunity', *Georgia Law Review*, 16, 821–832.

Le Vine, L., 2016, 'Gwyneth Paltrow Wonders How She's a More Hated Celebrity than Chris Brown', *Vanity Fair*, 30 June 2016.

Perloff, R.M., 2010, *The Dynamics of Persuasion: Communication and Attitudes in the 21st Century*, Routledge, New York.

Sheehy, G., 1987, 'The Road to Bimini', *Vanity Fair*, 1 September 1987.

Smith, M.R., 2008, *Advanced Legal Writing: Theories and Strategies in Persuasive Writing*, 3rd edn., Wolters Kluwer, New York.

Stanchi, K.M., 2008, 'Playing With Fire: The Science of Confronting Adverse Material in Legal Advocacy', *Rutgers Law Review*, 60, 383–434.

Stanchi, K.M., 2014, 'What Cognitive Dissonance Tells Us About Tone in Persuasion', *Journal of Law and Policy*, 22(1), 93–133.

19

THE TRAP OF ATTACK

Imagine a custody case in which one parent tries to gain custody by listing all the reasons why the other parent would be a terrible guardian. As misguided as this strategy is, it is all too common. Quite simply, it is much easier to criticize someone else's parenting than it is to list and substantiate what makes you a good parent. Affirmative reasons require creating arguments – and argument creation takes hard work, research, and careful thought. Reaction requires only a reflexive destruction of what someone else has already created.

No matter how easy it is to disparage the other side, it is a trap worth avoiding. Attacking the other side results in advocacy that sounds negative and defensive. No employer is going to hire a candidate because all the other candidates are terrible. Moreover, because attacking focuses on the other side's facts or arguments, it can have the paradoxical effect of reinforcing those arguments in the decision maker's mind. For example, if a mother in a custody battle spends significant time in her argument on how the father is a workaholic, the decision maker may very well remember what a hard worker the father is and conclude that he works hard to provide financial security for the family.

As with an unduly positive one-sided argument, moreover, arguments focused on why the other side is wrong are likely to evoke skepticism about the message and the trustworthiness (ethos) of the advocate making them. An advocate simply does not have much credibility with the decision maker when saying negative things about the other side. The decision maker knows the advocate is biased and is therefore likely to discount any attacks on the other side as the result of that bias.

Finally, just like a too positive one-sided argument, advocacy that aggressively focuses on disparaging the other side's case can stimulate reactance and over-correction. When an advocate "piles on" the other side, readers naturally come to the defense of the person being attacked. People tend to sympathize with the underdog, and if the advocate creates a rhetorical situation in which the other side looks like the underdog, the decision maker is likely to feel defensive on the other side's behalf. This can cause the decision maker to generate arguments in favor of the other side, the precise opposite from the result that the advocate desires.

Decision makers can also have a strong reactance response to excessive attacks on the other side because these kinds of arguments appear to be manipulative and designed to create bias. Whenever advocates argue in a way that leads the audience to feel manipulated or controlled, they risk a reactance response, which can result in the decision maker's rejection of the entire message. (Stanchi 2014).

∞ Case study: reactance caused by adopting "attacking" tone in brief

In this case study, an attorney's aggressive tone in an appellate brief caused the decision maker's reactance response. Professor Jim Stratman asked an appellate lawyer in a real case before the Commonwealth Court in Pennsylvania to tape record his thoughts on strategy while he was drafting his brief. (Stratman 1994). After the attorney filed the brief, Professor Stratman asked the Commonwealth Court clerks to record their reactions to the brief as they read it. This is one of the only studies that give insight into how an actual legal audience reacted to legal advocacy in real time.

In the recording by the attorney, notice how many times he uses the word "attack":

> I think I will make, yes, the attack on the lower court opinion,
> [I] can attack its failure to deal with Philadelphia Eagles and Barsky,
> I can attack its reliance on Meta v. Yellow Cab [cases cited by the lower court],
> I can attack its reliance on the right to jury trial cases,
> I can attack its failure to address Conestoga Bank,
> and I can attack. . . .
>
> *(Stratman 1994)*

While it is certainly an attorney's job to point out error, the advocate in this case attacked almost every aspect of the court's decision, from the smallest point to the largest, and did so with an unwavering stridency. When one of the clerks read the attorney's brief, she became immediately critical of the attacks made by the brief:

> I didn't see [the court] assuming that –
> That's not really being fair to the Commonwealth Court –
> I didn't read that the Commonwealth Court opinion even suggests that . . .
> This is the typical mode of argument where you set up a straw man and then knock
>   it down.
>
> *(Stratman 1994)*

These comments indicate a reactance response. The clerk reacted negatively to the brief ("I didn't see") and she quickly defended the entity being attacked ("That's not really being fair. . . ."). After that, the clerk turned her attention away from the merits of the case to the advocate, focusing on her irritation at his rhetoric ("This is the typical. . . ."). The "straw man" comment shows that the clerk felt that the advocate was trying to mislead or dupe her, and she reacts with the anger typical of a reactance response. The attorney lost his appeal.

∞ Case study: backlash response caused by excessive attacks in trial

In a recent study of 250 dismissed jurors in the Philadelphia and Seattle areas, Professors Kathryn Stanchi and Deirdre Bowen noticed a possible backlash that occurred when defense counsel in a civil case made an aggressive argument about the plaintiff's prior criminal conviction. (Stanchi and Bowen 2014). In this study, dismissed jurors watched videos of a mock civil trial involving a car accident. Some groups of jurors heard evidence that the plaintiff had a prior conviction for theft by deception. Others did not. Jurors were asked to decide if the defendant was negligent.

Jurors who heard evidence of plaintiff's prior conviction were somewhat more likely to find the defendant negligent than jurors who did not. In other words, jurors who heard about the plaintiff's conviction were more likely to rule in his favor and against the defendant. The difference was not very great – a 10 to 15% spread – but it was statistically significant. The researchers hypothesized that the prior conviction evidence could have had a "boomerang" effect that made the jurors gravitate toward a verdict for the plaintiff. This "boomerang" could have been the result of jurors feeling sympathy for the plaintiff or their feeling angry with the defendant for harping on a piece of evidence they perceived as irrelevant, or some combination.

Moreover, the largest percentage of jurors who rated the prior conviction as "not important" in their decision making were clustered in the group who heard defense counsel's most aggressive argument about the plaintiff's conviction. Defense counsel's aggressive use of the prior conviction evidence seemed to have led jurors to discount the importance of the prior conviction. Again, the researchers hypothesized that this result could be based on jurors having a "boomerang" reaction to defense counsel's aggressive attack on the plaintiff's credibility. Another explanation is that jurors, perceiving defense counsel's attack as biasing, "over-corrected" for the perceived bias by discounting the importance of the biasing evidence.

Both the brief and the trial case studies show the "disconnect" that happens between advocate and decision maker when the advocate is overly aggressive or negative in his argument. Whether due to reactance or over-correction, or simply distrust of the advocate, the "disconnect" is similar to what happens when an advocate puts forth an unduly positive argument that ignores opposing views. The bottom line is that when the advocate pushes too hard, she may end up pushing the decision maker away.

Summary

This chapter covers a common problem in advocacy. Too often, legal advocates react to adverse arguments, playing a defensive game instead of mounting a good offense. While it is easier to knock down adverse arguments than to come up with affirmative ones, effective advocates should not just do what is easier. Playing a defensive game accepts the other side's framing of the issues and, paradoxically, focuses the decision maker on the other side's arguments. But more important, the tactic of bashing the other side is likely to backfire.

Connection – in the sense of mental associations and also in the form of personal relationships – is essential to persuasion, and aggression severs that connection. It is the rhetorical equivalent of a shove to the chest. Connection in the persuasion context, like connection in most other situations, requires some patience and forbearance. In other words, it requires advocates to walk the fine line of showing our zeal and our deep belief in our clients without looking like zealots.

Bibliography

Stanchi, K.M., 2014, 'What Cognitive Dissonance Tells Us About Tone in Persuasion', *Journal of Law and Policy*, 22(1), 93–133.

Stanchi, K.M. and Bowen, D., 2014, 'This Is Your Sword: How Damaging Are Prior Convictions to Plaintiffs in Civil Trials?', *Washington Law Review*, 89, 901–996.

Stratman, J., 1994, 'Investigating Persuasive Processes in Legal Discourse in Real Time: Cognitive Biases and Rhetorical Strategy in Appeal Court Briefs', *Discourse Processes*, 17, 1–57.

PART VI

Conclusion

20

PUTTING IT TOGETHER

In closing, we go back to the beginning to connect the pieces and parts of our theory of legal persuasion.

As we wrote in the opening chapter, the lawyer's ability to persuade an audience to make favorable mental connections and break unfavorable ones is at the heart of legal persuasion. And persuasion often requires the advocate to construct not just one connection but an entire network of relationships. The first and primary relationship is between the advocate and her audience, a relationship most often formed by identifying common ground. In this book, we argued that almost every advocacy situation presents multiple possibilities for advocates to connect with their audiences. By drawing on rhetorical theory and persuasion science, we provided a foundation intended to help guide advocates through the difficult choices among those possibilities.

To think most effectively about connecting with their readers and listeners, lawyers must understand more about their primary audiences and how those audiences observe, interpret, and decide. Because connection with an audience member always takes place within a particular context, the lawyer also needs to understand the effects of timing and setting, both those affecting the immediate conflict and those making up the cultural and historical context. From that starting point, the advocate begins to construct and arrange her arguments, considering their substance, the array of potential frameworks and organizational models, and the appropriate style and tone. Each of these decisions provides an opportunity for the lawyer to strengthen the connection with her audience.

In addition to encouraging lawyers to gather the information necessary to make conscious and thoughtful choices among the many available options, we encouraged lawyers to recognize and take into account the extent to which persuasive connections are made subtly, unconsciously, and emotionally. Even when we make an argument that looks purely logical, the argument may persuade a judge not because he deliberates long and carefully, but instead because he responds automatically and intuitively. Sometimes these intuitive responses are based on harmful stereotypes or outdated traditional categories. But often these responses can be prompted by the judge's empathetic reaction to an individual's triumph or sorrow or to concrete images and examples of similar conflicts – reactions that implicitly suggest to the judge what should be the right or the most just outcome. We recommended that lawyers consider this fleshed-out picture in their advocacy responses, remembering that all of decision making is characterized by this blend of intuition and reflection, a mixture of cognitive and emotional components.

The lawyer's invention of arguments is perhaps the most critical step in legal persuasion and so storytelling, metaphor making, and analogy construction take up a significant portion of the book. Research underlines the importance of these frameworks for creating legal arguments: for most humans, narrative is a preferred organizing and retrieving mental structure (Schank and Abelson 1995), and analogy and metaphor have been characterized as the core of human cognition. (Hofstadter 2001).

Our purpose in the invention chapters was first to emphasize the importance of understanding the master stories, stereotypical characters, and iconic images that already influence legal audiences by filtering and framing what they see and understand. Next, we proposed methods of working within the positive influences and overcoming the negative influences of implicitly accepted concepts. If, for example, it would be persuasive to emphasize the parallels between your client's situation and the prototypical hero's journey, your argument would likely adhere to the recognizable storyline. If you wanted instead to emphasize that rather than acting as a hero, your client was the victim of another's deception, your argument likely would raise alternative plots or characterizations.

Within the storytelling chapters, we discussed researchers' views of how narrative transportation makes narrative persuasion different from what we usually understand as analytical persuasion. The chapters also explained why it is important that stories "ring true" and "hold together," and how to achieve those qualities of plausibility and coherence. These discussions join with Chapter 4's explanation of kairos, an important expansion of the concept of timing in storytelling. Developing a sense of kairos helps the advocate recognize and match the most opportune moments with the best-fitting arguments.

In addition to stories shaping the facts for persuasive ends, the invention chapters reminded advocates that all laws emerge from stories of conflicts and problems and that the way we tell law stories may influence their future interpretation and application. If he is to use law stories effectively, the advocate's duty extends beyond merely researching what the law is; the advocate should also know the story of how and why the law came to be. All those tools we use to tell client's tales – timing, plot, character, setting, point of view – offer useful approaches for telling the story of the law as well.

As for metaphor and analogy, these chapters developed methods for inventing persuasive arguments in situations lacking precedential rules. When there is no statutory rule or analogous case on which to construct a syllogistic organizational structure, the decision maker often must turn to a fitting metaphor or factual analogy. In these chapters, we discussed three alternative rhetorical situations. First, when the audience's initial response to an advocate's position is likely to be neutral or uninterested, arguments should rely on very familiar or conventional analogies and metaphors so that the outcome follows from automatic assumptions rather than deliberative analysis. Second, when the initial response is expected to be favorable, the most persuasive argument for reinforcing that response would take the shape of an extended factual analogy that can withstand more deliberative analysis. And finally, when the audience's initial response to the advocate's position is unfavorable, novel metaphors and characterizations can be employed to shift perspectives and realign expectations.

While the substance of the arguments is, of course, essential to the network of persuasive connections, the presentation of those arguments is a powerfully persuasive way of connecting one point to another. Our goal in the arrangement, or organizational, chapters was, again, to illustrate the array of possibilities for the legal advocate. First, the lawyer has the choice of whether to use a traditional syllogistic structure or not, but even within that structure, the lawyer faces many choices about constructing categories, framing questions, arguing about analogies, and selecting words and phrases to express concepts and hint at interpretations.

Overlaying all those choices is the concept of priming: that is, how to present information in a way that encourages the audience to connect one step or idea to another. Priming is a fundamental concept that forms the basis of most advocacy decisions, including the structure of an entire document and the organization of a single argument or paragraph. Once you know what priming is, you will see it everywhere, and you will recognize the potential uses for it everywhere as well. Priming can be used in all parts of persuasion, from the most macro or "big picture" decisions like your theory of the case down to the most micro or small-scale decisions of what precise word to use where.

Finally, we discussed tone. We started with the premise that a reasonable tone, one that is not overly combative or argumentative, is the best choice. That may strike some as inconsistent with the duty of zealous advocacy, but persuasion science indicates that reasonableness is the best route for making connections that win over the decision maker. But perhaps more important is the exploration of what "tone" means in a written document. How can writing have a "tone" like speaking? Because most of us "hear" what we read in our heads, writing does have a tone, and just as it is jarring for the listener, the wrong tone is jarring for the reader. In the tone chapters, we explained how to cultivate a reasonable, moderate tone while still advocating strongly for the client. We explored as well ways to avoid a strident, off-putting tone that will push the decision maker away from the desired result.

As we wrote in the introduction, making connections is the core concept that links rhetorical theory and analysis to persuasion science and to the real-life practice of persuasion. In this book, we have illustrated many of the ways in which lawyers can help their audiences connect with their arguments, and we have provided supporting arguments for our suggestions and illustrations.

Finally, in our closing defense of the need for lawyers to know and use the methods and techniques of rhetoric and persuasion science, we offer James Boyd White's response to Socrates's criticism of the Sophists. When you understand the process in which the lawyer takes part, White wrote, the lawyer's life and methods are more than justified:

> [T]he lawyer's task will always be to make the best case he can out of the materials of his culture in addressing an ideal judge. By its very nature, this [task] is to improve his materials, both by ensuring their congruence with the world of facts outside the law and by moving them toward greater coherence, fairness, and the like.
>
> *(White 1983)*

We hope the ideas and methods that law students and lawyers take away from this book will help them make the best case they can on behalf of the people they represent.

Bibliography

Hofstadter, D.R., 2001, 'Epilogue: Analogy as the Core of Cognition', in D. Gentner, K.J. Holyoak and B.N. Kokinov (eds.), *The Analogical Mind: Perspectives From Cognitive Science*, pp. 499–538, MIT Press, Cambridge, MA.

Schank, R.C. and Abelson, R.P., 1995, 'Knowledge and Memory: The Real Story', *Advances in Social Cognition*, 8, 1–85.

White, J.B., 1983, 'The Ethics of Argument: Plato's "Gorgias" and the Modern Lawyer', *University of Chicago Law Review*, 50, 849–894.

INDEX